Oracle® 11g For Dum

SQL Commands

Create a tablespace

```
CREATE TABLESPACE users
DATAFILE '/u01/oracle/oradata/dev11g/users01.dbf' size 100M
autoextend on next 10M maxsize 4G;
```

Set up a user

```
CREATE USER ldehoff IDENTIFIED BY 'welcome1'
DEFAULT TABLESPACE users
QUOTA 10m ON users
PASSWORD EXPIRE;
CREATE ROLE developer_role;
GRANT CREATE SESSION, CREATE TABLE, CREATE SEQUENCE, CREATE VIEW to developer_role;
GRANT developer_role TO ldehoff;
```

Create a table

```
CREATE TABLE clients (
client_id     NUMBER(4) CONSTRAINT pk_client_id PRIMARY KEY,
last_name     VARCHAR2(128) NOT NULL,
first_name    VARCHAR2(64) NOT NULL,
acct_number   NUMBER(8) CONSTRAINT uk_acct_number UNIQUE,
advisor_id    NUMBER(4) CONSTRAINT fk_advisor_id
   REFERENCES advisors(advisor_id)
) TABLESPACE users;
```

Create a view

```
CREATE OR REPLACE VIEW client_vw AS
SELECT last_name||','||first_name "LAST, FIRST", client_id
FROM clients;
```

Use a sequence

```
INSERT INTO clients
VALUES (client_id.nextval, 'Schumacher', 'Michael', 1000, 1234);
```

Create an index

```
CREATE INDEX idx_last_name ON
clients(last_name)
TABLESPACE indexes;
```

Create a sequence

```
CREATE SEQUENCE client_id_seq
INCREMENT BY 10
START WITH 10;
```


For more information about Wiley Publishing, call 1-800-762-2974.

Oracle® 11g For Dummies®

Cheat Sheet

(continued)

Drop a table

```
DROP TABLE advisors CASCADE CONSTRAINTS;
```

Flash back to a table

```
FLASHBACK TABLE advisors TO BEFORE DROP;
```

Join two tables

```
SELECT last_name, acct_number, advisor_last_name
FROM clients JOIN advisors
USING (advisor_id);
```

Start Enterprise Manager Database Control from command line

```
emctl start dbconsole
```

Start listener from command line

```
lsnrctl start
```

My Login Chart*

Database Name Tool (e.g. SQL*Plus)	Username	Password

Warning: Don't put any production information here!

Command-Line Executables for Oracle Tools

Tool	Command
SQL*Plus	sqlplus
Listener Control	lsnrctl
Data Pump Export	expdp
Data Pump Import	impdp
Recovery Manager	rman
SQL Developer	sqldeveloper
Net Manager	netmgr
Network Configuration Assistant	netca

Daily Common Watchlist

- Space
- System logs
- Audit records
- Sessions
- Backups
- Batch jobs
- Enterprise Manager

Oracle® 11g FOR DUMMIES®

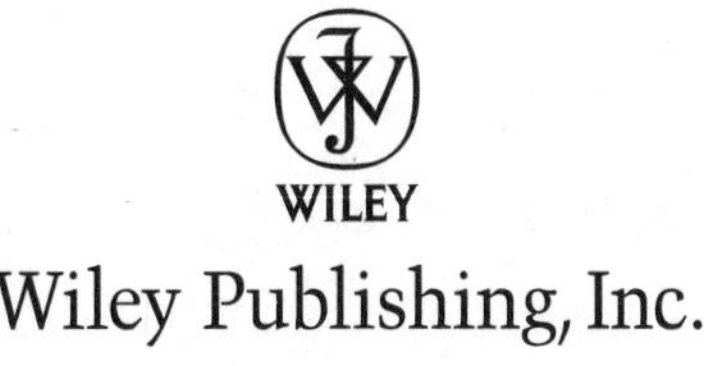

Wiley Publishing, Inc.

by Chris Zeis, Chris Ruel, and Michael Wessler

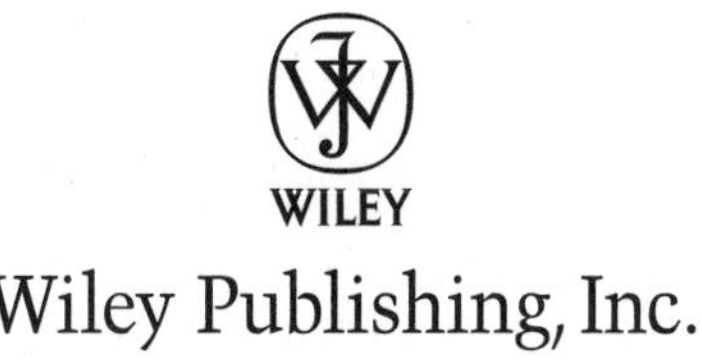

Wiley Publishing, Inc.

Oracle® 11g For Dummies®

Published by
Wiley Publishing, Inc.
111 River Street
Hoboken, NJ 07030-5774

www.wiley.com

Published by Wiley Publishing, Inc., Indianapolis, Indiana

Published simultaneously in Canada

For general information on our other products and services, please contact our Customer Care Department within the U.S. at 877-762-2974, outside the U.S. at 317-572-3993, or fax 317-572-4002.

For technical support, please visit www.wiley.com/techsupport.

Wiley also publishes its books in a variety of electronic formats. Some content that appears in print may not be available in electronic books.

Library of Congress Control Number: 2008942359

ISBN: 978-0-470-27765-2

Manufactured in the United States of America

10 9 8 7 6 5 4 3 2 1

About the Authors

Michael Wessler received his bachelor's degree in computer technology from Purdue University in West Lafayette, Indiana. He is an Oracle Certified Database Administrator for Oracle 8 and 8i, an Oracle Certified Web Administrator for 9iAS, and a 10g Database Technician. Michael also holds a CISSP security certification. He has administered Oracle databases on NT and various flavors of UNIX and Linux, including clustered Oracle Parallel Server (OPS) environments. He also performs database and SQL/PLSQL tuning for applications. Michael has worked in many IT shops ranging from small dot-com start-ups to large government agencies and corporations. Currently, Michael is a technical manager at Perpetual Technologies Inc., consulting for the U.S. government.

In addition to Oracle DBA consulting, Michael has worked extensively as an Oracle 10gAS Web Application Server Administrator. He manages multiple web applications for the Department of Defense and consults at various government agencies and in the private sector. Michael also frequently lectures on 10gAS and teaches Oracle Performance Tuning classes. Michael is the author of *Oracle DBA on UNIX and Linux* and coauthor of *Oracle Application Server 10g: J2EE Deployment and Administration, Oracle Unleashed,* Second Edition, *UNIX Primer Plus,* Third Edition, *COBOL Unleashed, UNIX Unleashed,* Fourth Edition, and *High Availablity: SuccessfulImplementation for the Data-Driven Enterprise*.

Chris Ruel lives in Indianapolis, Indiana. He graduated from Wabash College in 1997 and has been working with Oracle ever since. Currently, he is a consultant for Perpetual Technologies, Inc., a technology consulting firm with a focus on database management in the federal and commercial sectors. His clients range from Fortune 500 companies to Department of Defense contracts. He also serves as the vice president of the Indiana Oracle User's Group and speaks at many local events (Oracle Tech Days) hosted by his company. He served as an Oracle University Instructor from 2000–2004, traveling the country teaching Oracle's DBA curriculum. Chris is certified in Oracle 8i–10g. He recently received his 10g RAC Certified Expert qualification and is studying for his 11g OCP upgrade exam.

When not working on Oracle, Chris enjoys racing and restoring radio control cars. He is also a big fan of Formula 1 auto racing, grilling out with his friends, and watching the Indianapolis Colts play football.

Chris Zeis is the Chief Technology Officer and a partner at Perpetual Technologies, Inc. in Indianapolis, Indiana. Chris is the author or coauthor of four books on database technologies.

Dedication

Michael Wessler: For my Mom, Barb Wessler. A truly unique woman and loving mother; you're the best! Love always, Mike.

Chris Ruel: I dedicate this book to my parents who raised me well. If it wasn't for them, I don't know what I would be doing today. Well, my dad always said that I would be digging ditches when he scolded me for not applying myself.

Authors' Acknowledgments

Michael Wessler: I would like to thank all my family and friends for being so understanding of the time and commitment it takes when writing a book. It takes countless hours to write one of these and it's those closest to the authors who lose out during that time. In particular, I'd like to thank Angla Imel for understanding "Sorry, I have to write this weekend." I'd also like to thank my fellow authors, Chris Zeis and Chris Ruel, for bringing me into this exciting project. Finally, I'd like to thank Tony and Sue Amico not just for getting me into technical writing, but for being such wonderful family friends.

Chris Ruel: I appreciate the opportunity to be able to cooperate with the other authors of this book, Chris and Mike. A special thanks to the Wiley team (Kyle, Kelly, Tonya, and the mysterious "DB") for putting up with a newbie author who had a lot of questions and a writing style that had to be wrangled into submission.

Lastly, I want thank my lovely girlfriend, Angie, who put up with lots of lost weekends. Also, I apologize to my grilling buddies who wondered where I was half of the summer weekends!

Chris Zeis: I would like to personally thank my cowriters, Chris and Mike, for their support. I would also like to acknowledge the people and resources that helped me through this: my business partners Ron and Ryan at Perpetual Technologies, Inc. (PTI), my good friends and leaders at the Defense Finance and Accounting Serivces, The National Guard of Indiana PFO team (CW4 Ferguson and crew), the great folks at Wiley Publishing, and my Limey.

Publisher's Acknowledgments

We're proud of this book; please send us your comments through our online registration form located at `http://dummies.custhelp.com`. For other comments, please contact our Customer Care Department within the U.S. at 877-762-2974, outside the U.S. at 317-572-3993, or fax 317-572-4002.

Some of the people who helped bring this book to market include the following:

Acquisitions and Editorial

Project Editors: Tonya Maddox Cupp, Kelly Ewing

Acquisitions Editor: Kyle Looper

Technical Editor: Damir Bersinic

Editorial Manager: Jodi Jensen

Media Development Assistant Producers: Angela Denny, Josh Frank, Shawn Patrick, Kit Malone

Editorial Assistant: Amanda Foxworth

Sr. Editorial Assistant: Cherie Case

Cartoons: Rich Tennant (`www.the5thwave.com`)

Composition Services

Project Coordinator: Patrick Redmond

Layout and Graphics: Shawn Frazier, Christine Williams

Proofreaders: Laura Albert, John Greenough, Christine Sabooni

Indexer: Christine Spina Karpeles

Publishing and Editorial for Technology Dummies

Richard Swadley, Vice President and Executive Group Publisher

Andy Cummings, Vice President and Publisher

Mary Bednarek, Executive Acquisitions Director

Mary C. Corder, Editorial Director

Publishing for Consumer Dummies

Diane Graves Steele, Vice President and Publisher

Composition Services

Gerry Fahey, Vice President of Production Services

Debbie Stailey, Director of Composition Services

Table of Contents

Chapter 13: Monitoring and Managing with Enterprise Manager 299

Part IV: Inspecting Advanced Oracle Technologies 315

Chapter 14: Flashing Back and Replaying: Advanced Features 317

Chapter 15: Using High-Availability Options. 329

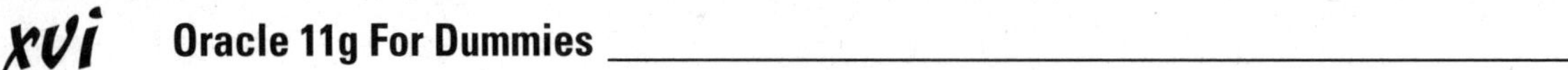

Introduction

If you are reading this text, chances are you're considering throwing yourself into the wonderful world of Oracle database administration. The good news is, you have come to right place. The bad news? Well, it's not really bad news . . . but you have quite an adventure ahead of you. Luckily, the authors of this book, your guides in this adventure, can help smooth out any bumpy roads. With over 35 years of combined Oracle experience, we hope to make understanding the Oracle database a fun, enlightening experience.

Oracle is large company with a diverse portfolio of software. It's constantly growing too. It seems like every other week Oracle releases some slick new product or acquires another company. Don't let the overwhelming nature of the big picture discourage you. This book imparts a fundamental knowledge of the basics of database administration. An Oracle career is a constant learning process. Establishing a solid understanding of the building blocks behind the database engine will vault you into a successful Oracle career.

You might be interested to know that the rock behind all of Oracle's products is almost always the database. Take comfort in knowing that in the database world, Oracle is the best. Learning the database is the first step to opening an awful lot of doors for you. Starting at this level is key. After reading this book, you will be well on your way to an interesting career filled with challenges and plenty of opportunity.

There will always be a need for managing information. Every year we see companies grow and accumulate data at a staggering rate. Databases are not a passing fad like some other areas of information technology. The concept of a relational database has been in circulation for almost 40 years and won't be going away anytime soon.

About This Book

Despite this book being titled *Oracle 11g For Dummies,* we focus on the tenets of Oracle database administration. Not only do we cover many of the features released with the 11g version of the database, but also cover the fundamental building blocks. Many of these concepts and techniques apply to past versions of the Oracle and almost certainly future releases.

Sometimes in the book we refer to directories and file locations on both Linux/UNIX and Windows. Essentially the two can be interchanged with a couple of things in mind. For example, here is an ORACLE_BASE value that you might come across on Linux/UNIX:

```
$ORACLE_BASE: /u01/app/oracle
```

In Windows, /u01 is much like a drive letter. They call it a *mount point* in Linux/UNIX.

Also, variables in Linux/UNIX are frequently prefixed with a dollar sign. Furthermore, the slashes are in opposite directions for each operating system. On Linux/UNIX you call / a *forward slash*. In Windows, you use a *back slash* \. Lastly, Windows encapsulates the variable in percent signs. The same previous setting might look like this in Windows:

```
%ORACLE_BASE%: C:\app\oracle
```

We try to give examples of both environments throughout this book.

Who Are You?

People who find themselves needing or wanting a skill set for Oracle databases come from all backgrounds. You might be an application developer, a system administrator, or even a complete newbie. Many of the folks that we come across in this industry became a *database administrator (DBA)* by accident. One day, your company finds itself without a DBA, and the next thing you know, that's you! One trick is to be ready. Above all else, learn on your own and *think* rather than just react.

What's in This Book

Oracle 11g has six different parts with six different major topics.

Part I: You Don't Have to Go to Delphi to Know Oracle

Part I helps prepare you for implementation by discussing why you'd choose Oracle in the first place, what's included in the architecture and how the elements work together, and what you need to do before starting Oracle database creation.

Part II: Implementing Oracle on Your Own

Part II gets you into the nitty gritty of Oracle database creation by discussing the tools and actual steps you'll take. The Database Creation Assistant (DBCA) is detailed here, as well as the SQL language. You can use either tool; automatic or manual setup is your choice. Finally, you read what to populate your Oracle database with.

Part III: Caring for an Oracle Database

You can't just create and populate an Oracle database: You have to protect it. Part III has the tools and tips you need to secure both the database and the data within. The less glamorous but no less crucial maintenance chores are detailed in this part, along with basic troubleshooting, should you need to do some. Enterprise Manager makes a star appearance here as well; keeping an eye on your database can keep you from having to troubleshoot in the long run.

Part IV: Inspecting Advanced Oracle Technologies

Part IV reveals some rare Oracle goods, including the flashback database, flashback data archive, and database replay. Rolling back for data recovery is detailed here, and high-availability options Real Application Clusters (RAC) and Data Guard are explained as well.

Part V: The Part of Tens

Avoid installation mistakes by reading Part V. Ten simple things to avoid (and another 10 to make sure you do) add up to 20 problem solvers. Head off trouble before it starts.

Icons in This Book

You see these icons throughout this book. They're a heads-up for different situations.

Warnings, if not heeded, will cause you to lose data. And maybe your job.

Remembering these bits of information can help you in the long run. And even the short run. Even on a brief walk.

Tips can save you time or energy or manpower or resources. We realize all these items are in short supply.

Technical Stuff icons indicate things we think are interesting and want to share with you, but can be skipped if you'd rather get straight to the nitty-gritty.

Where to Go from Here

Jump on in! Keep an open mind and try not to get overwhelmed. Like any skilled profession, it isn't always easy but you can do it and we think you'll find it rewarding. This book is written so you can avoid the "too-much-information" reaction. Look at each section as a piece of a big puzzle, and you will soon see how everything starts to take shape.

Part I

You Don't Have to Go to Delphi to Know Oracle

"One of the first things you want to do before installing Oracle 11g is fog the users to keep them calm during the procedure."

In this part . . .

Need to create a database? Considering Oracle? Already administering an Oracle database? Chapter 1 helps you with the first two by touting Oracle's advantages. Chapter 2 explains how Oracle database architecture works and Chapter 3 prepares you for actually implementing the Oracle database.

Chapter 1

A Pragmatic Introduction to Oracle

In This Chapter

- Getting familiar with Oracle
- Implementing grid computing
- Incorporating Oracle into everyday life

Oracle 11g is by far the most robust database software on the market today. It's also the leading database software used and sold all over the world. It has become an enterprise architecture standard for managing data, regardless of the data's size or complexity.

This chapter highlights the reasons to use Oracle 11g.

Introducing a New Kind of Database Management

Oracle is software that efficiently organizes data in a relational manner. Before Oracle, other database software ran on mainframes and used a *hierarchical data model* where data is stored in a tree-like structure as flat files — those crazy COBOL programmers!

The *relational model* is a concept where data is logically stored. These design elements are in the form of tables. Tables have columns, and the columns have attributes (character or number, for example). The tables are organized to store specific data. The tables relate to one another through primary keys.

For more clarity, Oracle, the company, was founded on the database software that transformed the industry into what it is today. Oracle, the company, owns many software products and applications that it has written or acquired, but the database software is still Oracle's core product.

This book focuses more on database administration rather than Oracle applications administration.

Decoding the *g* in Oracle 11g

Oracle has always had some creative marketing techniques. In the late 1990s, the Internet was booming, and everyone wanted Internet technology. Oracle released an upgraded version of Oracle 8 and labeled it 8i. *i* represents the Internet. This addition was a popular move because businesses realized the advantages of providing access via the Internet. Use of the Internet also reduced the labor and cost requirements for client server applications in which the client was installed onto the end user's PC.

As popular as the Internet boom was, grid computing is now the evolution of enterprise architecture management. (Hence the *g,* which stands for grid.)

Pooling Resources with Grid Computing

Grid computing offers a pool of distributed resources for computing services. It's simply described as computing as a service, similar to a utility-type model.

Oracle supports grid computing with its Real Application Clusters (RAC) capability and its Oracle Enterprise Manager (OEM):

- **RAC** uses Oracle's clustering software to manage a highly available environment. If you need additional hardware resources (such as memory or CPU), or experience hardware failure, you simply add another *node* (server) to the grid. (Truthfully, it's more complicated than that, but you get the point.)
- **EM** manages the databases and hosts, which are also called *targets.* It has a web interface that gives you a comprehensive view of each target's state. It handles all the monitoring requirements and provides other web-based tools to interact or perform maintenance with.

Together, RAC and EM make up the components to support true grid computing. RAC is a complex architecture that requires a fair amount of systems and database administrator knowledge, which is unfortunately beyond the scope of this book.

Chapter 13 covers the capabilities and configuration for EM and its lighter single database version, DB Console. You can find additional information about Oracle RAC at www.oracle.com/database/rac_home.html.

Anticipating Technology and Development Trends

Oracle's success is partially due to anticipating, adapting, and establishing database technology trends. You can choose from numerous designing tools and Integrated Development Environment (IDE) technologies, such as Service Oriented Architecture (SOA), Java, and Extensible Markup Language (XML).

These technologies are portable, which reduces hardware or software dependencies and suits standard *business-to-business (B2B)* processing and communication:

- **SOA** is a style of IT architecture that utilizes a build-once/deploy-many concept. Its root definition includes webcentric services that work together to sustain business processes. SOA separates the application function from the underlying software and hardware to allow better use (or reuse) of application processing. These functions or service units are written to be flexible by design and capable of service-to-service communication.

  SOA concepts eliminate hard coding and stove piping of applications for better use with other applications. Generally, SOA is engineered for large enterprise architectures that require a scalable, cost-effective approach to application development and maintenance.
- **Java** is a free programming language that standardizes applications across hardware platforms. This write-once/run-anywhere programming language supports *object-oriented programming (oop)* methodologies. Java is widely used for enterprise-level applications on the web and is very popular because it can run on any operating system without much tweaking. Oracle supported Java shortly after its creation.
- **XML** is an all-purpose language that helps share data across systems via the Internet. It standardizes the programming methods or calls, which allow for B2B communication. XML supports the SOA framework as well.

Meeting Oracle in the Real World

The Oracle 11g database can support any requirement you have for using and storing data. From financial institutions, such as banks, to human resources or manufacturing applications, Oracle can handle it. Its strengths lie in its vast number of software components and its ability to recover to any point in time.

General Oracle use supports a variety of applications that are labeled by type. The following list outlines the majority of database types:

- **Online Transactional Processing (OLTP):** Used for transaction-oriented applications where the response is immediate and records are modified or inserted regularly.
- **Decision Support System (DSS):** Used for processing data and making judgments on data for making decisions. A DSS database usually involves many ad hoc queries.
- **Online Analytical Processing (OLAP):** Used for analyzing data. Typically, OLAP is used for business intelligence or *data mining,* such as budgeting or forecasting.
- **Hybrid:** Acts as a multifunctional database. Most hybrid databases contain transactional, processing ad hoc querying, and batch processing. Larger databases that have service-level requirements are generally isolated to their own databases for performance and manageability reasons.

Uses for Oracle center around data and information. Industries leaders are particularly interested in information. Have you heard the motto "Information Drives Performance"? That motto basically suggests that the performance of a company is relative to the information it has and uses. This information assists in making more competitive and educated decisions.

A good example of this process is how Amazon and eBay use their information. They track user interaction on their Web sites to help define a user's shopping tendencies and interests. They then make programmatic recommendations based on that information to promote purchases, which in turn creates revenue. Information usage in this manner is known as *Business Intelligence* (BI) and is a common practice among many businesses today. Instead of saying, "Build it and they will come," Oracle can say, "Get their information and build them something they can't refuse."

Making the Oracle Decision

The decision to use Oracle over other technologies or database software can be a difficult one. Several things can influence your decision:

- Cost
- Available expertise
- Project scope
- Scale

Most of our clients decided to use Oracle based on available expertise because pricing is fairly competitive across database companies. In one case, Microsoft SQL Server was almost chosen because the developers had ASP/VB.NET experience. If the developers were Java eccentric, the database software would have never been discussed. Management, however, realized that it could use the pre-existing Oracle database infrastructure and still develop with Microsoft products.

Microsoft Access and even Microsoft Excel have their place, but if you want functionality, scalability, recoverability, and security, Oracle is the best choice. Linux gurus also use MySQL or PostgreSQL. Both are free for public use. The difficulty in using or managing MySQL or PostgreSQL is finding qualified expertise. You also need to consider the software support capability of the product. Oracle support provides a deep, mature group and a knowledge base for issues, such as bugs or general guidance.

In comparison to other database software products, Oracle has a similar level of complexity in installing, configuring, and maintaining it. Senior expert-level professionals are sometimes necessary for particular issues, but most novices to Oracle can achieve success without much training or guidance. We've trained many DBAs in our day, and they all had very little knowledge of Oracle but were eager to get their hands dirty. A good understanding of information technology and computers in general definitely helps with the learning curve.

Oracle runs on all the common and latest operating system versions of Linux, UNIX, Microsoft Windows, Mainframes, and Mac. It provides the same functionality and utilities regardless of the operating system or hardware. It also supports 64-bit architecture to add additional memory space for large applications. You can purchase licensing per CPU or per named user.

Additionally, Oracle provides lower-cost licensing for its standard editions. Oracle licensing information is available at www.oracle.com/corporate/pricing/technology-price-list.pdf.

Chapter 2

Understanding Oracle Database Architecture

In This Chapter

- Structuring memory
- Checking the physical structures
- Applying the irreducible logic of the logical structures

Understanding the Oracle architecture is paramount to managing a database. If you have a sound knowledge of the way Oracle works, it can help all sorts of things:

- Troubleshooting
- Recovery
- Tuning
- Sizing
- Scaling

As they say, that list can go on and on. That's why a solid knowledge of the inner workings of Oracle is so important.

In this chapter we break down each process, file, and logical structure. Despite the dozens of different modules in the database, you should come away with a good understanding of what they are, why they're there, and how they work together. This chapter is more conceptual than it is hands-on, but it gives you a solid base for moving forward as you begin working with Oracle.

Defining Databases and Instances

In Oracle speak, an *instance* is the combination of memory and processes that are part of a running installation. The *database* is the physical component or the files. You might hear people use the term *database instance* to refer to the entire running database. However, it's important to understand the distinction between the two.

Here are some rules to consider:

- **An instance can exist without a database.** Yes, it's true. You can start an Oracle instance and not have it access any database files. Why would you do this?
    - This is how you create a database. There's no chicken-or-egg debate here. You first must start an Oracle instance; you create the database from within the instance.
    - An Oracle feature called Automatic Storage Management uses an instance but isn't associated with a database.
- **A database can exist without an instance, but would be useless.** It's just a bunch of magnetic blips on the hard drive.
- **An instance can only access one database.** When you start your instance, the next step is to mount that instance to a database. An instance can only mount one database at a time.
- **You can set up multiple instances to access the same set of files or one database.** *Clustering* is the basis for Oracle's Real Application Clusters feature. Many instances on several servers accessing one central database allows for scalability and high availability.

Deconstructing the Oracle Architecture

You can break the Oracle architecture into the following three main parts:

- **Memory:** The memory components of Oracle (or any software, for that matter) are what inhabit the RAM on the computer. These structures only exist when the software is running. For example, they instantiate when you start an instance. Some of the structures are required for a running database; others are optional. You can also modify some to change the behavior of the database, while others are static.

- **Processes:** Again, Oracle processes only exist when the instance is running. The running instance has some core mandatory processes, whereas others are optional, depending on what features are enabled. These processes typically show up on the OS process listing.
- **Files and structures:** Files associated with the database exist all the time — as long as a database is created. If you just install Oracle, no database files exist. The files show up as soon as you create a database. As with memory and process, some files are required whereas others are optional. Files contain your actual database objects: the things you create as well as the objects required to run the database. The logical structures are such things as tables, indexes, and programs.

Maybe you could say that the Oracle architecture has two-and-a-half parts. Because files contain the structures, we lump those two together.

The following sections get into more detail about each of these main components.

Walking Down Oracle Memory Structures

Oracle has many different memory structures for the various parts of the software's operation.

Knowing these things can greatly improve how well your database runs:

- What each structure does
- How to manage it

In most cases, more memory can improve your database's performance. However, sometimes it's best to use the memory you have to maximize performance.

For example, are you one of those "power users" who likes to have ten programs open at once, constantly switching between applications on your desktop? You probably know what we're talking about. The more programs you run, the more memory your computer requires. In fact, you may have found that upgrading your machine to more memory seems to make everything run better. On the other hand, if you are really a computer nerd, you might go into the OS and stop processes that you aren't using to make better use of the memory you have. Oracle works in much the same way.

Trotting around the System Global Area

The *System Global Area (SGA)* is a group of shared memory structures. It contains things like data and SQL. It is shared between both Oracle background processes and server processes.

The SGA is made up of several parts called the *SGA components:*

- Shared pool
- Database buffer cache
- Redo log buffer
- Large pool
- Java pool

The memory areas are changed with initialization parameters.

- You can modify each parameter individually for optimum tuning (only for the experts).
- You can tell Oracle how much memory you want the SGA to use (for everyone else).

Say you want Oracle to use 1GB of memory. The database actually takes that 1GB, analyzes how everything is running, and tunes each component for optimal sizing. It even tells you when it craves more.

Shared pool

Certain objects and devices in the database are used frequently. Therefore, it makes sense to have them ready each time you want to do an operation. Furthermore, data in the shared pool is never written to disk.

The shared pool itself is made up four main areas:

- Library cache
- Dictionary cache
- Quickest result cache
- SQL result cache

A *cache* is a temporary area in memory created for a quick fetch of information that might otherwise take longer to retrieve. For example, the cache's mentioned in the preceding list contain pre-computed information. Instead of a user having to compute values every time, the user can access the information in a cache.

The library cache

The library cache is just like what it's called: a library. More specifically, it is a library of ready-to-go SQL statements.

Each time you execute a SQL statement, a lot happens in the background. This background activity is called *parsing*. Parsing can be quite expensive.

During parsing, some of these things happen:

- **The statement syntax is checked to make sure you typed everything correctly.**
- **The objects you're referring to are checked.** For example, if you're trying access a table called emp, Oracle makes sure it exists in the database.
- **Oracle makes sure that you have permission to do what you're trying to do.**
- **The code is converted into a database-ready format.** The format is called *byte-code* or *p-code*.
- **Oracle determines the optimum path or plan.** This is by far the most expensive part.

Every time you execute a statement, the information is stored in the library cache. That way, the next time you execute the statement not much has to occur (such as checking permissions).

The dictionary cache

The dictionary cache is also frequently used for parsing when you execute SQL. You can think of it as a collection of information about you and the database's objects. It can check background-type information.

The dictionary cache is also governed by the rules of the *Least Recently Used (LRU)* algorithm: If it's not the right size, information can be evicted. Not having enough room for the dictionary cache can impact disk usage. Because the definitions of objects and permission-based information are stored in database files, Oracle has to read disks to reload that information into the dictionary cache. This is more time-consuming than getting it from the memory cache. Imagine a system with thousands of users constantly executing SQL . . . an improperly sized dictionary cache can really hamper performance.

Like the library cache, you can't control the size of the dictionary cache directly. As the overall shared pool changes in size, so does the dictionary cache.

The quickest result cache

The result cache is a new Oracle 11g feature and it has two parts:

- **SQL result cache:** This cache lets Oracle see that the requested data — requested by a recently executed SQL statement — might be stored in memory. This lets Oracle skip the execution part of the, er, execution, for lack of a better term, and go directly to the result set, if it exists.

  What if your data changes? We didn't say this is the end-all-performance-woes feature. The SQL result cache works best on relatively static data (like the description of an item on an e-commerce site).

  Should you worry about the result cache returning incorrect data? Not at all. Oracle automatically invalidates data stored in the result cache if any of the underlying components are modified.

- **PL/SQL function result cache:** The PL/SQL function result cache stores the results of a computation. For example, say you have a function that calculates the value of the dollar based on the exchange rate of the Euro. You might not want to store that actual value since it changes constantly. Instead, you have a function that calls on a daily or hourly rate to determine the value of the dollar. In a financial application this could happen thousands of times an hour. Therefore, instead of the function executing, it goes directly to the PL/SQL result cache to get the data between the rate updates. If the rate does change, then Oracle re-executes the function and updates the result cache.

Least Recently Used algorithm

If the library cache is short on space, objects are thrown out. Statements that are used the most stay in the library cache the longest. The more often they're used, the less chance they have of being evicted if the library cache is short on space.

The library cache eviction process is based on what is called the *Least Recently Used (LRU)* algorithm. If your desk is cluttered, what do you put away first? The stuff you use the least.

You can't change the size of the library cache yourself. The shared pool's overall size determines that. If you think too many statements are being evicted, you can boost the overall shared pool size if you're tuning it yourself. If you're letting Oracle do the tuning, it grabs free memory from elsewhere.

Database buffer cache

The *database buffer cache* is typically the largest portion of the SGA. It has data that comes from the files on disk. Because accessing data from disk is slower than from memory, the database buffer cache's sole purpose is to cache the data in memory for quicker access.

Heap area

There aren't a lot of interesting things to say about the heap area within the context of this book. Basically, the *heap area* is a bunch of smaller memory components in the shared pool. Oracle determines their sizes and tunes them accordingly.

Only the nerdiest of Oracle DBAs will search the dark nether-regions of the Internet for heap area information. It's not readily available from Oracle in the documentation, and the information you do find may or may not be accurate. If all I have done was make you more curious, look at the dynamic performance view in the database called V$SGASTAT to get a list of all the other heap area memory component names.

The database buffer cache can contain data from all types of objects:

- Tables
- Indexes
- Materialized views
- System data

In the phrase *database buffer cache* the term *buffer* refers to database blocks. A *database block* is the minimum amount of storage that Oracle reads or writes. All storage segments that contain data are made up of blocks. When you request data from disk, at minimum Oracle reads one block. Even if you request only one row, many rows in the same table are likely to be retrieved. The same goes if you request one column in one row. Oracle reads the entire block, which most likely has many rows, and all columns for that row.

It's feasible to think that if your departments table has only ten rows, the entire thing can be read into memory even if you're requesting the name of only one department.

Buffer cache state

The *buffer cache* controls what blocks get to stay depending on available space and the block state (similar to how the shared pool decides what SQL gets to stay). The buffer cache uses its own version of the LRU algorithm.

A block in the buffer cache can be in one of three states:

- **Free:** Not currently being used for anything
- **Pinned:** Currently being accessed
- **Dirty:** Block has been modified, but not yet written to disk

Free blocks

Ideally, free blocks are available whenever you need them. However, that probably isn't the case unless your database is so small that the whole thing can fit in memory.

The LRU algorithm works a little differently in the buffer cache than it does in the shared pool. It scores each block and then times how long it has been since it was accessed. For example, a block gets a point each time it's touched. The higher the points, the less likely the block will be flushed from memory. However, it must be accessed frequently or the score decreases. A block has to work hard to stay in memory if the competition for memory resources is high.

Giving each block a score and time prevents this type of situation from arising: A block is accessed heavily at the end of the month for reports. Its score is higher than any other block in the system. That block is never accessed again. It sits there wasting memory until the database is restarted or another block finally scores enough points to beat it out. The time component ages it out very quickly once you no longer access it.

Dirty blocks

A modified block is a *dirty block.* To make sure your changes are kept across database shutdowns, these dirty blocks must be written from the buffer cache to disk. The database names dirty blocks in a dirty list or write queue.

You might think that every time a block is modified, it should be written to disk to minimize lost data. This isn't the case — not even when there's a *commit* (when you save your changes permanently)! Several structures help prevent lost data.

Furthermore, Oracle has a gambling problem. System performance would crawl if you wrote blocks to disk for every modification. To combat this, Oracle plays the odds that the database is unlikely to fail and only writes blocks to disk in larger groups. Don't worry; it's not even a risk against lost data. Oracle is getting performance out of the database *right now* at the possible expense of a recovery taking longer *later.* Because failures on properly managed systems rarely occur, it's a cheap way to gain some performance. However, it's not as if Oracle leaves dirty blocks all over without cleaning up after itself.

Block write triggers

What triggers a block write and therefore a dirty block?

- The database is issued a shutdown command.
- A full or partial *checkpoint* occurs — that's when the system periodically dumps all the dirty buffers to disk.
- A recovery time threshold, set by you, is met; the total number of dirty blocks causes an unacceptable recovery time.
- A free block is needed and none are found after a given amount of searching.
- Certain *data definition language* (DDL) commands. (DDL commands are SQL statements that define objects in a database. You find out more about DDL in Chapter 6.)
- Every three seconds.
- Other reasons. The algorithm is complex and we can't be certain with all the changes that occur with each software release.

The fact is the database stays pretty busy writing blocks in an environment where there are a lot changes.

Redo log buffer

The *redo log buffer* is another memory component that protects you from yourself, bad luck, and Mother Nature. This buffer records every SQL statement that changes data. The statement itself and any information required to reconstruct it is called a *redo entry.* Redo entries hang out here temporarily before being recorded on disk. This buffer protects against the loss of dirty blocks.

Dirty blocks aren't written to disk constantly.

Imagine that you have a buffer cache of 1,000 blocks and 100 of them are dirty. Then imagine a power supply goes belly up in your server and the whole system comes crashing down without any dirty buffers being written. That data is all lost, right? Not so fast. . . .

The redo log buffer is flushed when these things occur:

- Every time there's a commit to data in the database
- Every three seconds
- When the redo buffer is ⅓ full
- Just before each dirty block is written to disk

Why does Oracle bother maintaining this whole redo buffer thingy when instead, it could just write the dirty buffers to disk for every commit? It seems redundant.

- **The file that records this information is sequential.** Oracle always writes to the end of the file. It doesn't have to look up where to put the data. It just records the redo entry. A block exists somewhere in a file. Oracle has to find out where, go to that spot, and record it. Redo buffer writes are very quick in terms of I/O.
- **One small SQL statement could modify thousands or more database blocks.** It's much quicker to record that statement than wait for the I/O of thousands of blocks. The redo entry takes a split second to write, which reduces the window of opportunity for failure. It also only returns your commit if the write is successful. You know right away that your changes are safe. In the event of failure, the redo entry might have to be re-executed during recovery, but at least it isn't lost.

Large pool

We're not referring to the size of your neighbor's swimming pool. Not everyone uses the optional *large pool* component. The large pool relieves the shared pool of sometimes-transient memory requirements.

These features use the large pool:

- Oracle Recovery Manager
- Oracle Shared Server
- Parallel processing
- I/O-related server processes

Because many of these activities aren't constant and only allocate memory when they're running, it's more efficient to let them execute in their own space.

Without a large pool configured, these processes steal memory from the shared pool's SQL area. That can result in poor SQL processing and constant resizing of the SQL area of the shared pool. Note: The large pool has no LRU. Once it fills up (if you size it too small) the processes revert to their old behavior of stealing memory from the shared pool.

Java pool

The Java pool isn't a swimming pool filled with coffee (Okay, we're cutting off the pool references.) The *Java pool* is an optional memory component.

Starting in Oracle 8i, the database ships with its own *Java Virtual Machine (JVM),* which can execute Java code out of the SGA. In our experience, this configuration is relatively rare. In fact, we see this where Oracle-specific tools are installed.

However, don't let that discourage you from developing your own Java-based Oracle applications. The fact is, even though Oracle has its own Java container, many other worthwhile competing alternatives are out there.

Program Global Area

The *Program Global Area (PGA)* contains information used for private or session-related information that individual users need.

Again, this used to be allocated out of the shared pool. In Oracle 9i, a memory structure called the *instance PGA* held all private information as needed. This alleviated the need for the shared pool to constantly resize its SQL area to meet the needs of individual sessions. Because the amount of users constantly varies, as do their private memory needs, the instance PGA was designed for this type of memory usage.

The PGA contains the following:

- **Session memory**
  - Login information
  - Information such as settings specific to a session (for example, what format to use when dates are displayed)
- **Private SQL area**
  - Variables that might be assigned values during SQL execution
  - Work areas for processing specific SQL needs: sorting, hash-joins, bitmap operations
  - Cursors

Managing Memory

You have basically three ways to manage the memory in your instance:

- **Automatically** by letting Oracle do all the work
- **Manually** by tuning individual parameters for the different memory areas
- **Combination of automatic and manual** by using your knowledge of how things operate, employing Oracle's advice infrastructure, and letting Oracle take over some areas

First, a quick note on Oracle automation. Through the last three releases of Oracle (9i, 10g, and 11g) the database has become more automated in areas that were previously manual and even tedious at times. This isn't to say that soon it will take no special skill to manage an Oracle database. Exactly the opposite: When more mundane operations are automated, it frees you up as the DBA to focus on the more advanced features.

We've had great success implementing automated features for clients. It frees up our resources to focus on things such as high availability and security, areas that require near full-time attention. Thank goodness we don't have to spend hours watching what SQL is aging out of the shared pool prematurely.

We recommend that you manage memory automatically in Oracle 11g. For that reason, we only cover automatic management in this chapter.

Managing memory automatically

When you create your database, you can set one new parameter that takes nearly all memory tuning out of your hands: MEMORY_TARGET. By setting this parameter, all the memory areas discussed earlier in this chapter are automatically sized and managed. After you type this parameter in SQL*Plus — **show parameter memory_target** — (the SQL command-line interface available in Oracle), you see this output on the screen:

```
NAME TYPE VALUE
------------------------------------ ----------- ------------------------------
memory_target big integer 756M
```

Automatic memory management lets you take hold of the amount of memory on the system and then decide how much you want to use for the database.

It's never obvious what value you should choose as a starting point. Answer these questions to help set the value:

- How much memory is available?
- How many databases will ultimately be on the machine?
- How many users will be on the machine? (If many, we allocate 4MB per user for process overhead.)
- What other applications are running on the machine?

Before the users get on the machine, consider taking no more than 40 percent of the memory for Oracle databases. Use this formula:

> (GB of memory × .40) / Number of Eventual Databases =
> GB for MEMORY_TARGET per database

For example, if your machine had 8GB of memory and will ultimately house two databases similar in nature and only 100 users each, we would have this equation: (8 × .40) / 2 = 1.6GB for MEMORY_TARGET per database.

To help determine whether you have enough memory, Oracle gives you some pointers if you know where to look. It's called the Memory Target Advisor. Find it from the command line in the form of the view V$MEMORY_TARGET_ADVICE. As seen in Figure 2-1, find it in the Database Control home page by clicking Advisor Central➪Memory Advisors➪Advice.

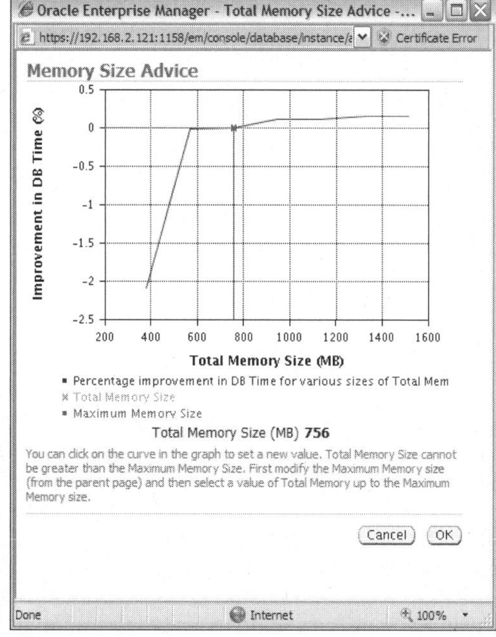

Figure 2-1: MEMORY_TARGET offers advice.

Whatever you choose for the MEMORY_TARGET setting isn't all the memory Oracle uses. That's why you should have an idea of how many sessions there will be *before* you make the final determination.

For instance, this parameter only covers memory used by the SGA and PGA. Every single session that connects to the database requires memory associated with its OS or server process. This adds up. One of our clients has nearly 3,000 simultaneous connections eating up about 16GB of memory outside the SGA and PGA. The client's machine has 64GB of memory and the MEMORY_TARGET is set at 16GB.

Following the Oracle Processes

When you start and initiate connections to the Oracle instance, many processes are involved, including

- The component of the Oracle instance that uses the Oracle programs
- Code to gain access to your data

There are no processes when the Oracle instance is shut down. Some of the processes are mandatory and others are optional depending on the features you've enabled. It can also depend on your OS.

Three types of processes are part of the instance:

- **Background processes** are involved in running the Oracle software itself.
- **Server processes** negotiate the actions of the users.
- **User processes** commonly work outside the database server itself to run the application that accesses the database.

Background processes

In Oracle 11g, you can have around 212 background processes. We say *around* because it varies by operating system. If this sounds like a lot, don't be scared. Many are multiples of the same process (for parallelism and taking advantage of systems with multiple CPUs). Table 2-1 shows the most common background processes.

By default, no processes have more than one instance of their type started. More advanced tuning features involve parallelism. To see a complete list of all the background processes on your OS, query V$BGPROCESS.

Table 2-1 Common Background Processes

Background Process Name	***Description***
PMON	The *process monitor* (or P-MOM, because it cleans up after you like your mother did when you were a kid) manages the system's server processes. It cleans up failed processes by releasing resources and rolling back uncommitted data.
SMON	The *system monitor* is primarily responsible for instance recovery. If the database crashes and redo information must be read and applied, the SMON takes care of it. It also cleans and releases temporary space.
DBW*n*	The *database writer's* sole job is taking dirty blocks from the dirty list and writing them to disk. There can be up to 20 of them, hence the *n*. It starts as DBW0 and continues with DBW1, DBW2, and so on. After DBW9, it continues with DBWa through DBWj. An average system won't see more than a few of these.
LGWR	The *log writer* process flushes the redo log buffer. It writes the redo entries to disk and signals a completion.
CKPT	The *checkpoint process* is responsible for initiating check points. A check point is when the system periodically dumps all the dirty buffers to disk. Most commonly, this occurs when the database receives a shutdown command. It also updates the data file headers and the control files with the check point information so the SMON know where to start recovery in the event of a system crash.
ARC*n*	Up to 30 *archiver* processes (0–9, a–t) are responsible for copying filled redo logs to the archived redo storage area. If your database isn't running in archive mode, this process shuts down.
CJQ0	The *job queue* coordinator checks for scheduled tasks within the database. These jobs can be set up by the user or can be internal jobs for maintenance. When it finds a job that must be run it spawns the following goodie.
J000	A *job queue process slave* actually runs the job. There can be up to 1,000 of them (000–999).
DIA0	The *diagnosability* process resolves deadlock situations and investigates hanging issues.
VKTM	The *virtual keeper of time* sounds like a fantasy game character but simply provides a time reference within the database.

Other background processes exist, as you can tell by the "around 212" number we stated at the beginning of this section. However, those described in Table 2-1 are the most common, and you will find them on almost all Oracle installations. When you engage some of Oracle's more advanced functionality, you'll see other processes.

It's very easy to see these background processes if you have an Oracle installation available on Linux or UNIX. In Figure 2-2, ps –ef |grep ora_lists the background processes. This works very well since all background processes begin with ora_.

```
oracle@classroom:~
[oracle@classroom ~]$ ps -ef |grep ora_
oracle   11125     1  0 12:05 ?        00:00:00 ora_w000_dev11g
oracle   11501     1  0 12:10 ?        00:00:00 ora_j000_dev11g
oracle   11648 10996  0 12:11 pts/1    00:00:00 grep ora_
oracle   18052     1  0 Jul31 ?        00:00:05 ora_pmon_dev11g
oracle   18054     1  0 Jul31 ?        00:00:00 ora_vktm_dev11g
oracle   18058     1  0 Jul31 ?        00:00:00 ora_diag_dev11g
oracle   18060     1  0 Jul31 ?        00:00:00 ora_dbrm_dev11g
oracle   18062     1  0 Jul31 ?        00:00:02 ora_psp0_dev11g
oracle   18066     1  0 Jul31 ?        00:00:00 ora_dia0_dev11g
oracle   18068     1  0 Jul31 ?        00:00:00 ora_mman_dev11g
oracle   18070     1  0 Jul31 ?        00:00:09 ora_dbw0_dev11g
oracle   18072     1  0 Jul31 ?        00:00:19 ora_lgwr_dev11g
oracle   18074     1  0 Jul31 ?        00:00:18 ora_ckpt_dev11g
oracle   18076     1  0 Jul31 ?        00:00:11 ora_smon_dev11g
oracle   18078     1  0 Jul31 ?        00:00:00 ora_reco_dev11g
oracle   18080     1  0 Jul31 ?        00:00:13 ora_mmon_dev11g
oracle   18082     1  0 Jul31 ?        00:00:04 ora_mmnl_dev11g
oracle   18084     1  0 Jul31 ?        00:00:00 ora_d000_dev11g
oracle   18086     1  0 Jul31 ?        00:00:01 ora_s000_dev11g
oracle   18094     1  0 Jul31 ?        00:00:03 ora_rvwr_dev11g
oracle   19303     1  0 Jul31 ?        00:00:01 ora_arc0_dev11g
oracle   19305     1  0 Jul31 ?        00:00:01 ora_arc1_dev11g
oracle   19307     1  0 Jul31 ?        00:00:01 ora_arc2_dev11g
oracle   19309     1  0 Jul31 ?        00:00:01 ora_arc3_dev11g
oracle   19311     1  0 Jul31 ?        00:00:00 ora_ctwr_dev11g
oracle   19348     1  0 Jul31 ?        00:00:00 ora_smco_dev11g
oracle   19350     1  0 Jul31 ?        00:00:01 ora_fbda_dev11g
oracle   19383     1  0 Jul31 ?        00:00:00 ora_qmnc_dev11g
oracle   19390     1  0 Jul31 ?        00:00:00 ora_q000_dev11g
oracle   19392     1  0 Jul31 ?        00:00:00 ora_q001_dev11g
oracle   19473     1  0 Jul31 ?        00:00:03 ora_cjq0_dev11g
[oracle@classroom ~]$
```

Figure 2-2: The Oracle background process list.

User and server processes

Because user and server processes are intertwined, we discuss the two together. However, they are distinct and separate processes. As a matter of fact, they typically run on separate machines. A very simple example: When you start SQL*Plus on a Windows client, you get a *user process* called sqlplus.exe. When a connection is made to the database on a Linux machine, you get a connection to a process named something like oracle<database_name> or ora_S000_<database_name>.

The *server process* serves. It does anything the user requests of it. It is responsible for reading blocks into the buffer cache. It changes the blocks if requested. It can create objects.

Server processes can be one of two types:

- Dedicated
- Shared

The type depends on how your application operates and how much memory you have. You're first presented with the choice of dedicated or shared when you create your database with Oracle's *Database Creation Assistant (DBCA)*. However, you can change it one way or the other later on.

Dedicated server architecture

Each user process gets its own server process. This is the most common Oracle configuration. It allows a server process to wait on you. If the resources can support dedicated connections, this also is the most responsive method. However, it can also use the most memory. Even if you're not doing anything, that server process is waiting for you.

Not that it's a bad thing. Imagine, though, 5,000 users on the system sitting idle most of the time. If your applications can't use connection pools (similar to shared server processes), your database probably won't survive and perform adequately for more than a day.

Shared server architecture

Just as the name implies, the *server processes* are shared. Now, instead of a server process waiting on you hand and foot, you only have one when you need it.

Think of a server process as a timeshare for Oracle. It's more cost-effective (in terms of memory), and you almost always have one available when you need it (provided the infrastructure is properly configured).

On a system with 5,000 mostly idle users, you might be able to support them with only 50 server processes. You must do these things for this to work properly:

- Make sure the number of concurrent database requests never exceeds the number of shared servers configured.
- Make sure users don't hold on to the processes for long periods. This works best in a fast transaction-based environment like an e-commerce site.
- Have a few extra CPU cycles available. All the interprocess communication seems to have small CPU cost associated with it over dedicated server processes.

The fact is shared server configurations are less common in today's environment where memory is cheap. Most applications these days get around the problems associated with too many dedicated servers by using advanced connection pooling on the application server level.

You should know about some other limitations: DBA connections must have a dedicated server. Therefore, a shared server environment is actually a hybrid. Shared servers can coexist with a dedicated server.

Getting into Physical Structures

The *physical structures* are the files that actually live on disk in the system. We call them *physical* because they have measurable physical properties (even though they're just magnetic blips on a rotating platter). However, they are present even if you completely power down the system.

The physical structures are accessed by way of the memory and processes of the running Oracle instance. In essence, the memory and processes are translators that convert the magnetic blips into something you can read and understand. Well . . . most of the time you can understand it.

Many different types of files are required (and optional) to run an Oracle database:

- Data files
- Control files
- Redo log files
- Archive log files
- Server and initialization parameter files

Knowing what each of these files does greatly increases your database management success.

Getting Physical with Files

Many types of files are created with your database. Some of these files are for storing raw data. Some are used for recovery. Some are used for housekeeping or maintenance of the database itself. In the next few sections, we take a look at the various file types and what they are responsible for storing.

Data files: Where the data meets the disk

Data files are the largest file types in an Oracle database. They store all the actual data you put into your database, as well as the data Oracle requires to manage the database. Data files are a physical structure: They exist whether the database is open or closed.

Data files are also binary in nature. You can't read them yourself without starting an instance and executing queries. The data is stored in an organized format broken up into Oracle blocks.

Whenever a server process reads from a data file, it does so by reading at the very least one complete block. It puts that block into the buffer cache so that data can be accessed, modified, and so on.

It's also worth noting that the data file is physically created using OS blocks. OS blocks are different from Oracle blocks. *OS blocks* are physical, and their size is determined when you initially format the hard drive.

You should know the size of your OS block. Make sure that it's equal to, or evenly divisible into, your Oracle block.

Most of the time Oracle data files have an extension of .DBF (short for database file?). But the fact of the matter is that file extensions in Oracle don't matter. You could name it .XYZ and it will function just fine.

We feel it is best practice to stick with .DBF because that extension is used in 95 percent of databases.

In every data file, the very first block stores the block header. To be specific, depending on your Oracle block size, the data file header block may be several blocks. By default, the header block is 64k. Therefore, if your Oracle block size is 4k, then 16 header blocks are at the beginning of the file. These header blocks are for managing the data file's internal workings. They contain

- Backup and recovery information
- Free space information
- File status details

Lastly, a *tempfile* is a special type of database file. Physically, it's just like a regular data file, but it only holds temporary information. For example, a tempfile is used if you perform sorts on disk or if you're using temporary tables. The space is then freed to the file either immediately after your operation is done or once you log out of the system.

Figure 2-3 shows that by executing a simple query against V$TEMPFILE and V$DATAFILE you can see a listing of the data files in your database.

```
oracle@classroom:~
SQL> select name
  2  from v$datafile
  3  union
  4  select name
  5  from v$tempfile;

NAME
--------------------------------------------------------------------------------
/u01/app/oracle/flash_recovery_area/DEV11G/datafile/o1_mf_users_47kn9j0z_.dbf
/u01/app/oracle/oradata/dev11g/example01.dbf
/u01/app/oracle/oradata/dev11g/sysaux01.dbf
/u01/app/oracle/oradata/dev11g/system01.dbf
/u01/app/oracle/oradata/dev11g/temp01.dbf
/u01/app/oracle/oradata/dev11g/undotbs01.dbf

6 rows selected.

SQL>
```

Figure 2-3: Data files listed.

Control files

The control file is a very important file in the database — so important that you have several copies of it. These copies are placed so that losing a disk on your system doesn't result in losing *all* of your control files.

Typically, *control files* are named with the extension .CTL or .CON. Any extension will work, but if you want to follow best practice, those two are the most popular.

Control files contain the following things:

- Names and locations of your data files and redo log files
- Recovery information
- Backup information
- Checkpoint information
- Archiving information
- Database name
- Log history
- Current logging information

Control files contain a host of other internal information as well. Typically, control files are some of the smaller files in the database. It's difficult to tell you how big they are because it varies depending on this:

- How many files your database has
- How much backup information you're storing in them
- What OS you're using

As mentioned earlier, it's important that you have several copies of your control files. If you were to lose all of your control files in an unfortunate failure, it is a real pain to fix.

Redo log files

Redo log files store the information from the log buffer. They're written to by the *Log Writer (LGWR).* Again, you can't read these binary files without the help of the database software.

Typically, redo log files are named with the extension .LOG or .RDO. It can be anything you want, but best practice indicates one of those two extensions. Also, redo log files are organized into groups and members. Every database must have at least two redo log groups.

Redo log files contain all the information necessary to recover lost data in your database. Every SQL statement that you issue changing data can be reconstructed by the information saved in these files.

Redo log files don't record select statements. If you forget what you selected, you're just going to have to remember that on your own!

The optimal size for your redo log files depends on how many changes you make to your database. The size is chosen by you when you set up the database and can be adjusted later. When the LGWR is writing to a redo log file, it does so sequentially. It starts at the beginning of the file and once it is filled up, it moves on to the next one. This is where the concept of *groups* comes in. Oracle fills each group and moves to the next. Once it has filled all the groups, it goes back to the first. You could say they are written to in a circular fashion. If you have three groups, it would go something like 1,2,3,1,2,3, . . . and so on.

Each time a group fills and the writing switches, it's called a *log switch operation.* These things happen during a log switch operation:

- The LGWR finishes writing to the current group.
- The LGWR starts writing to the next group.
- A database check point occurs.
- The DBWR writes dirty blocks out of the buffer cascade.

How fast each group fills up is how you determine its size. By looking at all the things that occur when a log switch happens, you might agree that it is a fairly involved operation. For this reason, you don't want frequent log switches.

The general rule is that you don't want to switch log files more often than every 15–30 minutes. If you find that happening, consider increasing the size of each group.

Because these redo log files may be involved in recovery operations, don't lose them. Similar to control files, redo log files should be configured with mirrored copies of one another. And, as with control files, each member should be on a separate disk device. That way, if a disk fails and the database goes down, you still have recovery information available. You should not lose any data.

Each copy within a group is called a *member.* A common configuration might be three groups with two members apiece, for a total of six redo log files. The group members are written to simultaneously by the log writer.

- **How many groups are appropriate?** The most common configuration we come across is three. You want enough that the first group in the list can be copied off and saved before the LGWR comes back around to use it. If it hasn't been copied off, the LGWR has to wait until that operation is complete. This can severely impact your system. Thankfully, we rarely see this happen.
- **How many members are appropriate?** It depends on how paranoid you are. Two members on two disks seems to be pretty common. However, it isn't uncommon to see three members on three disks. More than that and you're just plain crazy. Well, not really. It's just that the more members you have, the more work the LGWR has to do. It can impact system performance at the same time offering very little return.

We commonly get this question: If my disks are mirrored at the hardware level, do I need more than one member on each group? After all, if a disk fails, I have another one right there to pick up the slack.

Unfortunately, you get different answers depending on who you ask. Ask us, and we'll recommend at least two members for each group:

- Oracle still recommends two members for each group as a best practice.
- Depending on how your hardware is set up, you may have the same disk controller writing to your disk mirrors. What if that controller writes corrupt gibberish? Now both your copies are corrupted. Separating your members across two different disks with different controllers is the safest bet.

Moving to the archives

Archive log files are simply copies of redo log files. They're no different from redo log files except that they get a new name when they're created.

Most archive log files have the extension .ARC, .ARCH, or .LOG. We try to use .ARC as that seems most common.

Not all databases have archive log files. It depends on whether you turn on archiving. By turning on archiving, you can recover from nearly any type of failure providing two things:

- You have a full backup.
- You haven't lost all copies of the redo or archive logs.

There is a small amount of overhead with database archiving:

- **I/O cost:** The ARCn process has to copy each redo log group as it fills up.
- **CPU cost:** It takes extra processing to copy the redo logs via the ARCn process.
- **Storage cost:** You have to keep all the archive logs created between each backup.

Relatively speaking, each of these costs is small in terms of the return you get: recovering your database without so much as losing the dot over an *i*. We typically recommend that, across the board, all production databases archive their redo logs.

Sometimes, archiving isn't needed, such as in a test database used for testing code. You can easily just copy your production database to revive a broken test. We're not recommending *not* archiving on test databases. Sometimes the test database is important enough to archive. We're just saying that sometimes you can get by without incurring the extra overhead.

You should keep archive log files for recovery between each backup. Say you're doing a backup every Sunday. Now say that your database loses files due to a disk failure on Wednesday. The recovery process would be restoring the lost files from the last backup, and then telling Oracle to apply the archive log files from Sunday all the way up to the failure on Wednesday. It's called *rolling forward,* and we talk about it in Chapter 8.

Like control files and redo log files, it's best practice to have more than one copy of each of your archive log files. They should go to two different destinations on different devices, just like the others. You can't skip over a lost archive log.

Server and initialization parameter files

Server and initialization parameter files are the smallest files on your system:

- **PFILE**, or *parameter file,* is a text version that you can read and edit with a normal text editor
- **SPFILE**, or *server parameter file,* is a binary copy that you create for the database to use after you make changes.

Typically, these files with an .ORA extension. Personally, we have never seen anything but that. It's best practice for you to continue the tradition.

PFILEs and SPFILEs have information about how your running database is configured. This is where you configure the following settings:

- Memory size
- Database and instance name
- Archiving parameters
- Processes
- Over 1,900 other parameters

Wait, what was that? Over 1900 parameters to configure and tweak? Don't be frightened. The fact is 99 percent of your database configuration is done with about 30 of the main parameters. The other 1,900 are for uncommon configurations that require more expert adjustment. As a matter of fact, of those 1,900, over 1,600 are hidden. Sorry if we scared you a little there. We just want you to have the whole picture.

Whenever you start your database, the very first file read is the parameter file. It sets up all your memory and process settings and tells the instance where the control files are located. It also has information about your archiving status.

The PFILEs and SPFILEs are under the directory where you installed the database software. This directory is called the ORACLE_HOME:

- **Linux/UNIX:** $ORACLE_HOME/dbs
- **Windows:** %ORACLE_HOME\database

It should have a specific naming structure. For example, if your database name is dev11g, the files would be named as follows:

- The PFILE would be called initdev11g.ora.
- The SPFILE would be called spfiledev11g.ora.

By naming them this way and putting them in the appropriate directory, Oracle automatically finds them when you start the database. Else, you have to tell Oracle where they are every time you start the database; that just isn't convenient.

We recommend you keep the PFILE and SPFILE in the default locations with the default naming convention for ease of administration.

Applying Some Logical Structures

After you know the physical structures, you can break them into more logical structures. All the logical structures that we talk about are in the data files. Logical structures allow you to organize your data into manageable and, well, logical, pieces.

Without logical breakdown of the raw, physical storage, your database would

- Be difficult to manage
- Be poorly tuned
- Make it hard to find data
- Require the highly trained and special skill set of a madman

Figure 2-4 show the relationship of logical to physical objects. The arrow points in the direction of a one-to-many relationship.

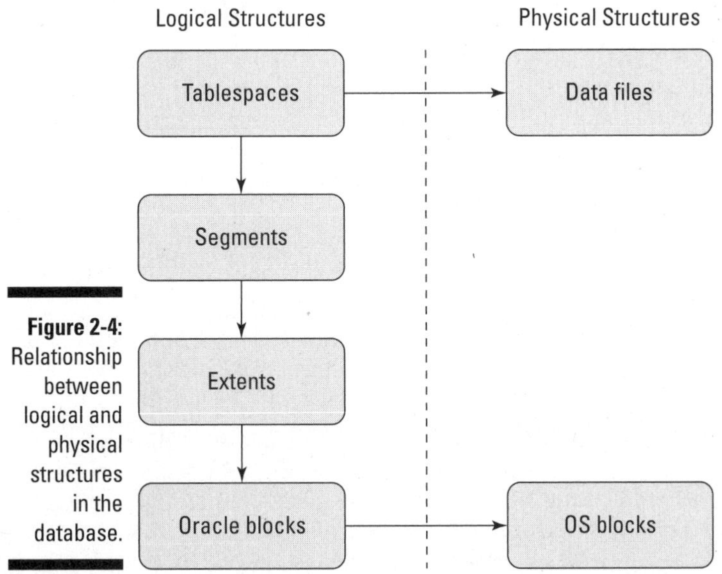

Figure 2-4: Relationship between logical and physical structures in the database.

Tablespaces

Tablespaces are the first level of logical organization of your physical storage.

Every 11g database should have the following tablespaces:

- **SYSTEM:** Stores the core database objects that are used for running the database itself.
- **SYSAUX:** For objects that are auxiliary and not specifically tied to the core features of the database.
- **UNDO:** Stores the rollback or undo segments used for transaction recovery.
- **TEMP:** For temporary storage.

Each tablespace is responsible for organizing one or more data files. Typically, each tablespace might start attached to one data file, but as the database grows and your files become large, you may decide to add storage in the form of multiple data files.

The next step to getting your database up and running? Creating some areas to store your data. Say your database is going to have sales, human resources, accounting data, and historical data. You might have the following tablespaces:

- SALES_DATA
- SALES_INDEX
- HR_DATA
- HR_INDEX
- ACCOUNTING_DATA
- ACCOUNTING_INDEX
- HISTORY_DATA
- HISTORY_INDEX

Separating tables and indexes both logically and physically is common in a database.

- Since tablespaces must have at least one data file associated with them, you can create them so data files are physically on separate devices and therefore improve performance.
- You can harden our databases against complete failure. Tablespaces can be backed up and recovered from one another independently. Say you lose a data file in the SALES index tablespace. You can take only the SALES_INDEX tablespace offline to recover it while human resources, accounting, and anyone accessing historical data is none the wiser.

We discuss actual tablespace creation in Chapter 7.

Keep in mind that when deciding on the logical organization, it pays to sit down and map out all the different activities your database will support. If possible, create tablespaces for every major application and its associated indexes.

If your database has especially large subsets of data, sometimes it pays to separate that data from your regular data as well. For example, say you're storing lots of still pictures. Those pictures probably never change. If you have a tablespace dedicated to them, you can make it read only. The tablespace is taken out of the checkpointing process. You can also back it up once, and then do it again only after it changes. That reduces the storage required for backups, plus it speeds up your backup process.

Segments

Segments are the next logical storage structure next to tablespaces. *Segments* are objects in the database that require physical storage and include the following:

- Tables
- Indexes
- Materialized views
- Partitions

These object examples are *not* segments and don't store actual data:

- Views
- Procedures
- Synonyms
- Sequences

The latter list of objects don't live in a tablespace with segments. They're pieces of code that live in the SYSTEM tablespace.

Whenever you create a segment, specify what tablespace you want it to be part of. This helps with performance.

For example, you probably want the table EMPLOYEES stored in the HR_DATA tablespace. In addition, if you have an index on the LAST_NAME column of the EMPLOYEES table, you want to make sure it is created in the HR_INDEXES tablespace. That way, when people are searching for and retrieving employee information, they're not trying to read the index off the same data file that the table data is stored in.

Extents

Extents are like the growth rings of a tree. Whenever a segment grows, it gains a new extent. When you first create a table to store items, it gets its first extent. As you insert data into that table, that extent fills up. When the extent fills up, it grabs another extent from the tablespace.

When you first create a tablespace, it's all free space. When you start creating objects, that free space gets assigned to segments in the form of extents. Your average tablespace is made up of used extents and free space.

When all the free space is filled, that data file is out of space. That's when your DBA skills come in and you decide how to make more free space available for the segments to continue extending.

Extents aren't necessarily contiguous. For example, when you create or items table and insert the first 1,000 items, it may grow and extend several times. Now your segment might be made up of five extents. However, you also create a new table. As each table is created in a new tablespace, it starts at the beginning of the data file. After you create your second table, your first table may need to extend again. Its next extent comes after the second extent. In the end, all objects that share a tablespace will have their extents intermingled.

This isn't a bad thing. In years past, before Oracle had better algorithms for storage, DBAs spent a lot of their time and efforts trying to coalesce these extents. It was called *fragmentation.* It's a thing of the past but we still see people getting all up in arms about it. Don't get sucked in! Just let it be. Oracle 11g is fully capable of managing such situations.

I also want to mention situations where you have multiple data files in a tablespace. If a tablespace has more than one data file, the tablespace automatically creates extents in a round-robin fashion across all the data files. This is another Oracle performance feature.

Say you have one large table that supports most of your application. It lives in a tablespace made of four data files. As the table extends, Oracle allocates the extents across each data file like this:

1,2,3,4,1,2,3,4,1,2,3,4 . . . and so on

This way, Oracle can take advantage of the data spread across many physical devices when users access data. It reduces contention on segments that have a lot of activity.

Oracle blocks

We have mentioned these at least twice before. They had to be mentioned when talking about the buffer cache and data files. Let's fill in a little more information.

An *Oracle block* is the minimum unit that Oracle will read or write at any given time.

Oracle usually reads and writes more than one block at once, but that's up to Oracle these days. You used to have more direct control but now of the option is automatically tuned. You can tune it manually to a certain extent, but most installations are best left to Oracle.

Regardless, blocks are the final logical unit of storage. Data from your tables and indexes are stored in blocks. The following things happen when you insert a new row into a table:

- Oracle finds the segment.
- Oracle asks that segment if there's any room.
- The segment returns a block that's not full.
- The row or index entry is added to that block.

If no blocks are free for inserts, the segment grabs another free extent from the tablespace. By the way, all this is done by the server process to which you're attached.

Oracle blocks themselves also have a physical counterpart as the data files do. They are made up of OS blocks. It is the formatted size of the minimum unit of storage on the device.

Oracle blocks should be evenly divisible by your OS block size. Oracle blocks should never be smaller than your OS block size. We discuss Oracle block sizing more in Chapter 4.

Chapter 3

Preparing to Implement Oracle in the Real World

In This Chapter

- Understanding Oracle Deployment Methodologies
- Verifying system requirements
- Planning server and disk configuration
- Post-installation setup steps

Before you create databases and store your data, you need to plan a few things that will make your implementation much easier. First and foremost, you need to determine your overall database architecture. Databases don't exist as standalone entities; they're part of an *information system,* and you need to understand how that system is laid out. This chapter looks at two of the most common deployment methodologies and helps you determine which method is right for you.

After you determine the right overall deployment plan, you need to make sure that your target environment meets the necessary requirements to host Oracle. This chapter not only looks at obvious requirements, such as server hardware and software, but it also looks at less reviewed (yet critical) requirements, such as user, configuration, and storage considerations. This chapter gives you the knowledge to make good judgments of where and how your Oracle database will be implemented.

Understanding Oracle Database Deployment Methodology

Oracle databases don't simply exist in isolation; they act as part of a computer system. Before installing your database, you need to know how your database fits into the overall system architecture. Some systems are more complex than others, but most fall into the following basic categories:

- Client-server
- Multi-tier
- Component configurations

Knowing which category your database fits into will make a big difference during your system setup because you'll know the specific needs of your database.

Client-server applications

Client-server applications (sometimes called *two-tier*) are those in which the user's workstation has the application program installed and, during execution, the program accesses data stored on a remote database server. Although you have some wiggle room here, the workstation handles the presentation and application logic, and the database server acts as a data store. Figure 3-1 shows how a client-server configuration works.

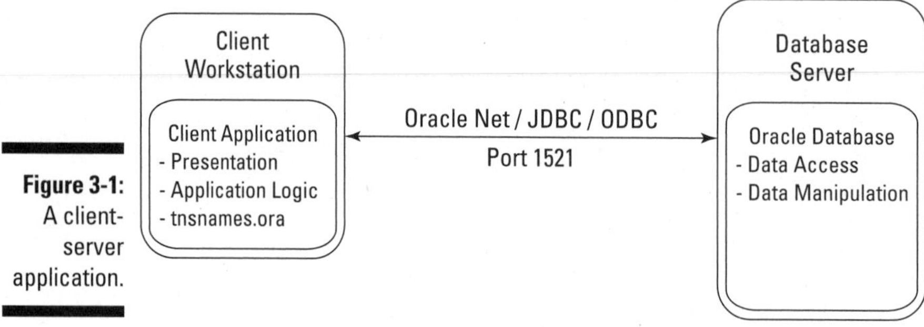

Figure 3-1: A client-server application.

In Figure 3-1, the workstation (client-tier) handles the application logic and presentation to the user. Application logic may be implanted via many different languages, but common examples include PowerBuilder, MS Visual Basic, Java applications, and even some versions of Oracle Forms and Reports. When these client-side applications need data, they access the database via ODBC (Open Database Connectivity), JDBC (Java Database Connectivity), or Oracle Net using client-side tnsnames.ora files. These database communication protocols allow connectivity from any client to any database, including Oracle.

On the database tier, the database stores the data and, via users, roles, and permissions, it provides that data to the application in response to SQL queries and data manipulation language (DML) statements (which are simply SQL statements that manipulate, or change, the data). Depending on whether you're using a *fat* or *thin* client, some of the application logic and processing may be off-loaded to the database tier. Processing on the database server often makes sense because a database server can do much more intensive processing and number-crunching than even the largest workstation. Data processing is commonly executed via database procedures, functions, and packages, which process the data into a smaller result set to be returned to the client for presentation to the user.

Many people have claimed that client-server is dead. If it is, why are so many client-server applications still out there? Sure, the client-server architecture is older, and many newer applications exist in the multi-tier world. However, a simple client-server application still meets the immediate needs of a business in some situations. Or the client-server application may be an existing legacy application that does its job — so the business has no need to upgrade. Regardless, while we don't recommend developing new, large-scale systems on this model, we can't deny that client-server applications still exist in many organizations.

Muli-tier applications

Multi-tier applications are the current industry standard and compose multiple web, application, and database servers providing content to thin clients with presentation via a web browser. Ever wonder what's behind the scenes when you login to a web application for online purchases or banking? Well, it looks something like Figure 3-2.

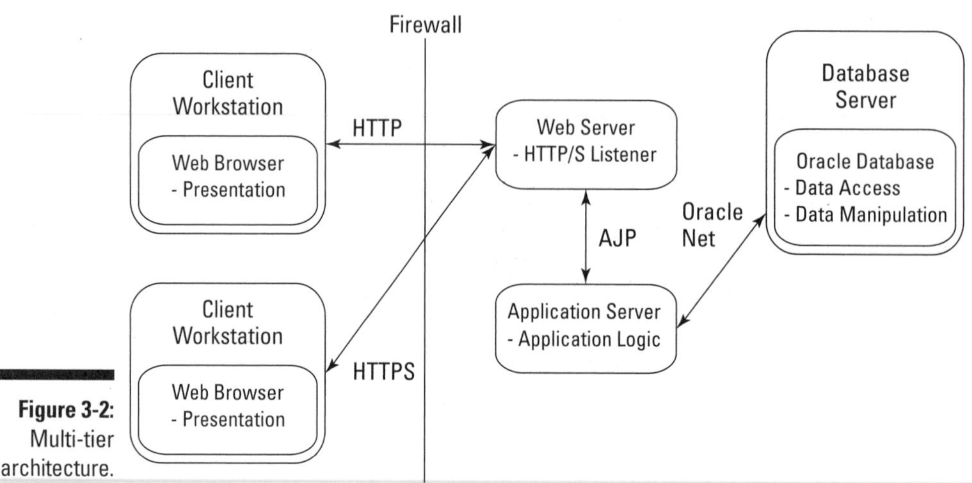

Figure 3-2: Multi-tier architecture.

In Figure 3-2, the client-tier is merely a web browser accessing a web server. Displaying content to the user is the primary purpose of the client in this architecture; no actual processing occurs at this layer within the browser. Presentation occurs most commonly via HTML (HyperText Markup Language), but it can also be within a Java Applet or ActiveX component and use JavaScript for more dynamic formatting and content.

Communication from the browser to the web server occurs via HTTP (HyperText Transfer Protocol) or HTTPS for secure (encrypted) data. Web servers conceptually act as web listeners; they receive requests from browsers and return formatted result sets with little processing on their own. Once on the web server, the browser request is parsed and sent to the appropriate application server for processing. The application server component may be on the same physical server as the web server, or it may be on another physical server. By far, the most common web server is Apache, or one of its commercial derivates, with 50 percent of the marketshare according to http://news.netcraft.com/archives/web_server_survey.html.

At the application server level, the user request is processed using the relevant application logic. One very common method is to use a Java application server, such as Tomcat, Orion, or Glassfish. In this case, the program logic is executed inside a Java Virtual Machine (JVM), which acts as the runtime environment for the program code.

Another popular tool is Oracle 10gAS (Application Server). Within 10gAS, the program may run as Oracle Forms, Reports, Discoverer, or even Java via Oracle Containers for J2EE (OC4J). Regardless of the product, it's within the application server component that the application logic is executed.

During processing on the application server, it's common to need database access to query, create, update, or delete data. The application server communicates with the database server via protocols, such as JDBC or Oracle Net, to access the data. During this time, the application server is accessing the database on behalf of the user making the application request. Rather than connecting as a named, distinct user such as JSMITH, the application server connects using a generic web account (such as WEB_USER). Multiple simultaneous connections from the application server to the database form a *connection pool* that allows any database connection to access data for a request. Connection pooling is a performance benefit because only a few database connections can service thousands of requests on behalf of many users.

Once logged into the database instance, the generic web user queries or executes DML on behalf of the application server, which is processing an actual user request. The connection pooled web user doesn't have schema ownership into the database; it has only those permissions needed to access or update data on behalf of the application server. During this time, normal database roles, permissions, and grants are utilized. Additionally, database program logic implemented in PL/SQL via procedures, functions, and packages is often executed.

After the data result set is generated on the database-tier, it's passed back to the application server for more processing. Next, the results are relayed back through the web server and across the network for presentation to the user via their web browser.

Sounds complicated with all the various components? You may think so at first, but good reasons exist for breaking the system into web, application, and database components:

- You can use components from different vendors in a "best of breed" configuration. For example, you can use a free Apache web server instance coupled with Tomcat or Glassfish for a cheap application server component. Then tie that to the power of the Oracle database, and you have yourself a solid system at lower costs!
- As more users come online, you can add more web, application, or database server instances to boost your processing power. Rather than buying bigger servers, just buy smaller servers.
- After you have a series of multiple servers, you gain fault tolerance. If a web server crashes or the application server needs maintenance, no problem — the redundant servers will pick up the workload.

Hopefully, these benefits show why muti-tier system architectures are the industry standard and have surpassed client-server systems.

Component configurations

In client-server and multi-tier systems, the Oracle database was the core of the system because it holds the data. Existing as the primary data store for the entire system is the most common use of an Oracle database, but it's not the only time you'll have to install Oracle. Often, these databases serve a support role by acting as secondary data stores for larger Commercial Off The Shelf (COTS) applications. In these cases, Oracle databases act as repositories storing specialized data for use within a larger system. During installation of the larger system, the Oracle database is installed as a supporting component.

One common example of an Oracle repository you may be familiar with is Oracle Designer. You can use this Oracle developer tool to design, create, and store application code (among other things), and it resides on the user's desktop. When the user starts Oracle Designer, it prompts for an Oracle repository to connect to, and the user specifies that information. It is within that repository that all the objects to be used by the Designer desktop are stored. In this case, Designer is following the client-server model described in the section "Client-server applications," earlier in this chapter.

Oracle Internet Directory (OID) is a more current example of Oracle acting as a subcomponent within a multi-tiered environment. OID is Oracle's implementation of an *LDAP (Lightweight Directory Access Protocol)*. LDAPs are hierarchically defined (not relational) data-stores (not databases) that allow systems quick lookup access of data. A common example is an email address book, which doesn't contain a lot of updates or deeply layered data — it's just a need for quick lookups of a piece of data, which is the core use of an LDAP.

Another common LDAP use is to store users and their credentials so that web application servers can simply look up a person to see whether she is authorized to access a system. After all, you don't want to allow just anyone into your system! This credential verification is a big need for Oracle's Application Server products (10gAS), and an LDAP is the solution. And, of course, with Oracle being a database company first and foremost, it opted to put its LDAP implementation inside an Oracle database, which is OID (see Figure 3-3).

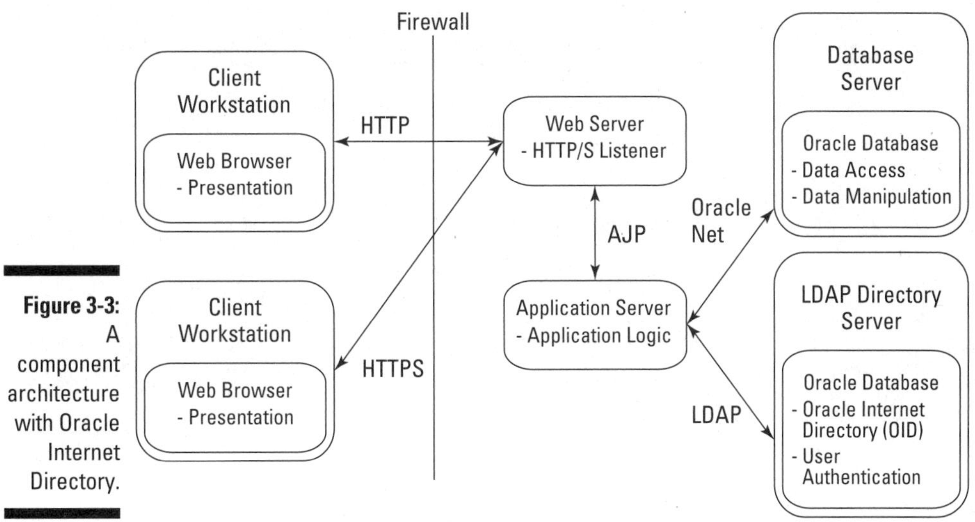

Figure 3-3: A component architecture with Oracle Internet Directory.

Figure 3-3 shows how a specialized Oracle database can provide authentication via OID/LDAP for a larger system that also happens to use Oracle for the backend database where traditional customer data is stored. The OID is just a necessary component in a larger system.

The idea of this section isn't to make you an authority on Oracle Designer or OID. Rather, it's to show you that Oracle is more than just "the database" for large applications; Oracle also appears in critical support roles. Your Oracle installation may be for one of these support components, but don't discount the importance of such a database. Without the supporting Oracle component database the overall system would not be functional.

Checking on the Requirements

Oracle databases are very good at storing and accessing data, but a little prep work will allow them to run even better. Before installing the Oracle software, you need to do a little homework to ensure that your server will support the software. (For installation information, see Part VI.)

Each release of Oracle databases is better than the previous one, but each version also has minor updates to the installation requirements. Oracle does a good job of documenting these detail updates for the myriad versions it supports and making them available on its web site at oracle.com/technology/documentation/database.html.

Pay particular interest to the Installation Guide and Quick Installation Guide for your *operating system (OS).*

You can avoid many of the installation problems people experience by just spending a few minutes reviewing the Oracle Installation Guide for your specific OS and meeting those requirements. A quick review of this guide before installing a new version can save you hours troubleshooting issues because you're not making mistakes that Oracle has already documented.

User and directory requirements

On UNIX- and Linux-based systems, you install and run Oracle as a specific user and group. In most cases, the user is called *oracle,* the primary group *oinstall,* and the secondary group *dba*. Here's a sample of how this user is defined:

```
$ id
uid=501(oracle) gid=501(oinstall) groups=501(oinstall),502(dba))
```

On Windows systems, the software should be installed by a member of the Local Administrators group for the machine.

It's common to have multiple versions of Oracle running on the same machine simultaneously. To avoid chaos, you need to organize how and where each version is installed. The framework commonly used to organize and install Oracle software is called *Optimal Flexible Architecture (OFA).* You can use this organizational hierarchy to install your Oracle software based on software versions and common directories used by all versions.

Key to the OFA are the directory environment variables ORACLE_BASE and ORACLE_HOME:

- ORACLE_BASE is where you can find common software used by all Oracle software versions; it's the base of underlying Oracle code trees.
- ORACLE_HOME is a subdirectory and denotes the location where a specific version of Oracle database software is installed, often associated with one or more database instances.

Here's the hierarchy:

```
/<directory name>/app/oracle/product/<version number>/<actual software>
```

Table 3-1 describes each level of the hierarchy.

Table 3-1 OFA Hierarchy

Level	*Description*
<*directory name*>	Base directory, file system, or drive name
app	Directory name denoting application software will be located in this tree
oracle	Owner of the software and is defined as ORACLE_BASE
product	Holding directory for software trees
version number	Directory with unique version number containing the actual software installation. Defined as ORACLE_HOME

Here's how this hierarchy exists on UNIX or Linux:

```
/u01/app/oracle/product/11.1.0
```

And on Windows:

```
d:\app\oracle\product\11.1.0
```

In both cases, the oracle is ORACLE_BASE, and 11.1.0 is ORACLE_HOME. The Oracle installation tool guides you through identifying these locations, but you need to understand why each location is defined so you can better organize your software installations.

In the ORACLE_BASE directory, an Oracle Inventory directory is created as *oraInventory*. Within this directory, Oracle logs a record of all Oracle software that has been installed, patched, and removed from the server. This information is used so that the Oracle *Universal Installer (OUI)* and the OPatch can track software dependencies during installation and patching operations. The Oracle Inventory is managed automatically by the OUI and OPatch utilities.

Underneath ORACLE_BASE is an admin directory with named subdirectories for each Oracle database, as well as backup, config tool logs, the flash recovery area, and product directories:

```
$ ls $ORACLE_BASE
admin  backup  cfgtoollogs  diag  flash_recovery_area  product
```

Of particular importance, under each ORACLE_BASE/admin/<*database name*> subdirectory are directories for auditing, data pump, configuration, and wallet files:

```
$ ls $ORACLE_BASE/admin/*
/u01/app/oracle/admin/db01:
adump  dpdump  pfile  wallet

/u01/app/oracle/admin/dev11g:
adump  dpdump  pfile  wallet
```

Table 3-2 shows you directories for auditing, Data Pump, configuration, and Oracle wallets.

Table 3-2 Database admin Directories

Directory	*Purpose*
adump	Audit file location. Can generate many files, but are generally not very large
dpdump	Location for Data Pump utility
pfile	Location for database startup configuration files
wallet	Oracle Wallets storage area

In previous versions of Oracle, bdump, cdump, and udump directories appeared underneath each database admin directory storing alert, trace, and core dump files. However, starting in Oracle 11g, these directories appear in trace, alert, and incident subdirectories under the diag/rdbms/<*database name*> directory. In Table 3-3, you see the location of key trace and alert files.

Table 3-3 Trace and Alert File Locations

Directory	*Purpose*
alert	Location of the ever important activity log file for your database.
cdump	Location of core dump files.
trace	Location of database or user-generated trace files reflecting an error event. Replaces bdump and udump directories.
incident	Location of additional trace files.

Oracle manages software installations based on their ORACLE_HOME. Multiple ORACLE_HOMEs can exist on a server, each corresponding to a different version of the database. Different versions can generally coexist without conflict as they only share the Oracle Inventory, `oratab` file, and database listener process. This separation of the software into different directories allows this separation and management to occur. Here's an example of multiple ORACLE HOMEs:

```
$ ls
11.1.0          10.2.0
                                                        9.2.0
```

In the preceding example, you see multiple ORACLE_HOMEs installed into different directories. Defining your environment variable settings to point to a specific ORACLE HOME determines which one you're using.

Database files (data, index, control, redo) are preferably stored in separate file systems allocated specifically for this purpose and separated by database names:

```
/u02/oradata/dev11g
/u03/oradata/dev11g
/u04/oradata/dev11g
```

The oracle user in group dba needs to be able to read, write, and execute to the ORACLE_BASE and ORACLE_HOME directories, subdirectories, and files, as well as the database files themselves. If other users on this server need to execute programs on the server side, such as SQL*Plus or export/import or SQL*Loader, they will need execute permissions on corresponding executables and, in some cases, libraries.

Hardware requirements

Oracle software requires a minimum amount of memory, virtual memory, CPU speed, and disk space to install successfully. If you lack these requirements, at best, the software will run slowly; at worst, it may not even install at all.

Don't forget to consider what other software is executing on the machine, too, both now and in the foreseeable future. It does little good to meet the database requirements and then add more software that will consume hardware resources beyond what the server can support.

Several vital server requirements to check include the following:

- **Memory:** The working area for programs as they execute, memory is key to fast performance. The kind you care about here is *Random Access Memory (RAM)*, and it's measured in megabytes (MB) or, more commonly, gigabytes (GB). Oracle database SGAs are memory pools. Having large amounts of memory available allows you to have larger SGAs. The more memory you have available, the more options you have when managing the ever important SGA.

- **Virtual memory:** When a program or data is being executed, it's stored in memory. When that same program isn't actively being executed but will be momentarily, it's stored in virtual memory (for MS Windows) or swap (for UNIX/Linux operating systems). This system administrator-defined disk area operates as a slower extension of memory. Generally, virtual memory is sized to between .75 to twice the size of installed memory.
- **CPU speed:** The clock speed of your *CPU (central processing unit)* is important. If the CPU is old (and slow) and is laboring just to keep the OS running, then adding an Oracle database isn't a good idea. Additionally, if so many other programs are running and consuming the CPU, you can have problems trying to run Oracle. For as much hype as you hear about CPU speeds, a better solution than having one fast CPU is having multiple CPUs; even if they are a little slower, more CPUs are better than fewer.
- **Disk:** The disk is where the Oracle database software is stored — essentially on your hard drive. The disk is only where your Oracle software itself is installed; it's not where your actual database files will exist with all your data. Oracle software installations take only a few gigabytes, but actual databases can take terabytes.

Like most software, a minimum value is listed by the vendor but more is generally better. Table 3-4 lists the *minimum* hardware requirements for 11g databases.

Table 3-4 Minimum Hardware Requirements

Operating System	*RAM*	*Virtual Memory/Swap*	*CPU*	*Disk*
Windows	1GB	2 times RAM	550 MHz	5GB
Linux	1GB	.75 to 2 times RAM	550 MHz	3.5GB

When identifying where you're going to install the software, make sure that you allow space for growth — don't just go with the minimum hardware requirements. After you install the software, you'll have patches to apply (which take space), and log files will grow as the software runs; you don't want to run out of space!

Software requirements

Your OS version must meet the Oracle requirements. Being close isn't good enough.

Oracle 11 is currently supported to operate on the following requirements in these specific Windows and Linux operating environments:

- Windows 2000 with Service Pack 1 or later (32 bit only)
- Windows 2003 and 2003 R2
- Windows XP Professional
- Windows Vista with Business, Enterprise, and Ultimate editions
- Asianux 2.0 and 3.0
- Oracle Enterprise LINUX 4.0 and 5.0
- Red Hat Enterprise LINUX 4.0 and 5.0
- SUSE LINUX Enterprise Server 10.0

Oracle is also supported on multiple UNIX operating environments such as Sun Solaris, HP HP-UX, and IBM AIX.

Furthermore, an OS has software bug fixes applied to it in the form of patches, which create a patch level. Patches aren't a negative reflection of any particular operating system; they're simply part of the software development life cycle. Oracle requires a specific minimum patch level per OS for the database software to even install.

It's common to have the system administrator apply software patches before the Oracle installer will execute. Hopefully, your system administrator routinely applies patches as they become available so that your OS is relatively current. Keep in mind that often a server needs to be restarted for the OS patches to take effect. The ramification is that if you need a patch applied, you may have to schedule time for a server to be restarted, which, depending on your organization's policies, may take several days or weeks.

How do you know what patches need to be applied? One way is to check the Oracle Installation and Configuration Guide as it lists the minimum requirements. Sometimes, though, the requirements change faster than the documentation, and you need to check the Release Notes for detailed updates. These notes appear on the Oracle web site under Installing and Upgrading for your specific OS version (oracle.com/pls/db111/homepage) or on the software installation media.

An easier method is to let the Oracle Universal Installer (executed via the runInstaller program) do the checking for you. With the –executeSysPrereqs option flag, the OUI program runs checks on the OS for version, patching, and hardware requirements prior to installing any software. It makes sure that at least the minimum requirements are met before software is installed, thus reducing problems during installation. The OUI is also a great way to generate a list of necessary patches so that you can have your system administrator install them. To run the OUI, execute it as

```
$ runInstaller -executeSysPrereqs
Starting Oracle Universal Installer...

Checking swap space: must be greater than 500 MB.   Actual 3813 MB    Passed
Checking monitor: must be configured to display at least 256 colors
```

Storage requirements

Your ORACLE_HOME directory will host your software files and binaries. Once installed, the ORACLE_HOME doesn't grow excessively except for patches. The ORACLE_BASE will grow some during logging operations and even more if trace and core dump files are generated. However, it's the actual database files that can take lots of space and grow rapidly.

Database files (data, index, redo, temp) should be stored separately from the installation files and binaries for management, growth, and performance reasons.

Many smaller databases are installed on whatever disk space is available on the server (called *internal drives*). Cramming multiple, smaller databases onto internal drives is often not optimal for several reasons:

- You have negative performance impacts when database files are on non-dedicated disks.
- Internal disks are often not as fast or flexible as external disk solutions.
- You need to consider special backup and recovery issues because these files have different backup requirements than other files (see Chapter 8).

Despite these issues, many people still cram their databases onto internal disks until their databases grow too large.

One downside of having a large or medium-sized database is that it takes a lot of disk space. Often the database will be larger than the internal disk that comes with your server, so you need another option, such as storing your database on a large disk farm or disk storage array attached to your database server.

Disk optimization basics

Planning and configuring storage for a large database is an art and science, but a few basic concepts should be understood by everyone. First, not all data files are accessed equally. Some types of files are read/written to far more often than others. Classify your files into either high- or low-utilization categories and then isolate the high-utilization files onto separate disks. The idea is not to have all your high-utilization files on the same physical disk; spreading them out over multiple disks balances the read/write operations to reduce contention and improve performance. Not all disks are the same speed, so make sure that your high-utilization files are on the fastest disks you have.

A second key item deals with disk redundancy and RAID levels. Redundancy Array of Inexpensive/Independent Disks is a categorization of how your data is spread across multiple disks. *Striping* is data written across multiple disks to speed up read/write access because there is less contention on an individual disk. *Mirroring* is maintaining multiple redundant copies of data on multiple disks so that if one disk fails, the data is still available (providing *fault tolerance*). *Parity* is a mathematical technique of maintaining special bits of data to recreate data if a disk is lost. The following table shows the most common RAID levels in use today.

RAID Level	***Description***	***Benefit***
0	Striping with no mirroring or parity	Performance benefit only
1	Mirroring with no striping	Improved fault tolerance
0+1	Striping and mirroring	Improved fault tolerance and performance
5	Striping with parity over multiple disks	Performance and fault tolerance without doubling needed disk space

Other RAID levels exist, but most times people use RAID 0+1 or RAID 5. You can achieve the best performance and fault tolerance with RAID 0+1, but it comes at the price of doubling your storage requirements because you're writing your data twice (mirroring). RAID 5 provides improved performance and fault tolerance while using less disk space, but the benefits aren't as pronounced due to the overhead of maintaining parity bits.

Storage arrays can be complex devices, but they offer many benefits. Using attached storage allows your database to grow because the storage administrator can allocate more space as needed. The reading and writing of data is often buffered in memory on the array to increase performance. Advanced configurations of disk mirroring and stripping are also available.

In addition to internal drives or attached storage, Oracle provides you three choices when determining what kind of disk to store your Oracle database files on:

- **Raw devices:** These unformatted *(uncooked)* disk partitions don't have an existing file system structure. While they're necessary for some advanced Oracle configurations and offer a performance improvement, they're difficult to manage and administer. Many people feel those negatives outweigh the benefits.
- **Automatic Storage Management (ASM):** A step up from raw devices, with ASM, Oracle manages the disk for you. It uses partitioned disks, but Oracle sets up the disk groups and spreads the data across them to improve performance by balancing disk Input/Output (I/O) operations. The idea is to offload the work of managing the disks from the system administrator and place it in control of Oracle.
- **File system:** The opposite of raw devices, these formatted disk partitions *(cooked)* have traditional mount points and directories like most people would expect. This disk is by far the most common type of disk configuration because it's easy to use, intuitive, and the standard for most servers. While raw and ASM-based systems offer benefits, traditional file systems are still the de facto standard.

Planning the storage for your database is one of the most critical factors for your database. If you get it right, performance will be fast, and management of the database growth will be simple. Mess it up or don't pay attention to it, and you'll have slow performance, and management will be difficult. You can almost always add more memory or CPUs if you need them, but if a large database is stored incorrectly, fixing it can be a large undertaking.

Other requirements

Oracle databases don't operate in isolation merely for the edification on the DBA; they operate to support a computer system, which in turn meets a business need. Identifying the details of the computer system the database must support will likely identify some unique requirements.

The following sections describe common examples of additional requirements and questions to ask before installation.

Oracle version

What version of Oracle is needed for this system? It's common to use the newest version of the database available, but is the application software certified for that version? Often times, a Commercial Off The Shelf (COTS) software package may not be tested and certified by the vendor to run with the latest version of a database. Although it may work fine, you don't know until it's tested. Plus, many organizations are mandated to operate only in *vendor-supported configurations.*

Oracle patches

Oracle software comes as a base release, such as 11.0, but then you're expected to apply patches to get a more stable and secure version, such as 11.1. These patches typically come in the form of Oracle Critical Patch Updates (CPUs), which are released quarterly (January, April, July, and October).

These patches fix both software bugs and security vulnerabilities. Oracle expects you to install the base version of the software first, and then apply whatever is the most recent CPU patch (such as July CPU 2008). You don't have to apply previous CPU patches; the fixes are cumulative, so the most recent CPU will do.

Although CPUs are the most common patch, sometimes Oracle provides what are commonly referred to as *one-off patches.* These patches fix only a specific bug and will likely be included in a future CPU.

Oracle patches are commonly applied using the OPatch *(opatch)* utility. This is an Oracle-provided Perl-based program that applies patches, but also runs dependency and conflict checks between your patches and can undo (rollback) patches. This utility stores a log of all patches applied in the oraInventory directory located in ORACLE_BASE. *opatch* is a critical part of databases, and the rollback feature is great, but the wise DBA will still run a good backup of the software and databases before running any patch!

Network connectivity

Who is connecting to the database and how? Connecting to the database has more to it than just updating the local tnsnames.ora files with the connection information.

If you're operating in the two-tier client/server model, people will be connecting to the database directly using Oracle Net protocol (sometimes still called SQL*Net) and connecting on port 1521 or 1526. If you're operating in a multitiered web architecture, the application server is connecting to the database on behalf of the users, probably via JDBC.

The question is, are these communication ports open on the firewalls for the users or application servers to access the database? Getting firewall ports open for users requires coordination with the network staff and security, which can sometimes be an issue.

Security

What security procedures must be followed before, during, and after installation, and has this procedure been followed? And is there an audit trail of this?

Many organizations have additional security procedures that need to be applied. You should consider these procedures before installation, as well as any impact they may have on the end product. It's not uncommon to have to uninstall some components, lock accounts, or change file and directory permissions after the installation.

Application

The database holds data, but it also contains PL/SQL packages, procedures, users, and grants/privileges to control access and processing of that data. Via SQL scripts and data loads, these objects and data must be loaded into the finished database itself. You generally have either a client-based application or a web application server that accesses the database. These components must be compiled, installed, and configured to access the database.

Automated batch jobs or programs may also be part of the build process. If the application is part of a commercial package, these steps are likely well documented along with any special requirements that need to be met. In cases of a home-grown application, that documentation needs to be developed and then executed to build the application. Once done, don't forget to test and validate that the system works properly before turning it over to the users.

Backups

No planning session would be complete if database backups weren't considered. The size and activity level of the database, sensitivity of the data, and availability and recovery requirements will drive the type and frequency of backups. In some cases, these backups take the form of traditional cold and hot backup scripts written in-house or downloaded off the web. In many other cases, you're using Recovery Manager to schedule and run various backups. And, of course, you need to store these backups somewhere or write them to tape or other media. (For more on backup methodology, see Chapter 8.)

One final note on backups: Planning and executing backups isn't enough; you need to actually test them to ensure that they work as planned before relying on them!

Part II
Implementing Oracle on Your Own

"This is your database software? This is what you've been running? Well, heck – this could be your problem!"

In this part . . .

You're ready to go. Chapter 4 leads you through the Database Creation Assistant's help so you can make your own Oracle database. Chapter 5 gets you up and connected. If the Database Creation Assistant isn't an option for you, Chapter 6 helps you manually build your database. Chapter 7 tells you what to populate with, no matter how you built your database.

Chapter 4

Creating an Oracle Database

In This Chapter

- Familiarizing yourself with the Oracle environment
- Configuring parameter files
- Making a database in Oracle with the DCBA

It takes a lot of work to create a database.

It's true, a graphical tool called the *Database Configuration Assistant (DBCA)* helps you point and click your way to victory. However, as it's named implies, it only assists. Just like any software wizard-type tool, it can't cover every option; it can't explain everything. It *does* cover up some of the ugly syntax and other required activities (like creating directories and setting permissions) commonly forgotten by someone new to Oracle. It truly is a wonderful tool . . . as long as you know what options to use and what values are appropriate for the questions that it asks you.

With that said, this chapter goes over some of the details necessary to make the right decisions up front when creating a database. This saves you from having to go back and do things twice . . . or even three times. In addition, when you understand why you make certain choices, it helps you create a robust and scalable database that serves you for a long time to come.

Feeling at Home in Your Environment

You should get familiar with a few things before working in your Oracle environment:

- Oracle software owner
- Oracle version
- Oracle base

- Oracle home
- Oracle SID (instance/database name)
- Path

Knowing how to find and work with these, you will better be able to manage not only your database, but databases and Oracle installations on other machines as well.

If Oracle was properly installed, these items should be relatively similar across most installations. Furthermore, if they're not similar, understanding what they are and how to find their values makes it easier for you to adapt.

Some slight differences exist between Oracle installations on Windows versus a Linux/UNIX environment. We point out some of those differences as well.

Finding the Oracle software owner

The Oracle software owner is a user on the operating system.

Linux/UNIX

On Linux/UNIX you typically create a new user to own the installation files. Most commonly, this user is called oracle.

In addition, you create two OS groups:

- **oinstall** should be the user's primary group. This group will contain any users whom you would like to allow the ability to install and patch the Oracle software.
- **dba** contains any users whom you would like to have the power to manage the database in its entirety. Be very careful who you put into these groups because they could wreak havoc on your system and/or have access to all your data.

Windows

Windows has gone a long way to simplify running complex software on their system, and Oracle developed its software to play along. Installing Oracle on Windows only requires that the user be a member of the Local Administrators group on the machine where Oracle is installed.

Consider these tips, however, which include more creation:

- You don't have to create a user specifically to own the software in Windows, but we do it anyway because Oracle runs on Windows through a series of services. This way you can start those services as a specific owner.

- If you use the Windows task scheduler, consider using the Oracle software account to run the jobs. Jobs are easier for people to identify when they're owned by a named account.
- In Windows you may sometimes want to map a drive for Oracle to use. It's easier if you assign it to a central Oracle management account so it isn't removed by someone else or forgotten about if passwords change.

You don't have to create any groups on Windows, but it creates a group on its own during the installation called ORA_DBA. This group behaves much the same way as the dba group on Linux/UNIX, so be careful who you add to it.

Oracle versions

Of course this book is about Oracle 11g. However, you may have to deal with environments that have multiple versions of Oracle installed. This version difference is especially evident when you're upgrading your database from one release to the next. You may also encounter it when you're testing new releases against existing applications.

When you upgrade a database to the same machine, you install the new version of Oracle in parallel with the existing one. It's important to know how to change the environments around and tell which one is active. You see how to do this on both Windows and Linux/UNIX in the following section "Sticking with the Oracle Universal Installer and oraenv."

Getting to home base

On systems where Oracle is installed, an important part of managing the Oracle installation is understanding environment variables. *Environment variables* tell

- The OS what software to run
- Oracle where to store certain files
- Oracle what database you want to connect to

The four most important variables are

- ORACLE_BASE
- ORACLE_HOME
- ORACLE_SID
- PATH

ORACLE_BASE

ORACLE_BASE is the top directory where all Oracle files on the machine are going to exist. If you have multiple versions of Oracle on the same machine, the ORACLE_BASE is likely the same.

Unless you have extraordinary circumstances and want everything to stay separate, we recommend having your ORACLE_BASE be the same for all installations.

A couple of common ORACLE_BASE settings follow:

```
/opt/oracle
/u01/app/oracle
/app/oracle
```

Oracle documentation uses /u01/app/oracle in most examples so we stick with that here.

A few of things you should consider when setting ORACLE_BASE:

- Don't install anything else under ORACLE_BASE.
- Choose a mount point that's not used for any other major OS or other third-party software.
- The final directory in the ORACLE_BASE should be oracle.

When you create your database, Oracle creates a series of directories underneath the ORACLE_BASE and uses them for management, logging, and troubleshooting.

ORACLE_HOME

ORACLE_HOME is where you have Oracle installed. Not only that, but it tells your session which Oracle installation you want to use.

If you have multiple Oracle installations on the same machine, set this variable to the location of the one that you want to work with.

Typically ORACLE_HOME values contain the major release number of the Oracle version installed in the directory. It's created as a subdirectory off ORACLE_BASE. For example

/u01/app/oracle/product/11.1.0

/u01/app/oracle/product/10.2.0

/opt/oracle/product/9.2.0

$ORACLE_BASE/product/11.1.0

The last example shows how you should use your ORACLE_BASE to define your ORACLE_HOME.

ORACLE_SID

ORACLE_SID is simply set to the name of the database that you want to connect to. If the database doesn't exist, set it to the name of the database you're about to create.

You can change the ORACLE_SID within your session if you're moving around to different databases. Just be very careful and note which database you're connecting to. I'd be lying if I said the authors of this book have never made that mistake.

PATH

The PATH variable is typically already set for all sessions on the system. However, when you're using Oracle, you have to add to the path. You simply have to remember to put ORACLE_HOME/bin in front of your path.

ORACLE_HOME/bin is where the Oracle binaries are located. It contains tools such as the DBCA, SQL*Plus, and Data Pump.

By putting ORACLE_HOME/bin in front of your path, you can execute these tools without always having to

- Be in the ORACLE_HOME/bin directory.
- Type the full path every time to want to launch a tool.

The OS checks your PATH locations sequentially to find the tool you're trying to launch. By putting your ORACLE_HOME/bin first, you guarantee not launching some other software package that has a tool with the same name as one of your Oracle tools.

Sticking with the Oracle Universal Installer and oraenv

All the environment settings are stored in your OS user profile on Linux/UNIX. That way, the appropriate parameters are configured every time you log into the system to use the database.

If you're constantly switching your environment to connect to different databases and different Oracle versions, it might suit you to create a script where you name your different environments and then run the script and input your choice.

Oracle provides a script to change the environment on Linux/UNIX installations: oraenv. (Windows has no such handy little script.) You simply run the script and it asks what database you want to connect to. Then, it sets the rest of your environment accordingly.

This output asks if you want to set the environment for the dev11g database. That happens to be the first database created on the machine by default. We override the default by choosing prod11g and it set the environment accordingly.

```
[oracle@classroom ~]$ oraenv
ORACLE_SID = [dev11g] ? prod11g
The Oracle base for ORACLE_HOME=
/u01/app/oracle/product/11.1.0/db_1 is /u01/app/oracle
```

Oracle 9i had the Oracle Home Selector. You launched the tool from the Start Menu folder, and then clicked which version you wanted to set as your environment tool. Oracle 10g took this tool away and put the functionality into the Oracle Universal Installer.

In 11g, this feature is hidden behind yet another Oracle Universal Installer screen. Here's the secret to switching between different Oracle installations on the same machine:

1. **Choose Start⇨Oracle 11g Home⇨Oracle Installation Products⇨Universal Installer.**

   The 11g Oracle Universal Installer launches.

2. **On the first screen, click Installed Products.**
3. **Click the Environment tab.**
4. **Click the installation you want to use.**

5. **Use the arrow keys on the right to move that installation to the top.**
6. **Click Apply.**

   Wait a few seconds. It always seems to take a too long for what it's doing.
7. **Click Close.**

   You're returned to the main screen.
8. **Click Cancel.**
9. **Tell the installer that you really want to exit.**

Figure 4-1 shows the screen where you move the Oracle installation you want to connect to up to the top of the list.

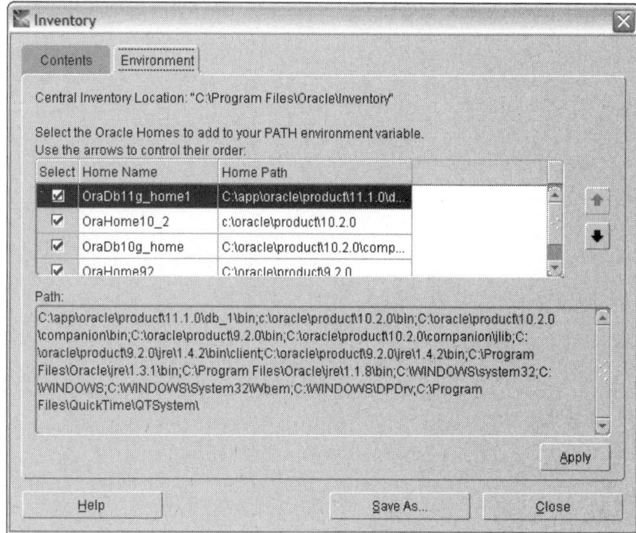

Figure 4-1: The home switch mechanism in the Oracle Universal Installer.

Seems kind of lengthy, doesn't it? We agree. If you want to accomplish the same thing without all the clicking, we recommend writing your own DOS script that works like the oraenv script.

One more thing regarding Windows: All of the environment settings are also set in the registry. You can override them by setting variables from the DOS command line or by setting system-level environment variables. Of course, if you're lucky enough to have only one environment and one database on your machine, you only have to mess with this once, when setting Oracle up. For most people, that doesn't seem to be the case.

Configuring an Instance

Certain files in the database can completely change the way your database behaves. They can influence everything from performance and tuning as well as troubleshooting. Maintaining and configuring these files are a major component of database administration.

Using PFILE and SPFILES

These are the files that set up your database operating environment:

- PFILE
- SPFILES

In Chapter 2 we talk a bit about PFILE and SPFILES. In this section we go through many of the common parameters you will find in these files that you can configure your database. The *parameter file* is the first file read when you start your database, so go through some of them first.

First, take a look at an example of a PFILE:

```
*.audit_file_dest='/u01/app/oracle/admin/dev11g/adump'
*.audit_trail='db'
*.compatible='11.1.0.0.0'
*.control_files='/u01/app/oracle/oradata/dev11g/control01.ctl',
                '/u02/app/oracle/oradata/dev11g/control02.ctl',
                '/u03/app/oracle/oradata/dev11g/control03.ctl'
*.db_block_size=8192
*.db_domain='perptech.com'
*.db_name='dev11g'
*.db_recovery_file_dest='/u01/app/oracle/flash_recovery_area'
*.db_recovery_file_dest_size=107374182400
*.diagnostic_dest='/u01/app/oracle'
*.memory_target=792723456
*.open_cursors=300
*.processes=150
*.undo_tablespace='UNDOTBS1'
```

The parameters have a * in front of them because you can use the parameter file to set parameters in more than one Oracle instance. In a file that serves multiple Oracle instances, you may see the instance name in front of some of the parameters, denoting that particular parameter only applies to one instance.

Follow these steps to see the parameters that are modified in your existing Oracle database:

1. **Log into SQL*Plus as a SYSDBA.**
2. **Type** create pfile from spfile; **(including the semicolon).**

   The command dumps a text version of your SPFILE.

Once you create your PFILE, you want to turn it into an SPFILE. Essentially, you do the reverse of what you did before:

1. **Log into SQL*Plus as a SYSDBA.**
2. **Type** create spfile from pfile; **(including the semicolon).**

   You get a file called spfileORACLE_SID.ora in the same directory as your PFILE, where ORACLE_SID is your instance_name.

Setting parameters in the pfile and spfile

Whether you use PFILES or SPFILES determines how you set your parameters. This next section explains the common parameters in Oracle 11g and how they're configured in the files themselves.

With a new database, you always start with a PFILE. If you end up wanting to use an SPFILE, you create it from the PFILE (shown at the end of the chapter).

The first thing you need to do is find your PFILE. For whatever reason, despite all the other similarities, Linux/UNIX and Windows store it in different locations.

Find your PFILE on Windows, where ORACLE_SID is your instance name:

```
ORACLE_HOME\database\initORACLE_SID.ora
```

Find your PFILE on Linux/UNIX, where ORACLE_SID is your instance name:

```
ORACLE_HOME/dbs/initORACLE_SID.ora
```

These parameters are some of the most commonly customized. Most parameters suit most databases at their default value.

The * means to apply the parameter to all instances that read this file.

- **audit_file_dest:** This parameter tells Oracle where to put auditing information on the file system. All connections to the database as SYSDBA are audited and put into this directory. Furthermore, if you're auditing other operations in the database, those audit records may be dumped here as well.
- **audit_trail:** This tells Oracle where you want audit records written. Audit records can be written to the database or the file system. They can be in text format or XML. Records written to the database are stored in the AUD$ system table. The valid values for this parameter follow:
  - **db:** Normal audit records written to the AUD$ table
  - **os:** Normal audit records written to the audit_file_dest directory
  - **db_extended:** Audit records written to the AUD$ table in extended format, including SQLTEXT and bind variable values
  - **xml:** XML-formatted normal audit records written to the database
  - **xml, extended:** Normal auditing and includes all columns of the audit trail, including SqlText and SqlBind values in XML format to the database
- **compatible:** Set it to force the database to behave like a version earlier than Oracle 11g. In Oracle 11g you can set it back as far as 10.0.0. However, it can only be set back before the database is created or before upgrading from an earlier version. Once you migrate this parameter to 11.1.0 and open the database, you can no longer go back. The parameter's useful for testing before an upgrade is complete. Most of the time you find it set on the latest version for your software. If you try using a feature from a database version later than what you've configured, it results in an Oracle error.
- **control_files:** Just what is says. It tells the instance where to look for the control files during the startup phase. If the instance doesn't find even one of them, you can't mount your database. Notice in the parameters listing that the controlfiles are spread across three different mount points.

- **db_block_size:** This parameter is really the only you can't easily change without recreating the database, so choose it carefully. It tells the database what block size you want your Oracle blocks to be formatted on disk. We discuss this more later on in the chapter.
- **db_domain:** If you want your network domain to be part of your database name for identification purposes, fill in the domain name here. This won't be your actual database name, but an alias to identify it from other databases with the same name that might exist in another domain.

- **db_name:** The database name. Think about this carefully. While it can be changed, it's a pain. The name can be up to eight alphanumeric characters. Avoid the urge to use special characters *other* than #, $, and _.
- **db_recovery_file_dest:** This sets what's known as the *flash recovery area.* The area can hold files such as
  - Backups
  - Archive log files
  - Control files
  - Redo log files

  We use it a lot for the first two tasks. While it can be done, to us it doesn't make sense to put redo and control files in here.
- **db_recovery_file_dest_size:** This determines how much space is dedicated to your flash recovery area. If it fills up, you get an error message and the database could come to a halt — especially if you're storing archive log files here. If archive log files can't be written, redo log files can't be overwritten. User sessions hang until the situation is resolved.
- **diagnostic_dest:** This location is known as the *Automatic Diagnostic Repository (ADR)* home. It contains files that Oracle Support may use to resolve issues with your database. This 11g parameter is new. You can use a new tool called ADRCI to access the files in this directory. It contains
  - Trace files
  - Core files
  - Alert logs
  - Incident files
- **memory_target:** This parameter sets the memory that the Oracle instance is allowed to use for all *system global area (SGA)* and program global area activities described in Chapter 2. It doesn't include memory consumed by server and user processes.
- **open_cursors:** Limits the number of open SQL cursors a session can have.
- **processes:** Limits the number of OS users' processes that can connect to the instance.
- **undo_tablespace:** This parameter tells the instance to which tables it will write its transaction undo. It must be an undo type tablespace.

Creating Your Oracle Database

You can create a database one of four ways:

- **Manually with SQL commands.** If you're on an ancient release like Oracle 8i, we recommend manual SQL commands; the DBCA wasn't as good back then. However, with Oracle 9i and up, it has really become a robust and useful tool. Furthermore, with more features being added to the database, the manual method isn't a laundry list of scripts. Back in the day you only had to run an SQL command and two scripts. Not anymore.

- **With the graphical tool called Database Configuration Assistant (DBCA).** We recommend Database Configuration Assistant (DBCA) to make your Oracle database. This is especially true for beginners. If you use DBCA to create the database, you don't have to make the PFILE; the DBCA creates it for you. You may want to alter your setting later, however.
- **A combination of SQL commands and DBCA.** Even old-timers like us prefer DBCA or SQL and DBCA. Using SQL to create the database gives you control over every aspect of the creation, but it also leaves open a lot of areas for mistakes and accidental omissions.
- **Cloning an existing database.** This book doesn't cover the topic because it's a more advanced topic for, uh, smarties?

Bossing the Database Configuration Assistant (DBCA)

Launch the Database Configuration Assistant (that's right; you're in charge) from the command line of the operating system where the database resides.

This set of steps chooses the Custom Database option (versus General Purpose or Data Warehouse options). This option is for when you really want to get your hands dirty and have complete control. We like this option.

- You don't have to install the features that you aren't going to use. They just take up more space and give you more things to manage.
- You can specify a lot more options that the other templates don't allow.
- Customizing isn't that hard. You're reading the book, right? It'll be easy.

The only drawback to the Custom Database method is the time it takes while creating the data files. How much time? We've seen it take anywhere from 2 to 30 minutes. It depends on

- The number of CPUs
- What features you select

Taking database control

Database control is an option you can choose during database creation. Don't get too attached to this invaluable resource. Take some time to learn the basic SQL commands for managing your database. I've seen Database Control crash and the only thing left was a blinking SQL prompt. A well-rounded DBA knows how to manage her database both ways.

Under the Database Control section you're asked whether you want to enable alert notifications. This is valuable on a production database, but I wouldn't enable alert notifications

- If you're just installing this for testing purposes
- On a production database until I configured what things I wanted alerts for; otherwise you're deluged with all kinds of frivolous alerts

Next, it asks if you want to enable automated backups of your system to disk. Again, if this is a test environment, you may not want to bother with this. After some time, your machine will probably start running out of space.

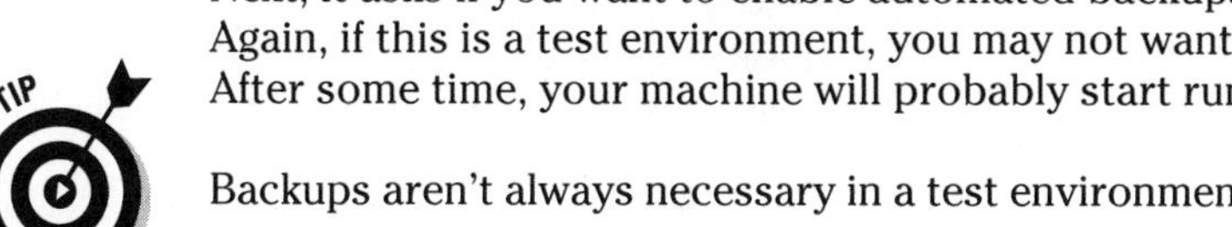

Backups aren't always necessary in a test environment.

Furthermore, even if this is a production database, I might wait until everything is in place before I start backups. We go over this extensively in Chapter 8.

DBCA steps

Not only does this tool create databases, it lets you delete and modify them, create database templates, and set up a feature called Oracle Automatic Storage Management. Notice at the top in the title bar it says 1 of 15 steps. We kid you not that in Oracle 9i it was 1 of 8 steps and in 10g it was 1 of 12 steps. This is what we mean: Creating the database with the DBCA is the way to go as Oracle gets heavier with features.

Taking the DBCA steps

If you're ever unsure about an option on the DBCA screen, click the Help button. It does a pretty good job of explaining what each thing does.

One of the things we have noticed in Oracle 11g is that Oracle has done a good job of speeding up the Help function. In past versions it took forever to load. Try it out!

The DBCA has a lot of screens with all kinds of information. The following steps take you through creating a database with the Database Configuration Assistant.

1. **Log in as the Oracle software owner.**
2. **Go to a command prompt.**
3. **Type** dbca.

   You see the welcome screen shown in Figure 4-2.
4. **Click Next.**

   You see another screen with several options.

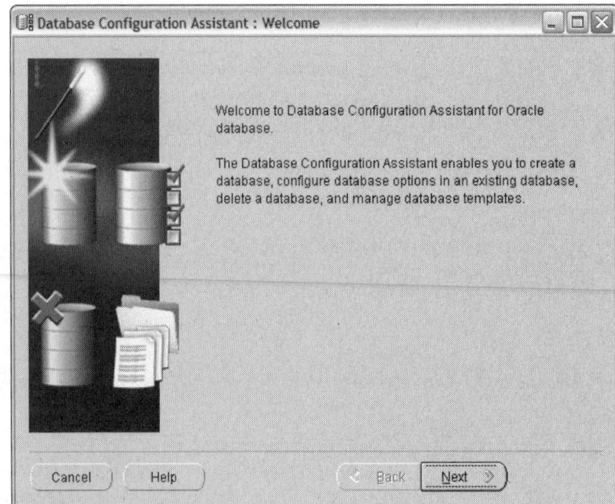

Figure 4-2: The Database Configuration Assistant welcomes you.

5. **Click Create a Database.**
6. **Click Next.**

   This time you see the output shown in Figure 4-3. Optional database templates are shown:

   • General Purpose
   • Data Warehouse
   • Custom Database

The first two include the data files. You supply a few custom settings and it unzips the database from the Oracle installation directory. Use these options only when you're new to Oracle and aren't sure what to do with some of the more advanced parameters. You should choose Custom here; we go over all the options in the rest of the steps.

7. **Choose Custom Database.**

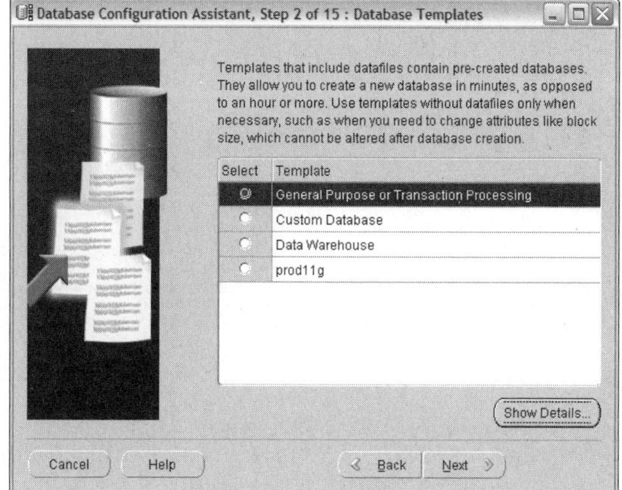

Figure 4-3: Database creation options require lots of steps.

Click Show Details if you want to see the features, parameters, and files chosen by default for each type of database.

8. **Click Next.**

   A screen asks you to choose the database name.

9. **Fill in these fields:**

   • **Global Database Name.** Your database name with your network domain attached. If you don't want to attach your network domain, leave this field blank. Doing so just sets the initialization parameter db_domain. It helps uniquely identify your database on the network. For example, you might have a database named prod in two different domains. A global database name allows that without confusing some of the Oracle networking features.

   • **SID.** This is the short name for your database. It equates to your environment variable ORACLE_SID.

10. **Click Next.**

    A screen asks if you want to manage your database with Enterprise Manager. See the output in Figure 4-4 and read more about Oracle Enterprise Manager in Chapter 13.

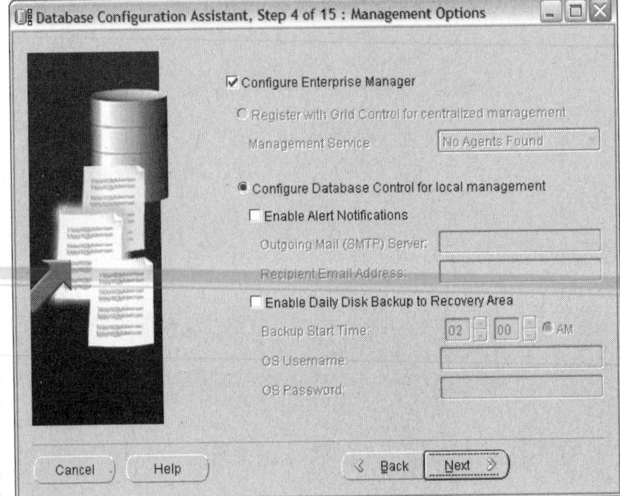

Figure 4-4: Your database management options come here.

It can be configured two ways:

- **Register with Grid Control for Centralized Management:** An Oracle software package that typically runs on its own server elsewhere on your network. It can manage many databases, many versions of Oracle, servers, application servers, and even other non-Oracle software such as Microsoft SQL server and firewalls. You must have the Grid Control Management Agent installed to get this option.

- **Configure Database Control for Local Management:** Database control is a management package that runs locally on the database machine and has many of the features of Grid Control. However, it only controls one database. We only caution you when configuring Database Control. If you're setting Oracle up on a machine with limited resources, you're going to feel Database Control, if you know what we mean.

11. **Choose Database Control.**

    Choose Database Control as your management option only if you're comfortable with your machine's resources. You can always stop when you're not using it and start it later.

If you see the error message because you haven't set up Oracle's listener network process (described in Chapter 5), open a prompt to the operating system as the Oracle software owner and type **lsnrctl start**.

Eventually you see `The command completed successfully` and get your prompt back.

12. **Click OK and then click Next.**

    It works this time. The next screen asks about passwords. Automatically included users are DBA users and users for Database Control.

13. **Decide on passwords.**

    - Use different password for each user. If this is a test database, it may not matter that much. Even if you want to keep it simple now and make all the passwords the same, you can easily go back change them later.
    - Set the same password for everyone. If this is production, it's in your best interest to have separate passwords for all the users.

14. **Click Next.**

    The following screen asks how you want to store your files:

    - **File System.** All your data files are put into formatted drives attached to your computer.
    - **Automatic Storage Management (ASM).** Don't choose this now. ASM has some great benefits but isn't as easy to set up as the DBCA leads you to believe.
    - **Raw Devices.** They're tough to back up and restore when problems arise. We aren't saying, "Don't use them." Just don't use them right now.

15. **Choose File System and click Next.**

    You're asked where you want the files stored and what to name them. Really, you're given one location.

16. **Choose a place to store your files:**

    - **File Locations from Template.** This option doesn't let you make any changes. Oracle chooses where to put the files.
    - **Common Location.** This option activates the grayed-out field. You choose type or browse for a location to store the files.
    - **Oracle Managed File.** You decide where to put files. You can't change the file names until after database creation. Oracle names them for you.

Separating files across multiple mount points is a best practice for performance and protection. If you create a test database or other non-production database, it's okay to put them all in one place if you have the space.

Filing that away

We could buy the argument that it's okay to put files in the same location if later on you were going to separate your application data files accordingly. Also, it's relatively easy to move them. The other possibility is that you're going to use a large chunk of storage on a SAN (a high-speed *storage area network*) that presents its storage to you as one location, and then manage the performance in the background by spreading the files across many disks.

17. **Choose File Locations from Template and click Next.**

    You're in the Flash Recovery Area (FRA) configuration. The FRA is a storage area that resides on disk which can house backups, archive logs files, control files, and redo log files.

18. **Choose to configure the FRA.**

    Doing so simplifies the storage of backups and archive log files. We typically use it for the control or redo. We manually separate those ourselves.

19. **Determine what FRA space you have available and increase it accordingly.**

    The default value is about 2GB. This might be okay for the archive log files of small databases. However, an FRA of this size will fill up very quickly. You can resize the FRA anytime without taking the database down.

20. **Choose to archive later and click Next.**

    It adds drain on the system while creating the database. It's easy enough to enable later on.

    You're asked what features you want to install on the screen. Depending on what software you installed, not all are available. Luckily, you can add later. Click the Help button if you want a more detailed description:

    - **Oracle Text:** This indexing feature allows custom indexing of large text-type documents. It can index pages of data. It also allows advanced searching against rich media objects.
    - **Oracle OLAP:** This is Oracle's business intelligence tool.
    - **Oracle Spatial:** This mapping tool is for geospatial mapping.
    - **Oracle Ultra Search:** Text-only indexing and searching mechanism.

- **Oracle Label Security:** Label security is for securing data in a way that gives users levels of access to restricted data.
- **Sample Schemas:** This bunch of test data that you can use for training or trying new features. We usually install this on test and training databases. It includes several schemas with varying degree of complexity.
- **Enterprise Manager Repository:** Just like it says, install this if you want to use Enterprise Manager Database Control with your database. If you're going to use Grid Control, leave this out.
- **Oracle Warehouse Builder:** Data warehouse tools for developing corporate metadata and consolidating data from various sources.
- **Oracle Database Vault:** Basically this locks down the database to extreme measure, disallowing activities we take for granted in a normal system. It protects your database against your own people, in essence. It significantly creates more management overhead. However, in a system that must remain ultra-secure, it's the price you pay.
- **Oracle Database Extension for .NET**: If you're going to develop Microsoft .NET apps to run against your database, this suite of utilities helps you integrate better with .NET's features.

21. **Click the Standard Database Components button and choose what you want installed:**
    - **Oracle JVM:** Oracle Java Container for running Java out of the database.
    - **Oracle XMLDB:** Contains XML extension for the database to better integrate with XML applications.
    - **Oracle Multimedia**: Extends Oracle's capabilities to offer better support for multimedia data.
    - **Oracle Application Express:** This is the kind of a development environment that allows you to develop applications in a web-based framework. It runs on top of the database and allows creating hosted applications that can be quite robust.

    If you're testing to get a basic environment up and running, deselect everything. However, if you're going to work with one or more of these options, install them. Remember that they take space and time during the database creation process — some more so than others.
22. **Click Next.**

    Figure 4-5 shows the screen where you begin choosing the initialization parameters discussed earlier in the chapter. The Memory tab has two options: Typical and Custom.

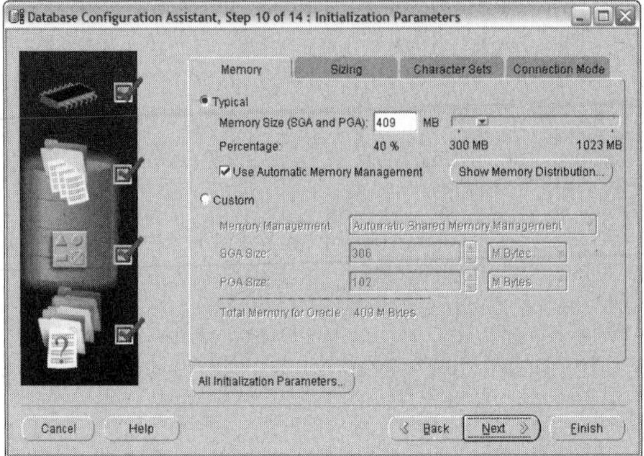

Figure 4-5: Choosing database initialization parameters.

23. **Choose Typical.**

    Since we're talking Oracle 11g, choosing Typical sets the memory target as one large chunk and lets Oracle figure out where everything goes.

24. **Click the Sizing tab.**

25. **Choose the block size.**

    If you get this wrong, your only option is to re-create your database (if the performance problems haven't gotten you fired).

    - If you're creating a database that will have many users with smaller quick transactions, go with a block size of 4k.
    - If you're creating a data warehouse-type database with large SQL queries that retrieve heaps of data at once for analysis, choose the largest block size you can. The largest block size you can choose is OS dependent.
    - If you're somewhere in the middle of the first two, go with 8k.
    - Make sure the block size is divisible evenly by the OS block size or OS I/O size. You don't want your OS to read a minimum of 8k but choose a 4k block size. That would waste 4k for every read.

26. **Click the Character Set tab.**

    You can change the character set after creating the database, but it's time consuming and tedious. Choose a character set that will house all the characters that your application may use.

    - **Database Character set.** For all the standard-language columns in your database. Also encompasses the character set that Oracle messages will display in, and the characters you may use in program code.

- **National Character set**. For special datatypes that may house data only used in your applications. For example, what if you work at a primarily English-speaking university and the Greek department wants to create an application to storage indexable, searchable Greek manuscripts? No programming or database message will be displayed in Greek.
- **Unicode Character sets.** Choose this if you're going to support multiple languages.

27. Click the Connection Mode tab.

- Dedicated Server Mode
- Shared Server Mode

We discuss this in Chapter 2. Most current systems use dedicated server connections. In most cases we recommend starting that way. If memory is constantly running short (while at the same time supporting thousands of users), investigate shared server configuration.

The All Initialization Parameters button lets you adjust all parameters discussed earlier in the chapter (as well as others we didn't); see Figure 4-6 for the All Initialization Parameters screen. By default the screen shows only what Oracle considers basic parameters. Oracle considers some parameters advanced. You don't need them but if you're curious, click Show Advanced Parameters.

28. Choose a security option:

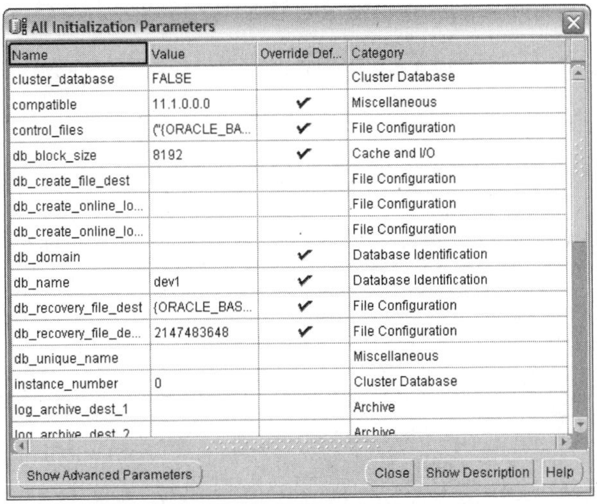

All Initialization Parameters

Name	Value	Override Def...	Category
cluster_database	FALSE		Cluster Database
compatible	11.1.0.0.0	✔	Miscellaneous
control_files	("{ORACLE_BA...	✔	File Configuration
db_block_size	8192	✔	Cache and I/O
db_create_file_dest			File Configuration
db_create_online_lo...			File Configuration
db_create_online_lo...			File Configuration
db_domain		✔	Database Identification
db_name	dev1	✔	Database Identification
db_recovery_file_dest	{ORACLE_BAS...	✔	File Configuration
db_recovery_file_de...	2147483648	✔	File Configuration
db_unique_name			Miscellaneous
instance_number	0		Cluster Database
log_archive_dest_1			Archive
log_archive_dest_2			Archive

Show Advanced Parameters | Close | Show Description | Help

Figure 4-6: The All Initialization Parameters page lets you make adjustments.

- **Keep the enhanced 11g default security settings (recommended)** if you want to take advantage of 11g's advanced security settings such as turning on auditing by default and enforcing stronger password.
- **Revert to pre-11g default security settings** and have very little password security and no auditing.

The 11g security profile enables more auditing by default and enforces more secure passwords. It makes passwords case sensitive.

29. **Breathe.**

    You're almost done.

30. **Choose Yes to automate certain maintenance tasks in the database.**

    If you choose Yes, Oracle automatically gathers performance-related statistics on your objects to speed up query execution. If you don't automate the tasks, you have to do them manually.

31. **Make storage adjustments.**

    Now is a good time to make sure the files spread across multiple mount points. Click each menu: Controlfile, Tablespaces, Datafiles, and Redo Log Groups. Change the directories (on the right) so they're not all in the same place.

    As you can see in Figure 4-7, the left pane lists the file and storage objects. The screen currently shows the Controlfile choices.

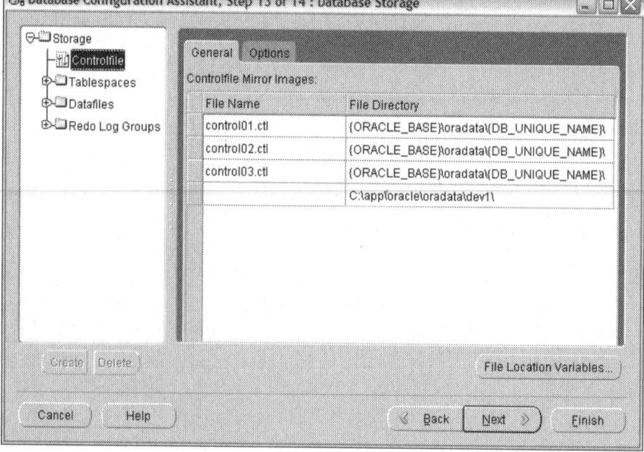

Figure 4-7: The storage configuration page lists file and storage objects.

    About file locations: In the past, we've encountered problems with some directories not being there when you change where the files are created. Sometimes Oracle complains about permissions.

Make sure the permissions on the directories where you store your files are set for the Oracle user to read and write. For example, if you move a control file to /u01/oradata/dev11g and that directory isn't there, some systems give an error and the database creation stops.

We create all the directories where files are going to go ahead of time. This might resolve some headaches when you launch the actual database creation.

32. **Decide if you want to create the database now.**
33. **Click Next to start creation.**

34. **Decide if you want to save your decisions as a template for future use.**

    If you think you may create a similar database again, this might be a good idea. You can give it a name and a description.

35. **Save everything you did in a set of scripts and decide where you want them.**

    It's a good idea to keep these around just in case. Also, if you're curious about all the scripting work you just avoided by using the DBCA, have a look.

36. **Click Finish.**

    A screen shows all the options you just chose and the parameters you set.

37. **Decide if you want to save your choices as a file.**

    If you do, the DBCA creates an HTML file summarizing your configuration. Then it starts creating the database. First, the template is made (if you chose one in Step 33); you also see the script creation screen (if you chose to save the creation as scripts in Step 34).

38. **Click OK to acknowledge the template and script screens.**

    The creation status screen appears. A status bar and options also appear. You can watch it go through everything until it's done.

    Once the database is complete, a screen shows the details. A Password Management button lets you unlock or change the passwords of the users that were created as part of the options you installed. All users except SYS, SYSTEM, DBSNMP, and SYSMAN are locked.

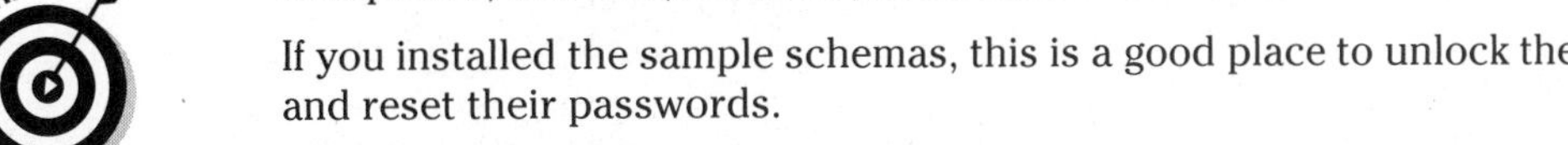

    If you installed the sample schemas, this is a good place to unlock them and reset their passwords.

39. **Click Exit to close the DBCA.**

Sharing (a) memory

Personally, we think a "typical" memory option is a bit of a misnomer. Nothing is typical about memory settings. It all depends on

- How much you have
- How many databases are going to be on the machine
- How many users you're expecting
- How much memory your users are going to require

Also, it is quite common to give yourself a starting point and then go from there. You see that Oracle suggests using 40 percent of your memory for the shared and private areas of your database. This is an interesting choice. What if this machine were destined to house ten databases? Hmmm....

Think about how the memory on this machine is going to be shared. These points might help you decide:

- Never start with the combination of shared and private memory areas of all your databases on the machine consuming more than half the memory. Therefore, if you have 8GB of memory and there will be two databases, both memory_target parameters combined *shouldn't exceed* 4GB. This gives plenty of room for error.

- If your database is going to be extremely large, figure out how many users will have server sessions at once. Take that number and multiply by 5MB. Add 2GB for your OS and then add 20 percent more of the available memory. Split what is left over amongst the rest of the databases.

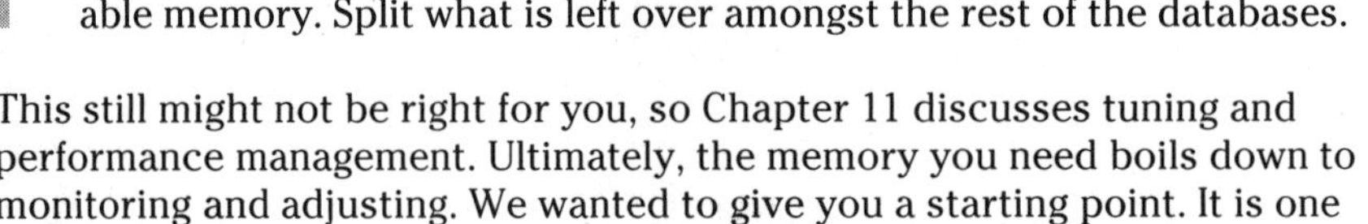

This still might not be right for you, so Chapter 11 discusses tuning and performance management. Ultimately, the memory you need boils down to monitoring and adjusting. We wanted to give you a starting point. It is one of the most common user questions yet is difficult to quantify without real application environment data.

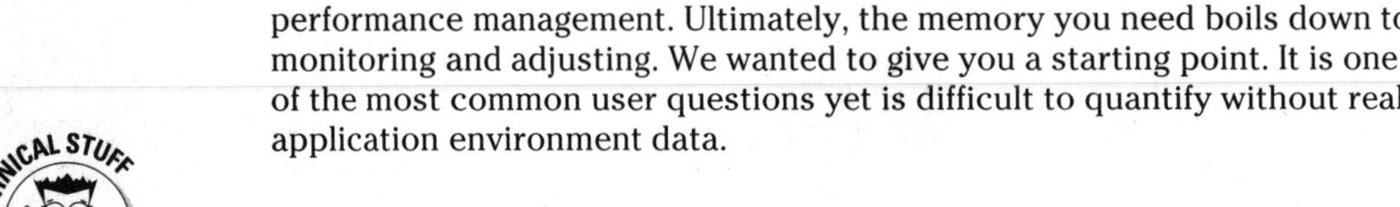

10g Memories

If you were on Oracle 10g, the Custom option on the Memory tab gives you a choice. You can set separate shared and private areas. It still gives you the typical 40 percent option, but it then sets the two in the background. If you were back in Oracle 9i, you'd have to set all the memory areas yourself. Man, how did we get by back in 2001? If you want to set everything yourself, or you want to see what it looked like in 9i just for the fun of it, select Custom and change the drop-down list to Manual Shared Memory Management. Ah the memories . . . .

Feeling the Post-Configuration Glow

When everything is complete, you might want to log into your database for the first time and check everything out.

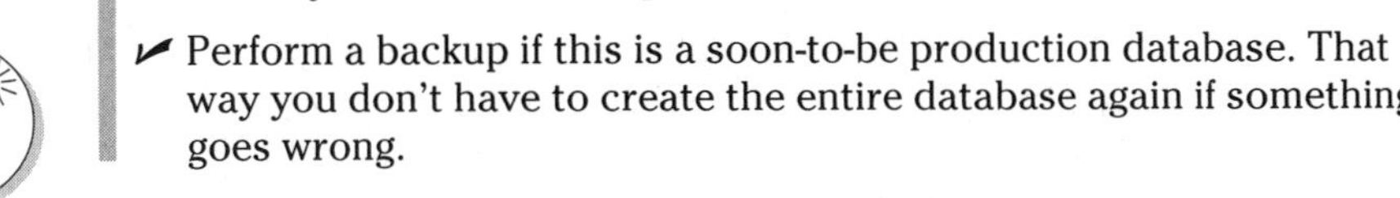

- Look in the directories where the files were supposed to go.
- Check your initialization parameters.
- Perform a backup if this is a soon-to-be production database. That way you don't have to create the entire database again if something goes wrong.

Chapter 5

Connecting to and Using an Oracle Database

In This Chapter

- Starting and stopping the database
- Connecting to the database instance
- Avoiding pitfalls

You can't use a database until it's running and you connect to it. In this chapter we cover how to make that happen. First, we cover the setup of your DBA environment so you can log in to the database and begin your startup work. Next, we cover the various startup modes and states that a database can be in depending on your type of work. Furthermore, shutting down a database can happen several different ways. We cover all the options so that you can start up and shut down with the proper parameters.

You can connect locally or remotely to a database with Oracle Net. We examine the role of the database listener process and how to configure, start, and stop it. Next, we show how to set up client-side connections to the database. Finally, we cover a few common problems you might encounter when setting up Oracle Net.

Starting and Stopping the Database

Before users connect to a database instance to do work, it obviously must be running. This entails starting up the database instance memory, processes, and opening the control and database files in a mode accessible and appropriate for the users. Depending on the type of work being done, there are several different states a database can be in for the users or DBA to access. Alternatively, it is sometimes necessary to shut down a database instance for a multitude of reasons. The key with shutdowns are what happens to users logged in and doing work when the shutdown occurs? Several different ways exist to handle existing users and the state of their work.

Environmental requirements

Before starting or stopping an Oracle database instance, a few environmental requirements must be met. These environment requirements get you logged into the server as the correct user with the right environment variables so that you can do your DBA work.

Log in to the database server

Log in to the server where the database resides to do your key *database administrator (DBA)* work. Yes, you can do some of this via Enterprise Manager but only after you've set up your environment and created your database in the first place.

Most critical DBA work occurs on the database server itself because it provides the most flexibility and is the simplest for starting DBAs.

Log in as the Oracle DBA account

You should be in the operating system DBA account that owns the Oracle software to start and stop the database. Commonly this is the oracle user account and is in the DBA group:

```
$ id
uid=501(oracle) gid=501(oinstall) groups=501(oinstall),502(dba))
```

The oracle user is in groups `oinstall` and `dba`.

Set up your environment variables

Many environment variables exist for your oracle user and we cover them in detail in Chapter 4. However, at a minimum you want to have these variables set:

- ORACLE_BASE
- ORACLE_HOME
- ORACLE_SID

```
$ echo $ORACLE_BASE
/u01/app/oracle
$ echo $ORACLE_HOME
/u01/app/oracle/product/11.1.0/db_1
$ echo $ORACLE_SID
dev11g
```

Be sure to verify the ORACLE_BASE, ORACLE_HOME, and ORACLE_SID variables before you do any type of DBA work. It is very easy to define the wrong ORACLE_HOME, in which case you work with the wrong database software. Worse yet, it's even easier to incorrectly define ORACLE_SID and stop the wrong database! If it occurs frequently, you're making what we refer to as a "career-limiting move."

Start SQL*Plus as a DBA

The command-line interface into Oracle databases is SQL*Plus. To do serious DBA work such as startup or shutdown, you need to be logged in as SYSDBA.

To log in this way, you must be the oracle operating system user as described earlier in this chapter. Then start SQL*Plus with the `"/ as sysdba"` option:

```
$ sqlplus "/ as sysdba"

SQL*Plus: Release 11.1.0.6.0 - Production on Wed Sep 24 07:46:53 2008

Copyright (c) 1982, 2007, Oracle.  All rights reserved.


Connected to:
Oracle Database 11g Enterprise Edition Release 11.1.0.6.0 - 64bit Production
With the Partitioning, OLAP, Data Mining and Real Application Testing options

SYS@dev11g>
```

An alternative: Once you're in SQL*Plus, issue `connect as sysdba` to log in as SYSDBA, provided you're on the database server as the oracle operating system user.

```
SYS@dev11g> connect / as sysdba
Connected.
SYS@dev11g>
```

Once connected as SYSDBA, you can begin your DBA work.

Database parameter file

Before starting the database, you must have a parameter file listing all the different runtime parameters, such as SGA configuration. This is covered in detail in Chapter 4, so we won't rehash the details here. However, we assume you have your SPFILE created and in a default location so that Oracle can find it. If it isn't in a default location, or you want to use a different parameter file, you may use the pfile='<PATH TO SPFILE/FILENAME>' syntax with your startup commands.

Improper environment setup is a common error and is something you should verify before beginning your database work. Doing so will save you time and frustration troubleshooting unnecessary errors.

Starting the database

You don't actually *start* a database per se; you start the instance.

A *database* is defined as the actual data, index, redo, temp, and control files that exist on the files system. The *instance* consists of the processes (PMON, SMON, DBWR, LGWR, and others) and the SGA (memory pool) that access and process data from the database files. The instance is what accesses the database, and it is the instance that users connect to. Thus, it is the instance (not the database) that you actually start.

Are we splitting hairs here? Not in this case; you need to understand the relationship between the instance and the database to understand startup and shutdown.

As an Oracle instance starts, it proceeds through various states until it and the database are fully open and accessible to users. At each state, different components are started and opened. Furthermore, at each state you may perform different types of DBA or user work. You may specify your startup command to take the database instance into a specific state depending on what you need to do.

In ascending order, during startup the database instance goes through these states:

NOMOUNT

- Read Parameter File
- Allocate SGA
- Start Background Processes
- Only SGA and Background Processes Running
- Used for CREATE DATABASE (Only SYS can access)
- Specified by STARTUP NOMOUNT

MOUNT

- Read Parameter File
- Allocate SGA
- Start Background Processes
- Open and Read Control File
- SGA and Background Processes Running and Control Files Open
- Used for database maintenance and recovery operations (Only SYS can access)
- Specified by STARTUP MOUNT

OPEN

- Read Parameter File
- Allocate SGA
- Start Background Processes
- Open and Read Control File
- Open All Database Files
- SGA and Background Processes Running, Control Files Open, All Database Files Open
- Default OPEN state for database and is accessible by users and applications
- Specified by STARTUP or STARTUP OPEN

Unless you're performing specialized maintenance, the default is as follows:

- STARTUP with the parameter file read
- Background processes and SGA started
- Control files open and read
- All database files open

In this open state, users access the database normally.

Here's what it looks like when starting the database into the default OPEN mode. Because we're using the default parameter file, we don't need to specify one.

```
$ sqlplus "/  as sysdba"

SQL*Plus: Release 11.1.0.6.0 - Production on Sat Sep 27 02:58:05 2008

Copyright (c) 1982, 2007, Oracle.  All rights reserved.

Connected to an idle instance.
SYS@dev11g> startup
ORACLE instance started.

Total System Global Area  789172224 bytes
Fixed Size                  2148552 bytes
Variable Size             557844280 bytes
Database Buffers          218103808 bytes
Redo Buffers               11075584 bytes
Database opened.
SYS@dev11g>
```

Although we normally go straight to the fully open mode, you can increment the modes. For example, you could do database maintenance with the database in MOUNT mode and, once done, issue ALTER DATABASE OPEN to take the database to open mode so users can start work.

That's what's done here:

```
SYS@dev11g> startup mount
ORACLE instance started.

Total System Global Area  789172224 bytes
Fixed Size                  2148552 bytes
Variable Size             570427192 bytes
Database Buffers          205520896 bytes
Redo Buffers               11075584 bytes
Database mounted.
SYS@dev11g> alter database open;

Database altered.

SYS@dev11g>
```

Note that you can only go forward to a more open state; you can't move to a more restrictive state without issuing a shutdown.

In most cases when you open a database, you want it open for every user. Sometimes, however, you want to block all or some users even though the database is in OPEN state.

To do this, put the database in RESTRICTED SESSION mode via one of these ways:

- STARTUP RESTRICT
- ALTER SYSTEM ENABLE RESTRICTED SESSION

```
SYS@dev11g> startup restrict;
ORACLE instance started.

Total System Global Area  789172224 bytes
Fixed Size                  2148552 bytes
Variable Size             570427192 bytes
Database Buffers          205520896 bytes
Redo Buffers               11075584 bytes
Database mounted.
Database opened.
SYS@dev11g>
SYS@dev11g> alter system enable restricted session;

System altered.
```

- When the database is OPEN, you must grant users CREATE SESSION to connect.
- When the database is RESTRICTED, users must have CREATE SESSION *and* they also must have RESTRICTED SESSION to connect.

The only backdoor is if the user was already logged in when an ALTER SYSTEM ENABLE RESTRICTED SESSION was issued; then the user can remain logged in.

Therefore, you should kill all user sessions after putting the database in RESTRICTED mode to kick them out. If they don't have RESTRICTED SESSION, they get this Oracle error when they try to log in:

```
$ sqlplus barb/test123

SQL*Plus: Release 11.1.0.6.0 - Production on Sat Sep 27 03:17:46 2008

Copyright (c) 1982, 2007, Oracle.  All rights reserved.

ERROR:
ORA-01035: ORACLE only available to users with RESTRICTED SESSION privilege
```

Why would you want to do this (other than just to frustrate your users)? While frustrating users is the secret pleasure of every administrator (especially security administrators), some valid technical reasons exist. Major data, table, or application updates often need a stable system with no updates or locks to contend with so they can process successfully. Some database maintenance operations also require restricted session.

If you need to allow in a subset of users or perhaps the application user processing a database job, you may grant them RESTRICTED SESSION:

```
SYS@dev11g> grant restricted session to barb;

Grant succeeded.

SYS@dev11g> connect barb/test123
Connected.
```

Revoke the RESTRICTED SESSION from any non-DBA user once the user's work is done. Also, don't forget to take the instance out of restricted session.

```
SYS@dev11g>alter system disable restricted session;

System altered.
```

Starting up database instances isn't terribly difficult and most times you use the default STARTUP command to take the database instance to the OPEN state. Only occasionally does the situation require a RESTRICTED SESSION.

If the database startup seems to take a few minutes, it may be because of a large SGA during which time memory is being allocated. Or there may be many database files to open.

If the database crashed or a SHUTDOWN ABORT occurred prior to the startup, database instance recovery is occurring, which can take time. If this occurs, leave your screen with the STARTUP command open; let it run. View the alert log with another window. We cover the alert log in Chapter 12. If more severe errors occur (such as media recovery), they appear both on the startup screen and in the alert log file. Of course, you can prevent much of this if you stop the database in a clean manner. Carry on to the next topic.

Stopping the database

Just as there is an order of events to starting a database instance, there is also an order for how a database instance is stopped. Ideally, this is what happens during a database shutdown:

- New connections to the database are denied.
- Existing transactions are either committed or rolled back with proper updates to online redo log files.
- User sessions are terminated.

- Database file headers are updated and files are closed.
- SGA is shut down.
- Background processes are terminated.

It is preferable for all the steps to occur naturally during shutdown. That ensures that

- All transactions are neatly committed or rolled back.
- Online redo log files are properly updated.
- All files are closed properly without corruption.

If the preceding steps *don't* occur during shutdown because of a server or database instance crash or SHUTDOWN ABORT, the cleanup operations must occur during startup in a phase called *instance recovery.*

During instance recovery, Oracle won't open a database instance until it's satisfied that all transactions are accounted for and all data files are opened. If it can't complete these tasks, error messages appear and the DBA must address them. Instance recovery is successful most of the time, but it may take several minutes to process the cleanup.

Shutdown types

When a database needs to be shut down, several methods exist to do so with varying effects on current users and their transactions.

SHUTDOWN [NORMAL]

- New connections to the database are denied.
- Existing transactions continue normally until either they roll back or commit.
- Users log out normally on their own.
- After the last user logs out, database file headers are updated and files are closed.
- SGA is shut down.
- Background processes are terminated.
- Specified by the SHUTDOWN or SHUTDOWN NORMAL command.

SHUTDOWN TRANSACTIONAL

- New connections to the database are denied.
- Existing transactions continue normally until either they roll back or commit.

- After an existing transaction is completed, user sessions are terminated.
- Database file headers are updated and files are closed.
- SGA is shut down.
- Background processes are terminated.
- Specified by the SHUTDOWN TRANSACTIONAL command.

SHUTDOWN IMMEDIATE

- New connections to the database are denied.
- Existing transactions are rolled back.
- User sessions are terminated.
- Database file headers are updated and files are closed.
- SGA is shut down.
- Background processes are terminated.
- Specified by the SHUTDOWN IMMEDIATE command.

SHUTDOWN ABORT

- New connections to the database are denied.
- Existing transactions are not rolled back.
- User sessions are terminated.
- SGA is shut down.
- Background processes are terminated.
- Specified by the SHUTDOWN ABORT command.
- Instance recovery is required on startup.

Shutdown decisions

When do you use each shutdown type?

- Generally, SHUTDOWN IMMEDIATE is what you want because it cleanly commits or rolls back existing transactions, terminates user sessions when they are complete, and then closes the database in a clean manner.

- Don't use SHUTDOWN NORMAL very often because even one user still logged in (after he's left for the day) can hang the shutdown.

- SHUTDOWN TRANSACTIONAL doesn't buy you much because it forces you to wait on users to finish their transactions. If you want to wait, you can just enter SHUTDOWN NORMAL. However, if you want to force them off the database instance, you use SHUTDOWN IMMEDIATE. There are times SHUTDOWN TRANSACTIONAL is useful, but it's not as common as you might think.

  Here's how a typical SHUTDOWN IMMEDIATE executes. Keep in mind that you must be logged in as SYSDBA to run the shutdown command.

```
SYS@dev11g> shutdown immediate;
Database closed.
Database dismounted.
ORACLE instance shut down.
SYS@dev11g> exit
```

- Only use SHUTDOWN ABORT when you have to. It essentially crashes the database and expects instance recovery to pick up the pieces. You may have to do that if the system is hung, but it shouldn't be your first choice (unless you want to do real database recovery sometime). If you are able to issue commands on the database instance, issue an ALTER SYSTEM SWITCH LOGFILE to force a checkpoint to close file headers and flush the online redo logs before issuing the SHUTDOWN ABORT. Forcing a check point will allow for an easier instance recovery during the next startup.

Connecting to the Database Instance

A database instance isn't much good if you can't connect to it. Establishing a reliable, persistent, and secure connection to the database from the client is essential.

Oracle has established a network architecture of protocols, processes, utilities, and configuration files to support communication into the database. Oracle Net (formally called SQL*Net or Net8) is Oracle's networking protocol.

Oracle Net is supported by

- DBA-managed listener processes
- Client- and server-side configuration files
- Command-line utilities
- Optional GUI administration tools

Additionally, connections can come into the database via several lighter-weight non-Oracle protocols such as ODBC or JDBC. However, even these non-Oracle protocols use the same underlying server-side Oracle components as Oracle Net connections. For these reasons, we focus on the Oracle specific components.

Local versus remote connections

Connections into the database can be one of two kinds:

- **Local (bequeath).** A local connection originates from the same server the database is on and doesn't use the database listener process. When you connect to SQL*Plus as `"/ as sysdba"`, you're connecting locally.
- **Remote.** All other connections from outside the database server or those from the server using the listener are remote connections. The easy way to determine if a user is connecting remotely is if you have @TNS_ALIAS in the connect screen. For example, `sqlplus scott@dev11g` indicates a remote connection to the dev11g database.

Communication flow

Connections to an Oracle database typically come across from a client located away from the database, over a network infrastructure, to the database server, through a database listener process and, finally, into the database itself.

On the client side, the program calling the database references tnsnames.ora to find the database server host and protocol to send the request to. The request then leaves the client and goes onto the network utilization Oracle Net. The standard port for Oracle Net communications is either 1521 or 1526, although that's configurable. Over this Oracle Net protocol is where database communications traffic flows between the client and database server.

After a client's communication request reaches the database server host, it's handed off to the listener. The database listener is a separate Oracle software process on the database server that listens for incoming requests on the defined Oracle Net port (1521 or 1526). When it gets a request, the listener identifies which database instance is targeted for that request and establishes a connection to that database instance. On the server side, the listener uses the listener.ora file to make this determination. When the connection is established and the session begins, the listener steps out of the picture and allows communication between the database and client. Each client session has a dedicated server process on the server side. Within this dedicated server process, the user's session code is executed. Figure 5-1 represents the communication flow.

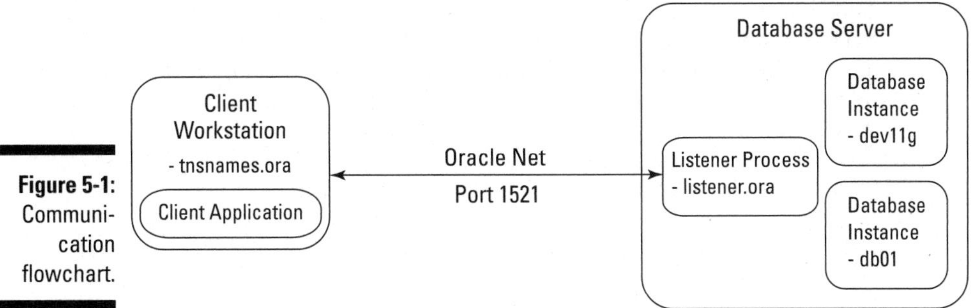

Figure 5-1: Communication flowchart.

The client contains the client application and tnsnames.ora file. It communicates to the database server over Oracle Net on port 1521. On the database server a listener process is configured by way of the listener.ora file. The listener routes the incoming request to the target database instance (either dev11g or db01) and establishes the initial connection handshake between the database instance and client.

Setting up tnsnames.ora

You must provide the address or location of the database you're trying to connect to. This information is often stored in the tnsnames.ora text file, which exists on the client you're connecting from. Other methods of locating your database exist such as referencing an Oracle Internet Directory (OID), but tnsnames.ora is the most common method for clients.

Note this "client" can be a user's workstation; it can be a web application server, or even another database server.

Here is a sample tnsnames.ora file:

```
dev11g =
  (DESCRIPTION =
    (ADDRESS_LIST =
      (ADDRESS = (PROTOCOL = TCP)(HOST = classroom.perptech.local)(PORT = 1521))
    )
    (CONNECT_DATA =
      (SERVICE_NAME = dev11g)
    )
db01 =
  (DESCRIPTION =
    (ADDRESS_LIST =
      (ADDRESS = (PROTOCOL = TCP)(HOST = classroom.perptech.local)(PORT = 1521))
    )
    (CONNECT_DATA =
      (SERVICE_NAME = db01)
    )
```

This particular tnsnames.ora contains 2 TNS (Transport Network Substrate) aliases, one for dev11g and one for db01. When connecting to a database instance, you actually specify the TNS alias (not database name). For example, `sqlplus barb@dev11g` uses `dev11g` as the alias. The TNS alias can be any name (such as dev11g or something more generic like dev or trainingdb); it doesn't have to be the actual database name. That flexibility means you can have a generic alias and not hardcode the database name.

Under HOST you specify either the DNS host name or the IP address of the server containing the database instance. Again, try to avoid hardcoded values such as IP address and use DNS names if possible.

PORT is the port the server-side listener process is listening on. It's also the port you connect across the network on for your Oracle Net traffic (thus the firewalls must be open on that port).

SERVICE_NAME is the service name of the database instance you are attempting to connect to. You can also use SID, although Oracle is promoting the use of SERVICE_NAME instead.

The tnsnames.ora file is text based, and you can edit it by hand. After making changes, it's not necessary to restart the database or listener process.

Configuring the database listener with listener.ora

The key file to the listener process is the listener.ora configuration file. This file identifies two things:

- Each database it will listen for
- On what ports (usually 1521 or 1526)

The file is located in ORACLE_HOME/network/admin or under the Automatic Diagnostic Repository (ADR) infrastructure in ADR_BASE/diag/tnslsnr tree.

Here's a sample listener.ora file:

```
# listener.ora Network Configuration File: /u01/app/oracle/product/11.1.0/db_1/
               network/admin/lis
tener.ora
# Generated by Oracle configuration tools.

SID_LIST_LISTENER =
  (SID_LIST =
    (SID_DESC =
      (GLOBAL_DBNAME = db01)
      (ORACLE_HOME = /u01/app/oracle/product/11.1.0/db_1)
```

```
      (SID_NAME = db01)
    )
    (SID_DESC =
      (GLOBAL_DBNAME = dev11g)
      (ORACLE_HOME = /u01/app/oracle/product/11.1.0/db_1)
      (SID_NAME = dev11g)
    )
  )

LISTENER =
  (DESCRIPTION_LIST =
    (DESCRIPTION =
      (ADDRESS = (PROTOCOL = TCP)(HOST = classroom.perptech.local)(PORT = 1521))
    )
    (DESCRIPTION =
      (ADDRESS = (PROTOCOL = IPC)(KEY = EXTPROC1521))
    )
  )
```

In the preceding code you see two main sections: SID_LIST_LISTENER and LISTENER. The SID_LIST_LISTENER section identifies each database instance that the listener will service connections for. It lists the global database name, ORACLE_HOME, and SID.

As you need more databases, simply add the following section and then customize the relevant information:

```
    (SID_DESC =
      (GLOBAL_DBNAME = dev11g)
      (ORACLE_HOME = /u01/app/oracle/product/11.1.0/db_1)
      (SID_NAME = dev11g)
    )
```

The LISTENER section identifies what host the database exists on and what port it accepts connections on:

```
    (DESCRIPTION =
      (ADDRESS = (PROTOCOL = TCP)(HOST = classroom.perptech.local)(PORT = 1521))
    )
```

Here you see the listener will listen on the HOST (server) classroom.perptech.local and the port is 1521. Requests on other ports will not be acknowledged.

You can add more databases, even if they're different database versions to the listener.ora. If you have multiple database versions, run your listener with the highest version of the database software you have. You can also add additional LISTENER processes (if you want to listen on multiple ports, for example).

You should be aware of one configuration option we don't necessarily recommend: *Shared Servers* (also known as *Multi-Threaded Servers* — MTS). With this method, each user connection uses a shared process rather than a dedicated server process on the database server. In theory, having connections share a server-side process reduces memory use and is good for systems with lots of concurrent users. However, we've never seen it provide a noticeable benefit, and we wouldn't consider it a common configuration.

Note that this is different from connection pooling with application servers, which is something we *do* recommend. What we outlined earlier, in the "Communication flow" section, is the *dedicated server* mode which is more common, provides better performance, and is required for DBA connections.

The sqlnet.ora file is one additional configuration file. It can be client or server side, usually located with the listener.ora or tnsnames.ora file. The sqlnet.ora file is a *special options* file where you can add parameters to the Oracle Net architecture. This file can exist both on servers to impact the listener process and on clients to influence TNS settings. For example, you can

- Add commands to force increased tracing, logging options, or encryption.
- Tell the listener to add a domain name to each database
- Direct the listener to look up connection information in an LDAP instead of a tnsnames.ora file.

Here is a simple sqlnet.ora file:

```
$ more sqlnet.ora
NAMES.DIRECTORY_PATH=TNSNAMES
```

The setting simply tells the client to use the tnsnames.ora file instead of any other resource (such as an LDAP).

If you're experiencing connection issues and your tnsnames.ora and listener.ora files look fine, don't forget the sqlnet.ora. There may be a forgotten setting there causing issues.

Starting and stopping the database listener

The database listener process reads the listener.ora and sqlnet.ora files for its configuration; the DBA manages it using the `lsnrctl` command-line utility. You can use the utility to do these things to the listener:

- Start
- Stop

- Check status

There is no direct relationship between the listener process and the database itself; the processes operate independently. That means you can start the listener before or after the database.

But remember that the listener must be started before the database can service remote connections.

To start the listener, issue the lsnrctl start command:

```
$  lsnrctl start

LSNRCTL for Linux: Version 11.1.0.6.0 - Production on 27-SEP-2008 03:04:48

Copyright (c) 1991, 2007, Oracle.  All rights reserved.

Starting /u01/app/oracle/product/11.1.0/db_1/bin/tnslsnr: please wait...

TNSLSNR for Linux: Version 11.1.0.6.0 - Production
System parameter file is /u01/app/oracle/product/11.1.0/db_1/network/admin/
               listener.ora
Log messages written to /u01/app/oracle/diag/tnslsnr/classroom/listener/alert/
               log.xml
Listening on: (DESCRIPTION=(ADDRESS=(PROTOCOL=tcp)(HOST=classroom.perptech.
               local)(PORT=1521)))
Listening on: (DESCRIPTION=(ADDRESS=(PROTOCOL=ipc)(KEY=EXTPROC1521)))

Connecting to (DESCRIPTION=(ADDRESS=(PROTOCOL=TCP)(HOST=classroom.perptech.
               local)(PORT=1521)))
STATUS of the LISTENER
------------------------
Alias                     LISTENER
Version                   TNSLSNR for Linux: Version 11.1.0.6.0 - Production
Start Date                27-SEP-2008 03:04:49
Uptime                    0 days 0 hr. 0 min. 0 sec
Trace Level               off
Security                  ON: Local OS Authentication
SNMP                      OFF
Listener Parameter File   /u01/app/oracle/product/11.1.0/db_1/network/admin/
               listener.ora
Listener Log File         /u01/app/oracle/diag/tnslsnr/classroom/listener/alert/
               log.xml
Listening Endpoints Summary...
  (DESCRIPTION=(ADDRESS=(PROTOCOL=tcp)(HOST=classroom.perptech.local)
               (PORT=1521)))
  (DESCRIPTION=(ADDRESS=(PROTOCOL=ipc)(KEY=EXTPROC1521)))
Services Summary...
Service "dev11g" has 1 instance(s).
  Instance "dev11g", status UNKNOWN, has 1 handler(s) for this service...
The command completed successfully
$
```

If you need to stop the listener, you can issue the lsnrctl stop command :

```
$ lsnrctl stop

LSNRCTL for Linux: Version 11.1.0.6.0 - Production on 27-SEP-2008 03:04:19

Copyright (c) 1991, 2007, Oracle.  All rights reserved.

Connecting to (DESCRIPTION=(ADDRESS=(PROTOCOL=TCP)(HOST=classroom.perptech.
              local)(PORT=1521)))
The command completed successfully
$
```

After changing the listener.ora file, you must restart the listener process. You can do this via the stop and start commands. An easier method is the lsnrctl reload command. It effectively restarts the listener process without the explicit stop and start.

To determine what databases the listener is configured to service requests, you can read the listener.ora configuration file. Or, more easily, you can issue the lsrnctl status command:

```
$ lsnrctl status

LSNRCTL for Linux: Version 11.1.0.6.0 - Production on 27-SEP-2008 03:03:23

Copyright (c) 1991, 2007, Oracle.  All rights reserved.

Connecting to (DESCRIPTION=(ADDRESS=(PROTOCOL=TCP)(HOST=classroom.perptech.
              local)(PORT=1521)))
STATUS of the LISTENER
------------------------
Alias                     LISTENER
Version                   TNSLSNR for Linux: Version 11.1.0.6.0 - Production
Start Date                17-SEP-2008 23:24:21
Uptime                    9 days 3 hr. 39 min. 10 sec
Trace Level               off
Security                  ON: Local OS Authentication
SNMP                      OFF
Listener Parameter File   /u01/app/oracle/product/11.1.0/db_1/network/admin/
              listener.ora
Listener Log File         /u01/app/oracle/diag/tnslsnr/classroom/listener/alert/
              log.xml
Listening Endpoints Summary...
  (DESCRIPTION=(ADDRESS=(PROTOCOL=tcp)(HOST=classroom.perptech.local)
              (PORT=1521)))
  (DESCRIPTION=(ADDRESS=(PROTOCOL=ipc)(KEY=EXTPROC1521)))
  (DESCRIPTION=(ADDRESS=(PROTOCOL=tcp)(HOST=classroom.perptech.local)(PORT=8080))
              (Presentation=HTTP)(Session=RAW))
```

```
Services Summary...
Service "dev11g" has 2 instance(s).
  Instance "dev11g", status UNKNOWN, has 1 handler(s) for this service...
  Instance "dev11g", status READY, has 1 handler(s) for this service...
Service "dev11gXDB" has 1 instance(s).
  Instance "dev11g", status READY, has 1 handler(s) for this service...
Service "dev11g_XPT" has 1 instance(s).
  Instance "dev11g", status READY, has 1 handler(s) for this service...
The command completed successfully
$
```

This code shows listening for connections for the dev11g database.

Logs for the listener process are stored in the listener.log file. Depending on database setup, the listener.log may be in one of these two spots:

- In ORACLE_HOME/network/admin
- Under the ADR infrastructure in ADR_BASE/diag/tnslsnr tree

For more information on this file, see Chapter 12.

Testing the connection

The best way to test a connection is via the application, but that isn't always possible. Preferably, you're on the client tier and actually go through the same network path as the client applications. If you don't do that, you may not be executing a valid test.

To execute a connectivity test, follow these steps to determine whether you can connect to the database instance:

1. **Go to the client tier.**
2. **See if Oracle client software such as SQL*Plus and tnsnames.ora is installed.**
3. **Execute a sqlplus username@tns_alias such as sqlplus barb@dev11g.**
4. **Enter the password to connect to the database.**

Using the tnsping utility is an even faster method that doesn't require a password. This connects over the network via the listener and establishes a handshake. It then terminates the connection and reports the results, which you see here:

```
$ tnsping dev11g

TNS Ping Utility for Linux: Version 11.1.0.6.0 - Production on 18-SEP-2008
            21:22:45

Copyright (c) 1997, 2007, Oracle.  All rights reserved.

Used parameter files:
/u01/app/oracle/product/11.1.0/db_1/network/admin/sqlnet.ora


Used TNSNAMES adapter to resolve the alias
Attempting to contact (DESCRIPTION_LIST = (DESCRIPTION= (ADDRESS_LIST= (ADDRESS=
            (PROTOCOL=tcp) (HOST= classroom.perptech.local) (PORT=1521)))))
OK (20 msec)
```

Testing connections is a good verification step for the DBA. If problems occur, it lets you catch them first instead of relying on users to report them later.

Oracle Net Configuration Assistant

It's important to understand how the listener works and what different files control the communication process; that's why we explain those parts first in this chapter.

Many DBAs simply copy the same template files from one server to the next making only minor changes. However, Oracle does provide a GUI database assistant tool called Oracle Net Configuration Assistant to preconfigure tnsnames.ora and listener.ora for you on the server side. It can also be executed on the client side. It walks you through generating your configuration files and even tests the connection for you.

We encourage you to test the Oracle Net Configuration Assistant and see if it's easy for you, but we caution you to understand the files themselves. Through that understanding, you can better fix problems and gotchas.

Sidestepping Connection Gotchas

Setting up connections to an Oracle database doesn't have to be difficult, but sometimes initial setup can be tough. Most of the time you, as the DBA, review the configuration and figure out the issue. In other cases, you need to work with the network people to trace connections or open firewalls. In still other cases, you work with the application experts and determine who the client application is attempting to connect to the database.

Many people fall into several gotchas:

- **Remember to start the listener.** This sounds obvious, but it's not uncommon to start the database and forget to start the listener process. Scripting these steps helps eliminate these errors.
- **Keep open the firewall on port 1521.** It is common to have a firewall separating the database server from the users or web application servers. That means Oracle Net traffic may be blocked; in fact, you should assume that you need to have the firewall opened on port 1521 until proven otherwise. Using the `tnsping` utility can help test these connections.
- **Watch out for multiple tnsnames.ora files.** On users' workstations, multiple installations of Oracle client software are likely to have multiple tnsnames.ora files. That becomes a problem when an update to tnsnames.ora is necessary, but not all the tnsnames.ora files are updated. This manifests itself in some applications working and others that don't. Either have one common file or a script to update all the files.
- **Copy and paste existing entries and change only the key parameters.** Because tnsnames.ora is a text file, it invites people to edit it by hand. That is fine, but it's easy to transpose a number (1512, for instance), misspell a server name, or insert an extra) somewhere. Also, avoid using IP addresses for host information unless you really need to. Use the DNS server name instead and you won't have to worry about the IP address changing without warning.

None of these errors is insurmountable, but checking these items may save you some time.

Chapter 6

Speaking the SQL Language

In This Chapter

- Using SQL and the SQL*Plus Tool
- Getting help from SQL*Plus
- Using the Oracle data dictionary
- Seeing an overview of PL/SQL

This chapter shows you some useful SQL and PL/SQL syntax and usage (that literally span over 1,000 pages that Oracle 11g has documented). With that understanding, we provide some helpful tricks by explaining and illustrating standard DBA commands and scripts that should be useful for everyday maintenance. We cover some SQL Developer examples too. And hey, you don't want to be perceived as Microsoft SQL Server DBAs of the royal GUI echelon do you? I guess that depends on the pay.

If you're somewhat familiar with SQL or Oracle's SQL*Plus, you might consider skimming through this chapter. If you find yourself feeling a little lost, consider ramping up on some SQL fundamentals first.

Almost all good DBAs are proficient in SQL*Plus, Oracle's SQL command-line executable. That is always the quickest and most efficient way to finding what you're looking for. Several other tools help execute SQL commands. Those on the market include but aren't limited to Toad, Embarcadero, SQL Worksheet, DB Console, and (my free favorite) Oracle's SQL developer.

Try to bear down and accept command-line interfaces before you get spoiled with what you might think is a simpler way.

Using SQL in Oracle

You might be asking what SQL is. Hopefully you know that it's pronounced *sequel* and that it stands for Structured Query Language.

SQL is an *American National Standards Institute (ANSI)* standard for communicating with relational database systems. Database software like Oracle, MS SQL Server, DB2, MySQL, and others try to use the ANSI-compliant version of SQL. Today, you find many ANSI SQL-like versions but they all have their own tweaks. That's where SQL*Plus comes in with Oracle.

SQL*Plus is an ANSI-compliant SQL executable that has additional functionality for Oracle use like the following:

- Formatting
- Translating
- Calculating for reports or queries

SQL*Plus is considered an interpreted language compiled on-the-fly like Java. Normally you install it with the Oracle database or client software. Its main uses include the following:

- Select data
- Insert
- Update data
- Delete data
- Create objects
- Drop objects
- Write procedural SQL (PL/SQL)

Sharpening the SQL*Plus Tool

First some definitions:

- A *client* is considered a user's desktop PC used to do user stuff. The client interacts with the server.
- A *server* is considered a big-iron host that would contain the database software and the database files. The server processes requests with its massive muscle.

Oracle software installed on a server can also be considered a client because like a client, Oracle's tools can interact with many databases on the local server or on remote servers through the network; therefore, a command-line SQL*Plus client is usually available on both.

Generally, you don't want to install SQL*Plus clients on all user PCs. Having SQL*Plus or other Oracle tools on an end user's PC is often considered a security or data integrity risk since that PC could be used to bypass the application's built-in edit functionality and security.

Users and applications normally only require the SQL*Net components, which allow client-side applications to communicate with the database. Modern applications and web servers have their own Oracle client installed on them and are web based, which would require a client-side Java runtime engine like Oracle's J-Initiator or nothing at all.

Chapters 4 and 5 cover environment variables and network configurations, respectively. If SQL*Plus does not work for you, then it's not installed or simply not in your environment path. To troubleshoot this, start by reconnecting with Chapters 4 and 5.

One final point: Oracle's SQL*Plus has many faces (different looks and feel). For example, it can look a little different depending on your OS but the functionality is the same as long as the SQL*Plus versions are the same. MS DOS command-line SQL*Plus has some different OS functionality than the MS GUI SQL*Plus executable. Often you can't find a SQL*Plus client version that matches the database release version. Keep that in mind when you jump into SQL*Plus, but don't sweat it too much. That's what testing is for.

Using SQL Connection Commands

To connect and execute SQL commands against the database, use SQL*Plus running on the client or the local host.

Follow these steps to execute the SQL*Plus program from your PC or server:

1. **Open a command prompt and type** <sqlplus>.
2. **Enter your username and press Enter.**
3. **Enter your password and press Enter.**

   The Oracle SID (also known as *Host String* or *Connect Descriptor*) can follow after the username with an @ and is optional. If the instance is running on your machine, then the environment variable ORACLE_SID determines which database you connect to if you don't use a Host String.

Here is an example of some connection types:

```
[oracle@classroom ~]$ sqlplus
SQL*Plus: Release 11.1.0.6.0 - Production on Sun Sep 7 11:40:06 2008
Copyright (c) 1982, 2007, Oracle.  All rights reserved.
Enter user-name: hr
Enter password:
Connected to:
Oracle Database 11g Enterprise Edition Release 11.1.0.6.0 - 64bit Production
With the Partitioning, OLAP, Data Mining and Real Application Testing options
SQL>
```

Here is an example of connecting to a remote database:

```
Enter user-name: system@dev11g
Enter password:
Connected to:
Oracle Database 11g Enterprise Edition Release 11.1.0.6.0 - 64bit Production
With the Partitioning, OLAP, Data Mining and Real Application Testing options
SQL>
```

SQL*Plus Profile Scripts glogin.sql and login.sql

SQL*Plus uses two profile scripts when you log in to Oracle using SQL*Plus.

- **glogin.sql:** This file resides in the $ORACLE_HOME/sqlplus/admin directory. If it exists, it's executed first when you log in.
- **login.sql:** This file can be found in many places but Oracle looks for it after glogin.sql based on your OS PATH variable, which usually begins in the present working directory (pwd). After that, it looks for it based on the SQLPATH operating system variable.

Both are found and executed from the local environment you're using (not the remote database software environment). Their purpose is to set SQL*Plus environment variables like the following:

- Line size
- Page size
- Text editor (notepad, vi, and so on)
- The SQL*Plus prompt

It can also run SQL statements that tell you what database you just logged into.

You can do several cool things with the glogin.sql and login.sql scripts. Here is an example of a login.sql script we use regularly:

```
--define _editor=notepad  *for Windows
define _editor=vi
column tablespace_name format a40 truncate
column file_name format a45 truncate
column username format a20 truncate
set lines 132
set pages 55
set termout on
set time on
SET SQLPROMPT '&_USER@&_CONNECT_IDENTIFIER> '
select instance_name dbname, version from v$instance;
```

There are operating system environment variables and SQL*Plus environment variables. For example, SQLPATH is an operating system variable and is set in the user profile on the OS. EDITOR is another OS-specific variable that you can set in the OS profile; or you can define another editor in the login.sql file with define _editor=vi.

Use caution when updating the glogin.sql script on a shared server. Doing so affects every user's SQL*Plus session if they're not overriding it with a login.sql script. It's an easy beginner's mistake and it only shows peers that you're a novice.

SQL*Plus buffer and commands

The *SQL*Plus buffer* is a session memory area that contains the most recent SQL statement or PL/SQL block and all SQL*Plus session environment settings. The most recent statements are in memory until the next statement is run or the session is terminated. It's common practice to save the statements to a file if they're large enough. Routinely, you will bounce from buffer session statements to files depending on the complexity of the statement.

You can show the contents of the latest statements with the LIST command (or abbreviate it with L). You can also see all of the environment settings with the show all command.

SQL*Plus commands

Table 6-1 shows most of the commands and their abbreviations used to manipulate text within the SQL*Plus buffer. We recommend a hands-on approach to learning these commands.

SQL*Plus buffer commands are *not* case sensitive.

Table 6-1 SQL*Plus Commands and Abbreviations

Command	*Abbreviation*	*Usage*
APPEND *text*	A *text*	Adds text to end of the current line
CHANGE/*old*/*new*	c/*old*/*new*	Changes old text to new text on current line
CLEAR BUFFER	CL BUFF	Erases the buffer
CONNECT user	CONN user	Connects as user
DEL	none	Deletes the current line
DEL *n*	none	Deletes the line number *n*
DEL LAST	none	Deletes the last line
EDIT	ED	Opens buffer into the default editor (vi/ notepad)
EDIT filename	ED filename	Opens file with default editor
GET filename	none	Loads filename into buffer; does not execute
INPUT	I	Adds one or more lines after current line
LIST	L or ;	Lists all lines in the buffer
LIST *n*	L *n* or *n*	Lists line *n*
SAVE filename	SAV filename	Saves buffer contents to file
SET	SET option	Sets many available SQL*Plus options
SPOOL	SPO filename	Saves output to a file on the operating system
START	STA, /, ; or @	Runs the current statement in the buffer
START *filename*	STA *filename*	Loads file into buffer and executes
QUIT or EXIT	—	Quits SQL*Plus

You can abbreviate most SQL*Plus buffer and set commands to be more efficient. These abbreviations appear when possible in this section. Additionally, these commands are exclusive to Oracle's SQL*Plus so some commands might not be available using third-party vendor products.

The following listing shows some SQL*Plus commands. Notice the *, which denotes the current line.

```
SYS@dev11g> select username from v$session where username is not null;
USERNAME
--------
DBSNMP
HR
ZEISC
SYSMAN
SYS
SYSMAN
DBSNMP
SYSMAN
SYSMAN
SYSMAN

10 rows selected.

SYS@dev11g> c/name/name, program
  1* select username, program from v$session where username is not null
SYS@dev11g> /
USERNAME     PROGRAM
-------------------- ------------------------------------------------
HR                                                        MS ACCESS.EXE
ZEISC                                                     SQL Developer
SYSMAN                                                              OMS
SYS                      sqlplus@classroom.perptech.local (TNS V1-V3)
SYSMAN                                                              OMS
SYSMAN                                                              OMS
SYSMAN                                                              OMS
SYSMAN                                                              OMS

8 rows selected.
SYS@dev11g> l
  1* select username, program from v$session where username is not null
SYS@dev11g> i
2  and username = 'SYS'
3  /

USERNAME     PROGRAM
-------------------- ------------------------------------------------
SYS                      sqlplus@classroom.perptech.local (TNS V1-V3)

1 row selected
SYS@dev11g>
```

Getting Help from SQL*Plus

When you're connected to SQL*Plus, you can get help from the SQL*Plus executable but help must be installed. Generally, you do that during database creation.

To see if help is available, simply type **help define** while in a SQL*Plus.

A large number of set commands available in SQL*Plus should be listed. If not, load information manually. The following steps and information guide you through the process:

- **hlpbld.sql** drops and create new help tables.
- **helpdrop.sql** drops existing help tables.
- **helpus.sql** populates the help tables with the help data.

To load the command-line help, run the following help commands in an active SQL*Plus session. The following two examples use the help feature to explain the SQL*Plus DEFINE and COLUMN commands.

1. **To install the help functionality, log in to SQL*Plus and type this:**

```
<start ?/sqlplus/admin/help/hlpbld.sql helpus.sql>
```

2. **Look at the help entry for the DEFINE command:**

```
<help define>
```

You should see something like this:

```
DEFINE
------
 Specifies a substitution variable and assigns a CHAR value to it, or
 lists the value and variable type of a single variable or all variables.
 DEF[INE] [variable] | [variable = text]
```

3. **Look at the help entry for the column command:**

```
<help column>
```

You should see something like this:

```
COLUMN
------
Specifies display attributes for a given column, such as:
    - text for the column heading
    - alignment for the column heading
    - format for NUMBER data
    - wrapping of column data
```

```
Also lists the current display attributes for a single column
or all columns.

COL[UMN] [{column | expr} [option ...] ]

where option represents one of the following clauses:
    ALI[AS] alias
    CLE[AR]

…output snipped

    WRA[PPED] | WOR[D_WRAPPED] | TRU[NCATED]
```

SQL language elements

SQL has language elements that support the intention of the SQL statement.

The following have implicit commits so there's no use, ability, or reason to roll back or commit:

- Data Query Language (DQL)
- Data Control Language (DCL)
- Data Definition Language (DDL)

You can use Transaction Control Language (TCL) in conjunction with DML. A commit or rollback is required if you change data within a table by inserting, deleting, or updating the data.

By default, a commit is executed when you exit SQL*Plus properly with the EXIT or QUIT commands. Killing the SQL*Plus program or session automatically rolls back any DML that you haven't committed.

Be sure to commit transactions that you want to make permanent.

Data Query Language (DQL)

DQL is often used to select data from the database in the form of columns. At the least, it contains the key words SELECT and FROM with an optional WHERE, GROUP BY, and ORDER BY.

```
select first_name, last_name, to_char(hire_date,'YYMMDD') from hr.emp
where substr(last_name,1,1) = 'S'
order by first_name;
```

Data Manipulation Language (DML)

DML adds, updates, or deletes data. Its three key words are INSERT, UPDATE, and DELETE.

```
update hr.emp
set last_name = 'Walsh'
where last_name='Smith'
and first_name = 'Lindsey';
```

Data Definition Language (DDL)

DDL defines objects in a database. Its most used key words are CREATE, DROP, ALTER, and TRUNCATE. It creates, drops, or alters objects in the database like tables, views, or stored procedures.

```
create table hr.certifications
(employee_id        number(6),
 cert_type          varchar(30),
 date_completed     date);
truncate table hr.certifications;
```

Data Control Language (DCL)

Used to define privileges in a database to objects with key words like GRANT or REVOKE.

```
revoke dba from hr;
```

Or

```
grant connect, resource to hr;
```

Transaction Control Language (TCL)

Used with DML, TCL defines transactional processing for record changes with the key words ROLLBACK, COMMIT, and SAVEPOINT.

DQL, DCL, and DDL have implicit commits, therefore there is no use ability or reason to roll back or commit. You can use TCL with DML. If you change data within a table by inserting, deleting, or updating the data, then a commit or rollback is required.

By default, a commit is executed when you exit from SQL*Plus properly with the EXIT or QUIT commands. Killing the SQL*Plus program or session automatically rolls back any DML that hasn't been committed.

Be sure to commit transactions that you want to make permanent.

Using the Oracle Data Dictionary

You don't want to get into the thickness of SQL itself (only because there is another *SQL For Dummies* book for that). Check these regular DBA SQL statements that you can use to get familiar with Oracle's Data Dictionary. The *Oracle Data Dictionary* is data about the data in the database (also known as *metadata*).

Data dictionary views

You might have access to four basic types of data dictionary views: DBA, USER, ALL, and V$. Each view is preceded by one of these key names:

- **DBA_viewname:** DBA dictionary views contains relevant information about the entire database. DBAs query these views to conduct maintenance research and are for DBAs only. A few examples are DBA_TABLES, DBA_USERS, DBA_TABLESPACES, DBA_DATA_FILES, DBA_FREE_SPACE, DBA_OBJECTS, and DBA_SEGMENTS.
- **ALL_viewname:** ALL dictionary views contains information accessible to the current user to which you're connected. The view information available is determined by the roles or privileges the user has been granted. A few examples are ALL_TABLES, ALL_OBJECTS, and ALL_SYNONYMS.
- **USER_viewname:** USER dictionary views only have information about the current user (schema) to which you're connected. Examples are USER_TABLES, USER_OBJECTS, and USER_INDEXES. USER views are normally used by developers that are creating applications under their own account. Because they have this information available, they don't need DBA privileges.
- **V$_viewname:** These *dynamic performance views* read from the database control file and from memory. They contain information about how the database is currently operating. Typically they're helpful for troubleshooting and performance tuning. Some examples are V$SESSION, V$LOCK, V$SGASTAT, and V$SQL.

The Oracle database has many dictionary views so it's easy to forget the exact name of the view you need to query. Use the following query to find these DBA views:

```
<set pages 55
set lines 80
select table_name
from dictionary;>
```

Using desc

As a DBA, it's sometimes difficult to find what you're looking for and to know what tables or views have the data you need. That's why the describe command is helpful. Use the following information to build simple queries that pull information from the data dictionary views.

The following listing uses the describe command (desc) as a shortcut. The describe command summarizes database objects and their attributes. It's useful for finding column names and data types of tables or views.

```
SYS@dev11g> desc dba_users
 Name                          Null?    Type
 ----------------------------- -------- --------------------
 USERNAME                      NOT NULL VARCHAR2(30)
 USER_ID                       NOT NULL NUMBER
 PASSWORD                               VARCHAR2(30)
 ACCOUNT_STATUS                NOT NULL VARCHAR2(32)
 LOCK_DATE                              DATE
 EXPIRY_DATE                            DATE
 DEFAULT_TABLESPACE            NOT NULL VARCHAR2(30)
 TEMPORARY_TABLESPACE          NOT NULL VARCHAR2(30)
 CREATED                       NOT NULL DATE
 PROFILE                       NOT NULL VARCHAR2(30)
 INITIAL_RSRC_CONSUMER_GROUP            VARCHAR2(30)
 EXTERNAL_NAME                          VARCHAR2(4000)
 PASSWORD_VERSIONS                      VARCHAR2(8)
 EDITIONS_ENABLED                       VARCHAR2(1)


SYS@dev11g> desc dba_role_privs
 Name                          Null?    Type
 ----------------------------- -------- --------------------
 GRANTEE                                VARCHAR2(30)
 GRANTED_ROLE                  NOT NULL VARCHAR2(30)
 ADMIN_OPTION                           VARCHAR2(3)
 DEFAULT_ROLE                           VARCHAR2(3)
```

If you get an Oracle error like `ORA-04043: object "DBA_USERS" does not exist` when selecting from DBA views, then you don't have DBA access or the role SELECT_CATALOG_ROLE. Also, it's probably not a good idea to run DBA queries on a database at work; you could get into big trouble. You're better off doing this at home on a test database. If the DBAs at work like you well enough, they might give you the role SELECT_CATALOG_ROLE for data dictionary access in a development or test database.

It's important to have a good understanding of the data dictionary view relationships.

Using l

Here is an example of selecting unlocked users from the dba_users data dictionary view. The l in this example is a shortcut for the command LIST, which lists the SQL in your session's buffer. To get a list of UNLOCKED users, type this:

```
<select username, account_status from dba_users
 where account_status = '%LOCKED%';>
```

You see something like this:

```
USERNAME        ACCOUNT_STATUS
------------------------------ --------------------------------
OPS$ORACLE                                              OPEN
ANONYMOUS                                            EXPIRED
MGMT_VIEW                                               OPEN
OE                                                      OPEN
APEX_PUBLIC_USE                                         OPEN
SCOTT                                                   OPEN
SYSMAN                                                  OPEN
XDB                                                     OPEN
SYS                                                     OPEN
SYSTEM                                                  OPEN
DBSNMP                                                  OPEN
HR                                                      OPEN

12 rows selected.
```

To list the command you just executed, type this:

```
<l>
```

You should see this:

```
1  select username, account_status from dba_users
2* where account_status = '%LOCKED%'
```

Creating a join

A simple join can create a relationship between two views called DBA_USERS and DBA_ROLE_PRIVS. Create the file by typing the key word EDIT (ED to abbreviate):

```
<edit dba_user.sql>
```

If you're in Windows, by default you're taken to a notepad editor. In Linux/UNIX, you're most likely taken to a vi editor.

Follow these steps to create your program:

1. **Type the following:**

```
set linesize 132
set pagesize 55
column username format a12
column granted_role for a10
select u.username, r.granted_role, u.account_status
from sys.dba_users u, sys.dba_role_privs r
where u.username = r.grantee
  and u.account_status = 'OPEN'
  and r.granted_role = 'DBA';
```

2. **Save the file.**
3. **Execute the program:**

```
<start dba_user.sql>
```

You should see something like this:

```
USERNAME     GRANTED_ROLE ACCOUNT_STATUS
------------ ----------   --------------------------------
SYSTEM      DBA                                       OPEN
SYS      DBA                                          OPEN
SYSMAN      DBA                                       OPEN
HR      DBA                                           OPEN
```

In normal practice, a schema/owner *shouldn't* have DBA privileges. For obvious reasons it can lead to data integrity issues if the developer or the application owner has DBA access; he could do something dreadful. Schemas should have the least amount of privileges necessary to get the job done. See Chapter 9 for more information about roles and privileges.

In Chapter 2 we discuss logical structures or objects (tables, indexes, synonyms, views, tablespaces, and so on). *Segments* are objects like tables and indexes that take up physical hard-drive space. *Tablespaces* are logical areas where segments reside. *Data files* are the physical space where segments are stored.

During normal DBA proactive maintenance, you might want to track how fast a segment is growing. Here's an example of finding out how big a segment currently is, what type it is, and in what tablespace it resides. Notice the abbreviations for linesize, column, and format.

```
<set lines 132
col meg for 9999999.99
col segment_name for a25
col segment_type for a25
col tablespace_name for a25
```

```
select sum(bytes/1024/1024) meg, segment_name, segment_type, tablespace_name
from dba_segments
where owner not in ('SYS', 'SYSTEM')
group by segment_name, segment_type, tablespace_name
order by meg, segment_type
/>
```

Getting a PL/SQL Overview

Oracle provides a method for writing complex procedures and functions that don't rely on third-party compilers and languages like C, COBOL, Fortran, ADA, or Pascal. Although some of these compilers are compliant and authorized by Oracle, PL/SQL is the native favorite for procedural type applications.

As a query tool, SQL*Plus can't make data-driven decisions like "if this is true then do this else do that." The SQL*Plus DECODE, TRANSLATE, and CASE commands only scratch the surface of what PL/SQL can do in the business rule decision-making process.

PL/SQL has lots of advantages:

- **SQL*Plus friendly.** It inherits data types and attributes.
- **More secure.** It groups SQL commands into programs so users are executing raw SQL commands against your objects. You have better control over what they can do this way. Plus, they only need the execute privilege against the PL/SQL program — not the individual privileges against the tables the program acts upon.
- **Fast.** PL/SQL procedures, packages, triggers, and functions can be stored within the database as compiled code. This allows client programs to pass only necessary variables to the PL/SQL code to process the request. This reduces network traffic and allows the server to do the processing.
- **Array processing with cursors.** *Cursors* are a subset of data that can be defined using a query and then loaded into variables one record at a time. This allows Oracle to cycle through each record and make business decisions based on the data. A good example is when a company's only interested in billing customers who are due for a bill. You could cycle through all records where the customer is due payment but only if they haven't already paid.

Blocking PL/SQL

PL/SQL has basic code known as a *block*. A block is broken down into four key Oracle words. These are broken down into the following structures:

- **DECLARE:** Used to declare input, output, and default values for variables, types, and other subprograms.
- **BEGIN:** Used to start the main body of the PL/SQL statement and can utilize the variables passed through the DECLARE section. This section of code does what you want it to do. It contains the SQL commands that work with your data.
- **EXCEPTION:** Used to handle exceptions or errors during the processing of the main body of the code. Sometimes exceptions can be used for debugging.
- **END:** Ends the statement. Nothing is put here; it's just a keyword signifying the end of the block.

The block structure breaks your program into distinct areas. Each area handles a specific portion of what you want the program to do. All PL/SQL programs use the block structure to organize the code.

Here's a program that selects an employee's last name and salary and then evaluates whether she makes a lot of money based on salary. The program then outputs a statement saying `makes a lot` or `doesn't make a lot` based on whether the salary is below $10,000. Note the use of the block structure.

```
set serveroutput on
DECLARE

        v_last_name     VARCHAR2(25);
        v_salary        NUMBER(8,2);

        CURSOR c1 IS
           SELECT last_name, salary
              FROM employees;

BEGIN
        OPEN c1;
           LOOP
              EXIT WHEN c1%NOTFOUND;
              FETCH c1 INTO v_last_name, v_salary;

                 IF v_salary < 10000 THEN
                    DBMS_OUTPUT.PUT_LINE(v_last_name||' does not make a lot.');
                 ELSE
```

```
                DBMS_OUTPUT.PUT_LINE(v_last_name||' makes a lot.');
             END IF;

        END LOOP;
     CLOSE c1;

EXCEPTION
     WHEN NO_DATA_FOUND THEN
        DBMS_OUTPUT.PUT_LINE('There are no rows in the table.');

END;
/
```

Chapter 7

Populating the Database

In This Chapter

- Making tablespaces
- Getting into users and schemas
- Knowing database objects

It's no secret that databases hold data: typically lots of it. However, data isn't just loose in the database; data lives in structures, which are owned by users. Furthermore, this isn't a random collection of data and objects; it supports a specific application.

In this chapter we focus less on the actual data itself and more on the structures that hold the data and control access to that data. We explain tablespaces and their role in object storage. Objects must have an owner, and we explain how users have schemas that contain objects. Database objects that a user can own include — but are not limited to — tables, indexes, and views.

A database application includes the tables, indexes, PL/SQL code, and other objects executing the program logic inside the database. Depending on the application's size and nature, building an application structure within a database can be complex.

Here is the general order of operations for building an application environment:

1. Create the tablespaces that will contain the tables and indexes for the application.
2. Create the database account who will own the database objects for the application.
3. Create the objects (tables, indexes, packages, and so on) in the application owner's schema.
4. Create any synonyms for object names and database roles to control access to the application schema owner's objects.

5. Load the data into the tables and generate indexes.
6. Create the application users and grant those users access roles so they can access the application objects.

The exact build instructions for an application environment should come from the vendor, or you should create them with the application developers. The requirements should be defined before the production environment is built; although in the "real world" the requirements are often subject to change.

In this chapter we give you knowledge and tools to perform the steps for building an application environment.

Creating Tablespaces

Database objects are logically contained within tablespaces. A *tablespace* is a logical storage container composed of physical data files in which database tables and indexes are stored.

In a database, tablespaces are created in two ways:

- By default for internal database structures
- By the DBA to store user objects

For example, a data tablespace has one or more database files on the OS's file system. Within that tablespace, one or more data table is created and the data is stored in the tablespace's corresponding data files. In Figure 7-1 you see a graphical example of a tablespace and its contents.

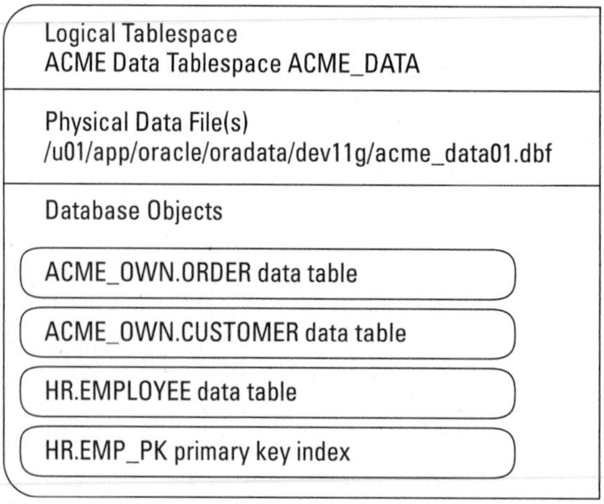

Figure 7-1: The data tablespace hierarchy.

Figure 7-1 includes the following:

- **Logical tablespace.** Stores data tables for the user.
- **Physical data file.** You can add data files as necessary.
- **Database objects.** Here you can see objects from different users.

Multiple users can store their objects in the same tablespace. Tablespaces are available to any user with objects in the database, although organizing different users in different tablespaces is better for performance and manageability. Also, try to separate data and index objects into separate tablespaces (and thus database files) to reduce disk contention as index and table segments for the same object are accessed.

Database tables are stored in each tablespace, but in Figure 7-1 you see an index for a primary key stored in the tablespace.

As you add objects and tables grow, Oracle manages the size of these things:

- *Segments* are any objects requiring storage.
- *Extents* are the unit of storage Oracle uses to allocate space for segments.

Oracle tracks the growth of segments and extents and knows where each object is stored. This *segment management* is covered in greater detail in Chapter 10.

These standard tablespaces are listed with their corresponding data files:

```
SYS@dev11g> SELECT TABLESPACE_NAME, FILE_NAME FROM DBA_DATA_FILES
  2  ORDER BY TABLESPACE_NAME;

TABLESPACE_NAME  FILE_NAME
---------------- ---------------------------------------------
EXAMPLE          /u01/app/oracle/oradata/dev11g/example01.dbf
MY_DATA          /u01/app/oracle/oradata/dev11g/my_data01.dbf
SYSAUX           /u01/app/oracle/oradata/dev11g/sysaux01.dbf
SYSTEM           /u01/app/oracle/oradata/dev11g/system01.dbf
UNDOTBS1         /u01/app/oracle/oradata/dev11g/undotbs01.dbf
USERS            /u01/app/oracle/oradata/dev11g/users01.dbf

6 rows selected.
```

The EXAMPLE tablespace is for Oracle demo objects and MY_DATA contains demo table. SYSTEM and SYSAUX are for internal database objects. UNDOTBS1 is for undo (rollback) objects. USERS is the default tablespace for objects created by users who didn't specify a tablespace when they created objects.

To see each tablespace, space available, type, and extent management, go to Enterprise Manager and choose Databases➪Tablespaces. Figure 7-2 shows this data.

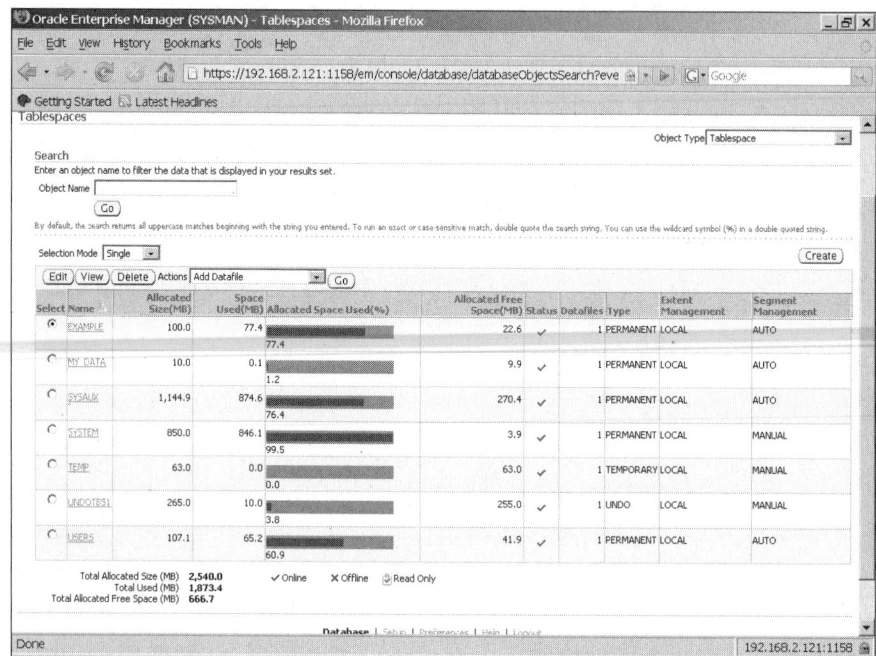

Figure 7-2: Tablespace management.

From the Tablespace management screen, you can click the Create button in the upper right to create a tablespace to store application data tables, as seen in Figure 7-3. Follow these steps:

1. **In the General Options screen, type a tablespace name.**

   In this example, we've named the tablespace ACME_DATA.

2. **Click the Storage tab and choose Extent Management:**

   - **Locally Managed: Default for most tablespaces; the recommended option because object definitions are stored and tracked at the local tablespace level.**
   - **Dictionary Managed: Method common in previous versions of Oracle in which object management is stored in the SYSTEM tablespace. Generally not recommended.**

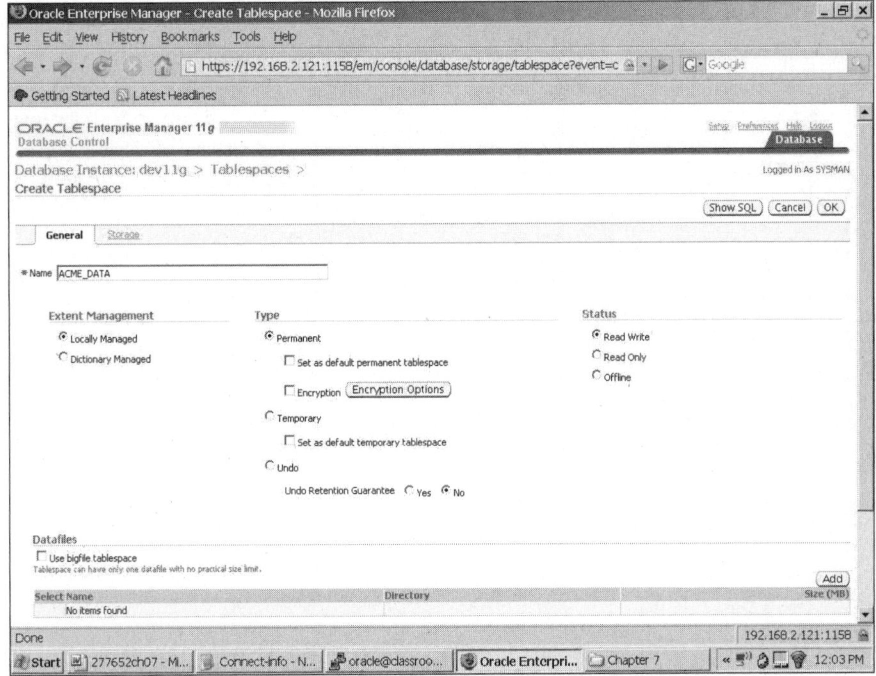

Figure 7-3: Create Tablespace general options.

3. **Select a Type:**
   - **Permanent:** Objects exist permanently
   - **Temporary:** Objects that exist temporary in database; not permanent
   - **Undo:** Undo (aka rollback) tablespace type
4. **Choose a Status:**
   - **Read Write:** If tables and data will be created in this tablespace.
   - **Read Only**: Data is in read only mode and can only be queried. It is also not backed up by standard backups.
   - **Offline**: Content is offline and cannot be accessed.
5. **Click the Add button.**

   In Figure 7-4 you can see an added data file and filename for acme_data01.dbf.
6. **Enter the file's name and path.**

Figure 7-4: Adding the ACME_DATA data file.

7. **Type the file size.**
8. **Choose units from the File Size drop-down menu.**

   In Figure 7-4 it's 100MB, which you can expand as objects grow. Also, you can add more data files to the tablespace if you want to grow onto separate disks. To add additional data files, click on the Add button at the bottom right of the Create Tablespace screen that was shown in Figure 7-3.

9. **Choose the Storage tab from the** Create Tablespace screen (refer to Figure 7-3).

10. **Choose a Segment Space Management option:**
    - **Automatic:** For ease of management, let Oracle manage the extent and segment growth.
    - **Manual: Manually specify the size of each unit of allocation.**

   Click the Show SQL button to see the actual SQL being executed:

```
CREATE SMALLFILE TABLESPACE "ACME_DATA" DATAFILE
'/u01/app/oracle/oradata/dev11g/acme_data01.dbf'
SIZE 100M LOGGING EXTENT MANAGEMENT LOCAL
SEGMENT SPACE MANAGEMENT AUTO DEFAULT NOCOMPRESS
```

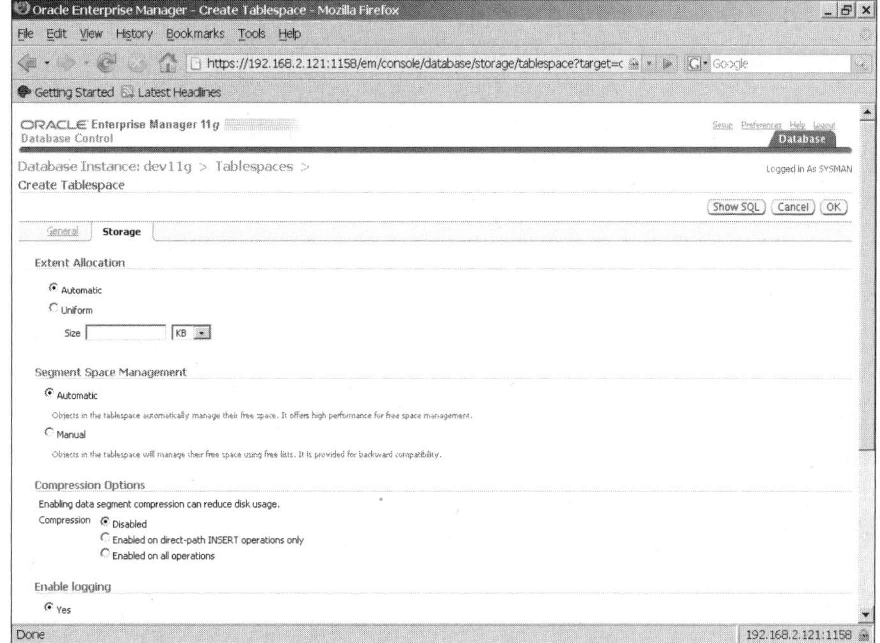

Figure 7-5: ACME_DATA storage options.

11. **When you are satisfied with your options, click the OK button.**

    The tablespace is created.

12. **Create another tablespace with the same options to be used for index storage. Repeat Steps 1 through 11 to create the index tablespace.**

    If the second tablespace is named ACME_INDEX, you have these options when it's created:

```
TABLESPACE_NAME  FILE_NAME
---------------- ---------------------------------------------
ACME_DATA        /u01/app/oracle/oradata/dev11g/acme_data01.db
ACME_INDEX       /u01/app/oracle/oradata/dev11g/acme_index01.d
EXAMPLE          /u01/app/oracle/oradata/dev11g/example01.dbf
MY_DATA          /u01/app/oracle/oradata/dev11g/my_data01.dbf
SYSAUX           /u01/app/oracle/oradata/dev11g/sysaux01.dbf
SYSTEM           /u01/app/oracle/oradata/dev11g/system01.dbf
UNDOTBS1         /u01/app/oracle/oradata/dev11g/undotbs01.dbf
USERS            /u01/app/oracle/oradata/dev11g/users01.dbf

8 rows selected.
```

    Now you have tablespaces and are ready to start creating users and objects.

Creating Users and Schemas

Users not only access data in a database, but they own the objects that contain the data. The set of objects owned by a user is its *schema*. Not all users own objects so schemas may be empty.

Other users can access or execute objects within a user's schema once the schema owner grants privileges. It is common practice to have one user own all of an application's objects (tables, indexes, views, and so on) and then provide access to those objects to all the application users within the database. This is done via database grants, roles, and synonyms.

For example, assume you have the ACME application. You'd create a user called ACME_OWN and create all objects as ACME_OWN. Then you'd create a database role called ACME_USER and grant SELECT, UPDATE, EXECUTE for the objects in ACME_OWN's schema to that role. Application users would be granted the ACME_USER role so they could access the ACME_OWN's objects. This way one user owns the objects, but the actual database or application users access the data. This separation improves both security and manageability.

Users fall into one of two categories:

- Application owners whose schemas contain multiple objects
- Application users with few or no objects

The syntax for each user creation is the same, but grants and privileges for each are what separate the two categories.

Here's the simple syntax for creating a user:

```
CREATE USER <USERNAME>
IDENTIFIED BY "<PASSWORD>"
TEMPORARY TABLESPACE <TEMPORARY TABLESPACE>
DEFAULT TABLESPACE <DEFAULT TABLSPAC>;
```

For username, use something descriptive (such as *DATABASE TITLE*_OWN) for the owner of objects for the application. If a connection pooled web user (as explained in Chapter 3) is going to access the application, a name appended with _WEB is appropriate. Normal application users should be descriptive such as first initial, last name, birth month, and birthday; an example is JSMITH0912.

The password for the user should have the following characteristics:

- Should be more than eight characters
- Should include numbers and special characters

- Should *not* be based on dictionary words

Placing the password in double quotation marks (" ") allows special characters without disrupting the SQL syntax.

Two tablespaces need to be identified when creating a user: temporary and default:

- TEMPORARY tablespace is where temporary segments are created. TEMP is the standard.
- DEFAULT tablespace is where tablespace objects (such as tables or indexes) are created if you omit the TABLESPACE storage clause during the object create statement. Ideally, every table or index creation statement lists a tablespace. If a tablespace is missing, these objects go to the tablespace defined as DEFAULT. Generally the USERS tablespace is defined as DEFAULT.

A user needs system privileges to be able to connect to the database and create objects. Granting the CREATE SESSION privilege or CONNECT role allows a user to log in to the database. Giving a user the RESOURCE role enables the user to create database objects. Roles and privileges are explained in greater detail in Chapter 9.

In the following steps you create a user with SQL*Plus and grant the necessary roles and privileges to connect to the database:

1. **In SQL*Plus, type the following to create a user:**

   ```
   SYS@dev11g> create user acme_own
     2  identified by "acme_own2008!!"
     3  temporary tablespace temp
     4  default tablespace users;

   User created.
   ```

   In this example, the user is schema owner ACME_OWN. The default tablespace is defined as USERS, although the TABLESPACE storage clause is expected to specify ACME_DATA when objects are created.

2. **Grant the user CONNECT and RESOURCE roles so that the user can log in to the database and create objects:**

   ```
   SYS@dev11g> grant connect to acme_own;

   Grant succeeded.

   SYS@dev11g> grant resource to acme_own;

   Grant succeeded.
   ```

3. **Create a new role:**

```
SYS@dev11g> create role acme_user;

Role created.

SYS@dev11g> grant create session to acme_user;

Grant succeeded.
```

   In this example, ACME_USER is created. That user will receive object grants from the ACME_OWN account as objects are created.

4. **Grant the appropriate INSERT, UPDATE, DELETE, and EXECUTE privileges for each object to the second role.**

   This lets you grant the role that has the grants to each application user. Each application user then has access to the ACME_OWN objects. This saves you from having to individually grant each user access to each object.

5. **Grant CREATE SESSION to the first role.**

   When users receive the role, they can log in to the database.

You can create individual application users by using SQL*Plus. Use Enterprise Manager to create users:

1. **Choose Security⇨Users to get to the user creation screen shown in Figure 7-6.**

2. **Click the Create button.**

3. **Enter the username, profile, password, and default and temporary tablespaces.**

   JSMITH0912 has DEFAULT profile and password authentication. The password you type appears as asterisks; you have to enter it twice to ensure you don't mistype it. The user has default USERS and TEMP tablespaces.

4. **Click the Roles tab to grant ACME_USER role to the JSMITH0912 user.**

   The tab is shown in Figure 7-7.

5. **Click OK to create the user with the information you specified.**

   The information added on the single screen is the same you specify through SQL*Plus.

Figure 7-6 is simply a GUI of the user using the same data as done via command line. The user JSMITH0912 has default USERS and TEMP tablespaces. In Figure 7-7 the ACME_USER role is granted to the new application user JSMITH0912.

Oracle Enterprise Manager - Create User - Mozilla Firefox

File Edit View History Bookmarks Tools Help

https://192.168.2.121:1158/em/console/database/security/user?event=create

ORACLE Enterprise Manager 11g
Database Control

Database Instance: dev11g > Users >
Create User

Show SQL Cancel OK

General Roles System Privileges Object Privileges Quotas Consumer Group Privileges Proxy Users

* Name JSMITH0912
Profile DEFAULT
Authentication Password
* Enter Password ***********
* Confirm Password ***********
For Password choice, the role is authorized via password.
Expire Password now
Default Tablespace USERS
Temporary Tablespace TEMP
Status Locked Unlocked

Database | Setup | Preferences | Help | Logout

Copyright © 1996, 2007, Oracle. All rights reserved.
Oracle, JD Edwards, PeopleSoft, and Retek are registered trademarks of Oracle Corporation and/or its affiliates. Other names may be trademarks of their respective owners.
About Oracle Enterprise Manager

Done 192.168.2.121:1158

Figure 7-6: Create an application user.

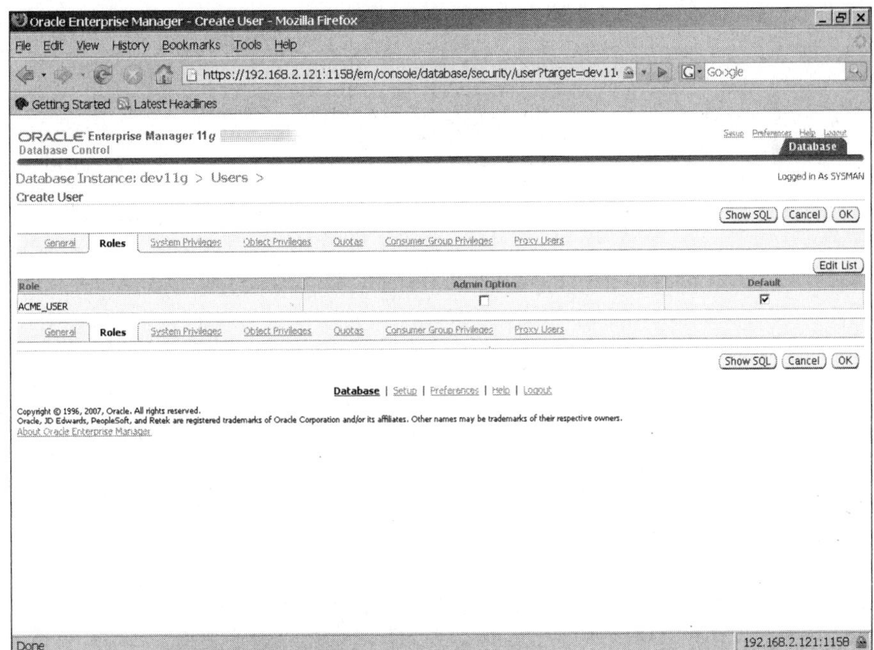

Figure 7-7: Grant the ACME_USER role.

If you need more application users, follow these steps:

1. **Right-click the user you want to use as a template.**
2. **Select CREATE LIKE.**
3. **Create a new user with the same roles and privileges but with a different username and password.**

   At this point you have an application schema owner account and a database role; grant object privileges to this role as you create objects. You also have an application user with a role. After the application objects are built and access has been granted to that role, the application user can access the objects.

Creating Database Objects

Multiple object types exist in a database, and it's important to know what's available. Periodically, Oracle adds new object types to extend functionality, and new options within each object type are regularly added, as well.

The multitude of objects in Oracle grows with every release, and the options available for each object grow even faster. To get the most up-to-date listing of syntax and options, visit the Oracle Database SQL Language Reference 11g documentation at http://download.oracle.com/docs/cd/B28359_01/server.111/b28286/toc.htm.

After you decide what type of objects to create, you need to know how to create them. The most common object creation methods are

- Via SQL*Plus with scripts or command-line statements
- Via a GUI tool such as Enterprise Manager

Creating objects via SQL*Plus is covered in Chapter 6. To use Enterprise Manager to create objects, you can see table creation in this chapter's "Object creation methods" section. But first we show you what object types are available.

Object types

The guts of a database are its objects; and tables are at the core because they contain the rows of data. However, other objects within the database are important. The following objects are common in an Oracle database.

Table

A *table* contains rows of data and is the core of the database. Tables are composed of column names, each with a defined data type. Data is loaded into the table as *rows.*

Create specific *constraints* on each column of data to restrict data. Create *primary keys* on one or more columns to enforce uniqueness for each row. *Foreign keys* generate relationships between rows in one table and rows in other tables.

Tables are contained within a tablespace and may be split between multiple tablespaces (called *partitioning*) to improve performance and manageability.

View

A *view* is a SQL statement that joins one or more tables to form a logical representation of data. Rather than the user or program unit issuing a complex statement on multiple tables, the view allows that data to already be joined. That way the user can select from the view to achieve the same result. Views provide the benefits of reduced complexity and improved performance when created as materialized views. A materialized view is one where data is already selected and stored.

Index

An *index* is an internal mechanism that allows fast access to selected rows within a table. Just as you look in a book's index to find a topic, a database index is a pointer to selected data within data tables.

You can use multiple types of indexes depending on the nature of the table and data:

- **B*Tree indexes** are the default and most common.
- **Bit mapped indexes** are used for data with low cardinality.
- **Function-based indexes** exist on functions on SQL statements.

Indexes are key to fast data access, but they come at a cost. The index must be updated every time data is inserted, updated, or deleted; this is a performance hit. Indexes also consume disk space and are commonly stored in tablespaces separate from the corresponding data tablespaces.

Like rows of data, you may partition indexes into multiple tablespaces to improve performance and manageability.

Procedure

A *procedure* is a PL/SQL program unit that executes program code to process rows of data. Application and business logic exist as procedures within a database.

A procedure can

- Standalone within a schema
- Be part of a package
- Be an anonymous PL/SQL block

Function

A *function* is a PL/SQL program unit that executes and returns a value to the program unit that called it. Conceptually, an Oracle function isn't unlike functions in other programming languages. Functions typically accept input parameters from the calling program, perform some type of processing on that input, and return a value to the calling program unit.

Functions come in two ways:

- Oracle provides many useful built-in functions (for example, time, date, and mathematical functions).
- The user can write customized functions.

A function can exist in the following ways:

- Standalone within a schema
- As part of a package
- As an anonymous PL/SQL block

Package

A *package* is a group of related PL/SQL procedures and functions that form a larger program unit. A package typically has procedures and functions related to a specific business purpose; that way the functionality is contained to that package. A package contains two things:

- A package *spec,* or *header,* which lists the publicly exposed program units
- The package *body,* which holds the actual PL/SQL program code for each contained procedure or function

Trigger

A *trigger* is a PL/SQL program unit that is executed when a table is updated, inserted, or deleted, or when other database events occur. A common trigger example: Assume an insert on the sales table. Delete the appropriate amount on the inventory table; if it drops to a certain level, then order new inventory.

Database link

A connection from one database to another is a *database link*. It allows a user or program unit to select or modify data from another Oracle database. The link specifies a TNS (Transport Network Substrate described in Chapter 5) alias to connect to a remote database. For example, if you execute

```
SELECT * FROM CUSTOMER@SWREGION;
```

you'd select all the data from the CUSTOMER table in the SWREGION database.

Synonym

A *synonym* in a database is just what it is in the English language: a different name for the same thing. Synonyms can be either of the following:

- **Private.** The name is available only to the owner of that synonym.
- **Public.** More common and provides a short name for all users within a database so they don't have to list the schema owner for each object in their queries.

By default, objects are accessed by SCHEMA_OWNER.OBJECT_NAME. For example, ACME_OWN.CUSTOMER is the customer table for ACME_OWN and is how any other application user must access that table (for instance, SELECT * FROM ACME_OWN.CUSTOMER). A public synonym allows you to drop the ACME_OWN from the query.

Object creation methods

As a DBA, you're expected to create objects — but you seldom create them from scratch. Normally the application developer or software vendor provides SQL scripts with the DDL and DML for the objects to be created. You simply log in via SQL*Plus and run the scripts provided.

SQL scripts are the recommended method for these reasons:

- A script isn't subject to typos.
- A script can be versioned, controlled, and reexecuted as necessary.

We cover many of the fine points of SQL and SQL*Plus in Chapter 6.

Odds are, if you're creating multiple objects by hand typing directly into SQL*Plus, something is wrong with your overall development process. Rarely is it okay to create ad-hoc objects.

The easiest way to create objects is with a GUI tool such as Enterprise Manager. You should understand the SQL being executed behind the Enterprise Manager scenes. We also recommend that you try these tools, as they're far less error prone than typing commands manually.

Within Enterprise Manager, choose Database⇨Schema to access the tool that is most useful for object review, creation, and management. This tool lists the different kinds of objects available. Clicking each type lists the owners to allow you to drill down for more details.

To create a database table in a schema, follow these steps

1. **Choose Schema⇨Table.**
2. **Use the CREATE TABLE option.**

   A wizard starts.
3. **Select Standard for table.**
4. **Enter tablespace and column information.**

   Figure 7-8 specifies a CUSTOMER table with multiple columns. The ACME_DATA tablespace is for storage, which means the table will be created in the ACME_DATA tablespace.
5. **Choose the Constraints tab shown in Figure 7-9.**
6. **Create any necessary primary keys.**

   Refer back to Figure 7-8, where a primary key is created on the CUST_ID column so that only unique, non-null values are allowed during inserts.
7. **Click OK to create the table.**
8. **Grant SELECT, INSERT, UPDATE, DELETE privileges for the user to view and insert, update, and delete data.**

   In this example, privileges are given to ACME_OWN.CUSTOMER and to the ACME_USERS role.

   ```
   ACME_OWN@dev11g> grant select, insert, update, delete on customer to acme_
             user;
   Grant succeeded.
   ```

   With this grant, anyone with the ACME_USERS role can select, insert (add), update, or delete data to the ACME_OWN.CUSTOMER table.
9. **From the main Enterprise Manager screen, click Schema tab⇨Indexes⇨Create.**

   The Create Index screen appears in Figure 7-10.

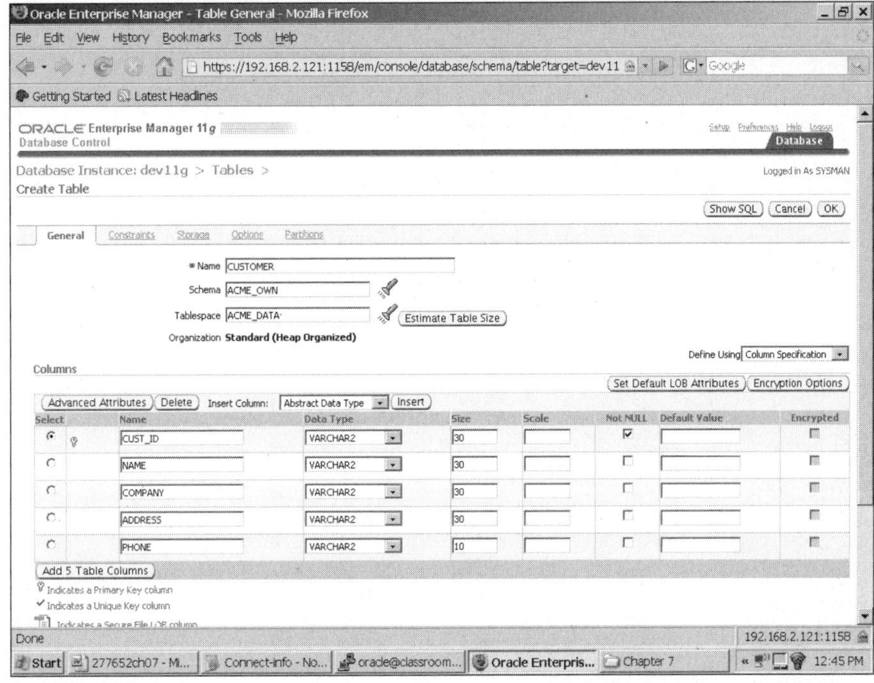

Figure 7-8: Creating the ACME_OWN CUSTOMER table.

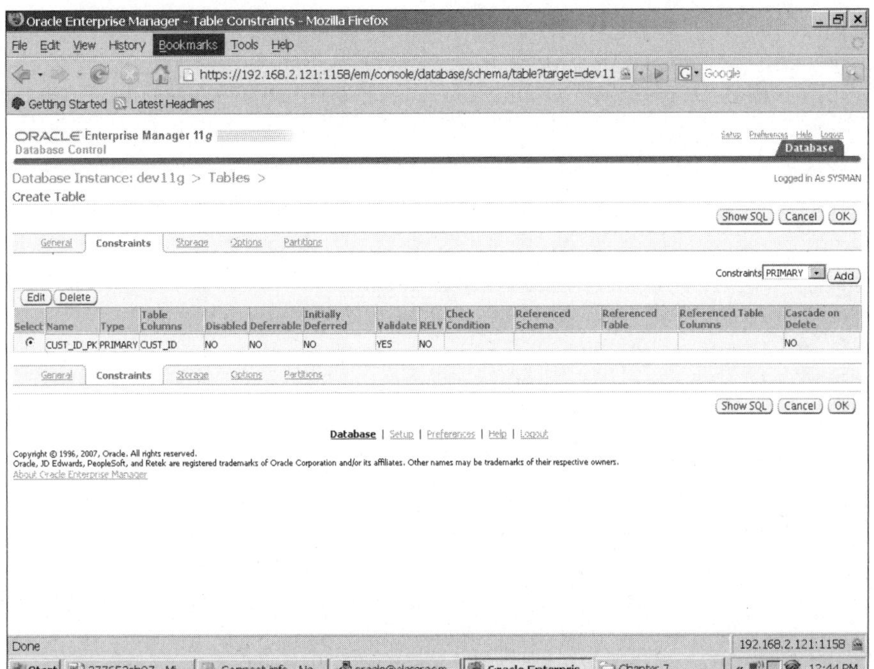

Figure 7-9: Primary key constraint.

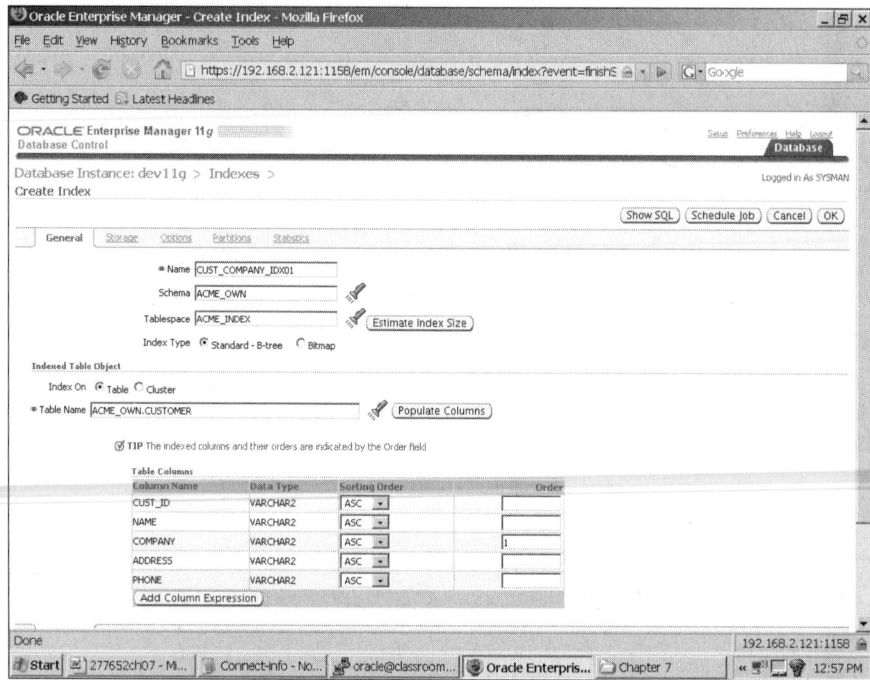

Figure 7-10: Creating an index on the CUSTOMER table.

10. Select Create Index and fill in the appropriate values.

In Figure 7-10 another index is being added to the CUSTOMER table on the COMPANY field (shown under the Table column). The index allows fast access to data where the SELECT statement uses the COMPANY column as part of a join or WHERE clause.

11. Decide in what tablespace to store the index information.

The ACME_INDEX is indicated in Figure 7-10.

Other third-party GUI tools provide a graphical view into the database. Here are two popular examples:

- SQL Navigator
- TOAD (Tool for Oracle Application Developers)

Both SQL Navigator and TOAD are made by Quest Software (quest.com). These tools are common for application developers because they provide nicely formatted output, particularly for PL/SQL program units. As a DBA, you should be familiar with the tools your developers use, but you also may find these tools beneficial.

Part III
Caring for an Oracle Database

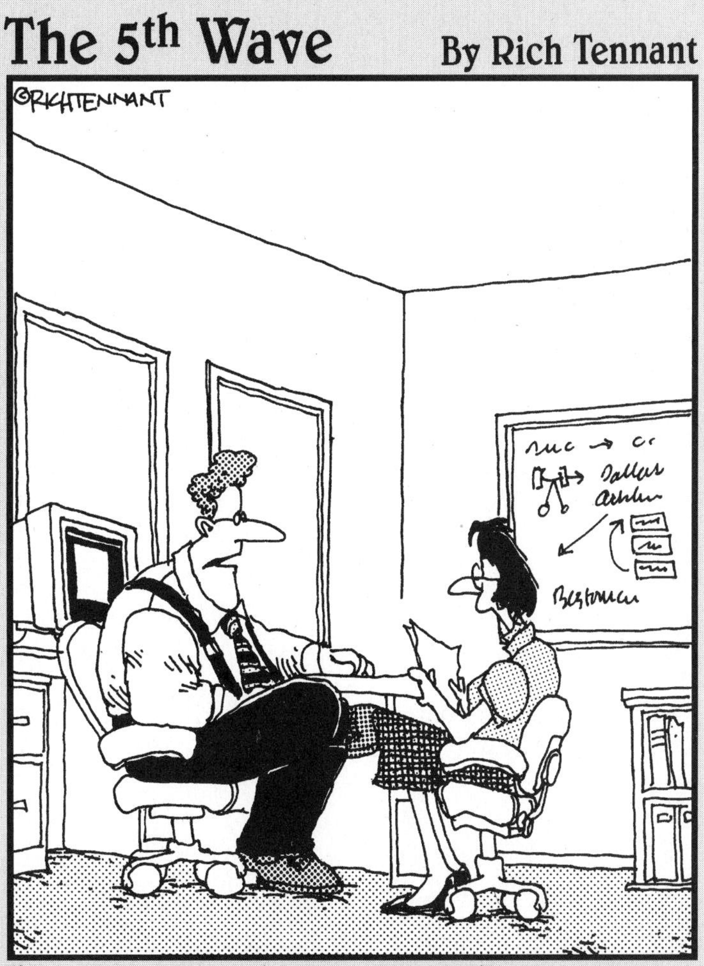

"Our automated response policy to a large company-wide data crash is to notify management, back up existing data and sell 90% of my shares in the company."

In this part . . .

Your database is up and running but you need to attend to some matters. Chapters 8 and 9, respectively, help you protect the database and the data it holds. Chapter 10 helps you keep things up and running with a daily maintenance checklist. Tuning is important; things change when users enter the daily grind. Chapter 11 helps you fine tune. Inevitably, snags appear; Chapter 12's troubleshooting information gets you out of the muck. Chapter 13 gives you a leg up and reveals Enterprise Manager.

Chapter 8

Protecting Your Oracle Database

In This Chapter

- Knowing the threats
- Backing up and recovering
- Getting an introduction to Oracle Recovery Manager

Forget the Boy Scouts. DBAs need to be prepared for anything. In addition to security, protecting your data is done with backups. All kinds of threats are out there waiting to destroy your database. Luckily, you have a number of ways to protect your data against those threats. But first you need to know what those threats are.

Assessing Database Threats

Backing up your Oracle environment involves putting processes and procedures in place to protect the database from any and all type of failures. Creating a backup strategy involves many steps. Unfortunately, you can push no singular button and make everything okay.

A good backup plan can guard against the following threats.

Instance failure

Instance failure occurs when Oracle, as a running program, crashes. The good news here is Oracle has provided a recovery mechanism for this so you get off easy. All you have to do is restart the database instance; Oracle automatically recovers from instance failure. However, you might want to investigate what caused the instance failure in the first place so you can prevent it from happening again.

Oracle code tree

The *Oracle code tree* has the files that you install when you put Oracle on your system. It includes the database files, any patchsets and patches you apply, and any other tools required to make your application run.

Losing files within the code tree may result in your database crashing. That's why it's important to make sure it not only is protected but that you are able to recover it in the event it is damaged. It's an often-overlooked portion of a solid backup and recovery strategy.

Make sure the code tree is backed up as part of the OS backup. Sometimes the loss of a file in the Oracle code tree can quickly be restored out of the OS backup instead of doing an entire reinstallation.

Keep all the software handy in case you need to reinstall it. Keeping it handy means having a hard copy of it ready to go, rather than storing it on the network. In the event of a disaster, you may not have access to those network resources. Don't rely on Oracle's web site to download it. Depending on how busy they are, it could take hours.

Dropped objects

Objects are dropped by humans, so this problem occurs when someone drops an object that they either didn't mean to drop or that they later decide they want back.

As a DBA, unless you are involved with application design, many times you are simply told what and when to remove something from the database. Always take a Data Pump export of that object before you drop it.

Media failure

Media failure is the loss of a file required for the database to operate. What files might you need to recover if media loss occurs?

- **Data files** store the bulk of your data. They typically have an extension of .dbf.
- **Control files** store information about how your database is configured. For example, are you in ARCHIVELOG mode? Or, how many data files are you allowed to have? Find control files by checking the initialization parameter control_files. Typically, they have an extension of .ctl or .con.

- **Archive logs** are created when you turn on archiving in the database. Find them by checking the initialization parameter log_archive_dest_n (with n being a number from 1–10). Else, look in at the parameter db_recovery_file_dest to find them in the Flash Recovery Area. Typically, they have an extension of .arc.
- **Parameter files** are PFILE or SPFILE. If your database uses an SPFILE, check the initialization parameter for spfile. Otherwise, by default, the file is in $ORACLE_HOME/dbs for Linux/UNIX or $ORACLE_HOME/database for Windows.

Being able to put these files — data, control, parameter, and archive logs — back into action quickly is the key to recovery.

We show you two operating system methods to recover these files, as well as Recovery Manager backup and restore operations, in this chapter's "Recovering Your Oracle Database." Chapter 2 has more information about these file types.

Corruption

Brrrr . . . shiver. Corruption is one of the most elusive and difficult types of failure to deal with. Figuring out why it occurred is often a considerable challenge. When things are *corrupted,* rows become unreadable in the database and report errors.

Corruption can be

- Physical
- Logical
- Your data
- In the data dictionary

You can use RMAN and Block Media Recovery as well as Data Pump to help recover from corruption problems. Luckily, this type of failure is rare.

If you are having corruption troubles in your database, consider contacting Oracle support for help. This is the type of issue where Oracle earns those hefty support contracts.

User error

This isn't actually a type of failure, but is probably the most common cause for recoveries. We mention it because you can protect against user error (even your own in case you're fallible).

Proper training, including training your users, can help reduce the chances of user error.

Getting Your Oracle Recovery Manager

Recovery Manager (RMAN as we lovingly refer to it) is Oracle's backup and recovery solution to protect the files in your database. It can recover from things like lost rows or lost objects, but its primary purpose is to restore and recover lost files.

RMAN is Oracle's replacement to Enterprise Backup Utility (EBU) from Oracle 7. RMAN first reared its head in Oracle 8.0.*x*, but it was not well received in its earliest versions. It was difficult to configure and to use. RMAN came of age with the release of Oracle 9.*x*. Further improvements in 10g and 11g have led it to become almost the de facto standard now for backup of Oracle files. The commands are more concise and meaningful than in previous versions of RMAN. Repeated operations and options can be pre-configured instead of being coded into every script. It's fast, efficient, and reliable. And most of all, it's easy to learn and implement.

Starting RMAN

You have a number of ways to launch RMAN:

- Launch the tool, then log in.
- Launch the tool and log in all at once.
- Launch the tool and have all the output go to a log file. This option is typically used when running RMAN as a scheduled task.

Here is an example of probably the simplest way to get RMAN going:

1. **Set your ORACLE_SID from the OS command line:**
   - For **Windows:**

```
<set ORACLE_SID=dev11g>
```

- For **Linux/UNIX:**

```
<export ORACLE_SID=dev11g>
```

This example uses dev11g for the ORACLE_SID. There will be no output for setting your ORACLE_SID.

2. **Launch RMAN:**

```
<rman>
```

The RMAN launches, as shown in Figure 8-1.

3. **Connect to the database you want to back up:**

```
RMAN> connect target /
```

You see something like this:

```
connected to target database: DEV11G (DBID=3869622232)
RMAN>
```

You have to connect to RMAN as SYSDBA. However, do not specify it. It is included by default.

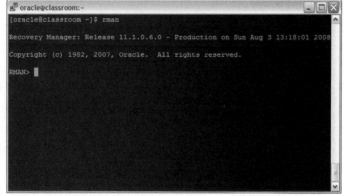

```
oracle@classroom:~
[oracle@classroom ~]$ rman

Recovery Manager: Release 11.1.0.6.0 - Production on Sun Aug 3 13:18:01 2008

Copyright (c) 1982, 2007, Oracle.  All rights reserved.

RMAN>
```

Figure 8-1: Use the Recovery Manager to back up and recover files.

Configuring RMAN

You can preconfigure RMAN some parameters. These parameters are primarily for options that you want to use for all your backups and recoveries. They can be overridden inside your scripts for one-off operations.

1. **Launch RMAN.**
2. **View a list of these parameters by typing the following:**

```
<show all;>
```

You see this:

```
using target database control file instead of recovery catalog
RMAN configuration parameters for database with db_unique_name DEV11G are:
CONFIGURE RETENTION POLICY TO REDUNDANCY 1; # default
CONFIGURE BACKUP OPTIMIZATION OFF; # default
CONFIGURE DEFAULT DEVICE TYPE TO DISK; # default
CONFIGURE CONTROLFILE AUTOBACKUP OFF; # default
CONFIGURE CONTROLFILE AUTOBACKUP FORMAT FOR DEVICE TYPE DISK TO '%F'; #
          default
CONFIGURE DEVICE TYPE DISK PARALLELISM 1 BACKUP TYPE TO BACKUPSET; #
          default
CONFIGURE DATAFILE BACKUP COPIES FOR DEVICE TYPE DISK TO 1; # default
CONFIGURE ARCHIVELOG BACKUP COPIES FOR DEVICE TYPE DISK TO 1; # default
CONFIGURE MAXSETSIZE TO UNLIMITED; # default
CONFIGURE ENCRYPTION FOR DATABASE OFF; # default
CONFIGURE ENCRYPTION ALGORITHM 'AES128'; # default
CONFIGURE COMPRESSION ALGORITHM 'BZIP2'; # default
CONFIGURE SNAPSHOT CONTROLFILE NAME TO 'SNCFDEV11G.ORA';
```

Sometimes you only want to see one parameter. If so, just choose one parameter name and type this:

```
<show retention policy;>
```

You see this:

```
using target database control file instead of recovery catalog
RMAN configuration parameters for database with db_unique_name DEV11G are:
CONFIGURE RETENTION POLICY TO REDUNDANCY 1; # default
```

To change a parameter, copy what you see from the SHOW command and change the value accordingly. For example, type:

```
<CONFIGURE RETENTION POLICY TO recovery window of 3 days;>
```

And you see this:

```
new RMAN configuration parameters:
CONFIGURE RETENTION POLICY TO RECOVERY WINDOW OF 3 DAYS;
new RMAN configuration parameters are successfully stored
```

Take a closer look at some of the configuration parameters:

- **Retention Policy:** Configuring a retention policy tells RMAN how long you want to keep your backup information. For example, if you reuse your backup tapes every two weeks, you can set your retention policy to expire those backups after 14 days. That way, you can purge them from RMAN to avoid cluttering the catalog of backup information that RMAN stores. Retention policies can be set two ways:

  - **Recover Window** specifies that after so many days the backup information will expire.
  - **Redundancy** tells RMAN that after you get so many backups of your files, they will expire. For example, if you set redundancy to 3, after taking the fourth backup, the first one becomes obsolete.
- **Backup Optimization:** If you turn on backup optimization and a backup fails half way through, RMAN picks up where it left off when you restart the backup. If it is turned off, RMAN starts from the beginning.
- **Default Device Type:** You can have RMAN back up files to disk or tape. This parameter configures what the default method is when the option is omitted from the backup command.
- **Control File Autobackup:** You can configure RMAN to take a backup of the control file and the spfile every time a backup runs. Also, if the database is in archive log mode, it will take a backup of the control file any time the database file structure changes such as renaming or adding a data file.
- **Control File Autobackup Format:** This tells RMAN the name and location you would like control file auto backups to take on.
- **Parallelism:** On a machine with many backup devices, such as tapes or disks, as well as multiple CPU's, you can set this parameter to use more resources in hopes of speeding up the backup. You can experiment with this to find the optimal setting.
- **Data file Backup Copies:** This parameter will tell RMAN how many copies to make when backing up files. The more you have the safer you are from losing a backup file. However, backups will take longer and require more space.
- **Archive Log Backup Copies:** Similar to data file backup copies, but applies to archive logs.
- **MAXSETSIZE:** This can be used when backing up to tape to make sure that the backup files don't span multiple tapes. This way, losing one tape won't nullify an entire backup. Typically, this is left to unlimited when backing up to disk.
- **Encryption for Database:** Typically, the backup files created will contain the character strings of data that reside in your data files. A clever hacker can extract this data and perhaps make sense out of it. By turning this parameter on, all the data in the backup file will be garbled.
- **Encryption Algorithm:** You can choose the level of encryption in Oracle. The higher the encryption level, the longer it can take to back up the database. Choices follow:
  - AES128 AES 128-bit key
  - AES192 AES 192-bit key
  - AES256 AES 256-bit key

- **Compression Algorithm:** New in 11g, you can choose the compression algorithm that RMAN uses to compress backups. You can choose between these two:
  - High compression (BZIP2)
  - CPU efficiency (ZLIB)
- **Snapshot Control File Name:** Tell RMAN where to put the control file and what to name it when a snapshot of the control file is taken.

RMAN catalog

When setting up your RMAN environment, consider the recovery catalog. A *recovery catalog* is a repository for all your RMAN configuration parameters, backup operations, and metadata. The catalog can store backup information indefinitely.

Selecting a catalog mode

RMAN provides two options for storing backup data:

- NOCATALOG mode stores backup data only in the control file for each individual database. This is the default.
- CATALOG mode stores backup data in both the control file and the catalog.

Storing backup data in only the control file has some limitations:

- By default Oracle stores seven days of backup data in the control file. The database parameter control file_record_keep_time can change the length of time. Still, it isn't recommended that you use your control file for long backup retention periods. It causes control file growth; and if you ever lose your control files, you've lost all your recovery information. It's doesn't make recovery impossible, but it's a real pain.
- Limits the type of reporting you can do on your backups. You can only query one database at a time after which you have to manually aggregate all the reports for multiple databases together.

Consider using a catalog if

- You have a lot of databases to back up
- All the databases you back up are different versions of Oracle
- You want to save your backups more than 60 days
- You know what kind of reporting you want to do

- You can afford the resources it requires to keep and maintain a catalog database

Suppose that at the end of every week you want a report that sums up all the backup information for 50 different databases ranging from Oracle 8i to 11g. You want that report to include things such as elapsed time, average piece size, compression info, and backup type. A recovery catalog can easily generate that report.

The recovery catalog has a set of views you can query, with SQL, to get backup information. This is next to impossible to do without a recovery catalog since all the backup information is stored separately in each database.

If you only have one or two databases to back up and want simple reports and short retention policy, perhaps the recovery catalog is overkill. After all, it has to go into its own database, be backed up, and be maintained just like any other application.

Creating the catalog

If you decide to create a catalog, it's easy:

1. **Create a tablespace to hold the RMAN data by typing in SQL*Plus:**

```
<create tablespace rman_data datafile
'C:\APP\ORACLE\ORADATA\ORCL\rman_data01.dbf' size 100M
autoextend on next 100M maxsize 2G
segment space management auto;>
```

   You see this:

```
Tablespace created.
```

2. **Type the following to create the catalog owner:**

```
<create user rmancat identified by rmancat
default tablespace rman_data
quota unlimited on rman_data;>
```

   You see this:

```
User created.
```

3. **Grant appropriate privileges:**

```
<grant connect, recovery_catalog_owner to rmancat;>
```

   You see this:

```
Grant succeeded.
```

4. **Log into the recovery catalog with the owner and create the catalog:**

```
<rman catalog rmancat@orcl>
```

You see output like this:

```
Recovery Manager: Release 11.1.0.6.0 - Production on Sun Feb 24 14:47:30
         2008
Copyright (c) 1982, 2007, Oracle. All rights reserved.
recovery catalog database Password:
connected to recovery catalog database
```

5. **Once connected to the catalog database, create the catalog repository:**

```
<create catalog;>
```

You see this:

```
recovery catalog created
```

6. **Type the following to connect to both the target database and the catalog:**

```
<rman catalog rmancat@orcl target /@dev11g>
```

Every time you back up a database, you need to connect to both the target and the catalog.

You see this:

```
Recovery Manager: Release 11.1.0.6.0 - Production on Sun Feb 24 14:52:00
         2008
Copyright (c) 1982, 2007, Oracle. All rights reserved.
connected to target database: DEV11G (DBID=3869622232)
recovery catalog database Password:
connected to recovery catalog database
```

Don't specify the password on the command line when you launch RMAN. It is not a secure way to log in because it can expose your password to other people on the system.

7. **Connect to both the target and the catalog and type this:**

```
<register database;>
```

Register any database that you will back up within the recovery catalog.

You see this:

```
database registered in recovery catalog
starting full resync of recovery catalog
full resync complete
```

Everything else in RMAN functions exactly the same whether you use a catalog or not.

Putting It in the Archives

Archiving is the database's ability to track all data changes. You can turn archiving on or off.

Chapter 2 discusses the processes and files associated with archiving, and confirms that running in archive mode has processing and storage overhead. Is this going to slow your database? Well, it depends.

- If you have a database with very few changes and is mostly read, archiving barely has an impact.
- If you have a database under a constant barrage of data changes and batch loads, you might feel it a little.

Luckily, Oracle has designed archiving to cause minimal overhead. In the end, the price is worth the piece of mind you have of having a 24/7 operation with darn near guaranteed-zero data loss.

Turning archiving on and off

With archiving off, you can only take backups of the database when it is closed (also called *consistent* backups). This is done by shutting down that database and starting it in mount mode. By doing this, no changes are allowed to the data. It allows you to take a consistent copy of the data as it exists at that point in time. If you ever have to restore this backup, your database will look exactly as it did when the backup was taken . . . even if it was a year ago.

You might begin to see some inconveniences:

- This is unacceptable if your database requires 24/7 availability. You can't just shut it down and disallow changes for as long as your backup takes.
- Even if you do consistent backups every day, what happens to the changes that occur between backups? They're lost if you have to restore from a previous backup.

With archiving turned on, you can do the following:

- All data changes are tracked.
- You can do backups with the database open and available to all users.
- If you ever have to restore a backup that was taken the night before, you can apply the archives that were tracked up until the point of failure.

In reality, archiving is a must for almost all live production databases. It's rare that you can afford to take the database offline for significant periods of time or afford to lose data in the event a backup has to be restored.

Archive logs

Besides the impact of the archiving process, you have to consider what to do with all the archive log files being created. Again, your database size and number of changes determine how much archive data you will create.

You have two choices on where to store the archive logs:

- **Flash recovery area:** If you store them here, Oracle neatly organizes them by database and date. This solution results in less work and fewer parameters to configure.
- **LOG_ARCHIVE_DEST_n initialization parameter:** This is actually ten parameters. The n represents a number from 1 to 10. That's right: You can store up to ten copies of your archive logs (but doing so would be a little overkill). However, DBAs commonly have two, maybe three copies. Here is an example of how you might set the LOG_ARCHIVE_DEST_1 parameter in your spfile:

```
alter system set log_archive_dest_1='LOCATION=/u01/oradata/dev11g/archive';
```

The bottom line is that you need to monitor the creation, storage, and backup of the archive logs. It's a fact of DBA life.

The good news is you only need to keep the archive logs for recovery between backups.

Does that mean if you back up every night, you can trash all archive logs created prior to that backup? *Do not* trash them every day.

We can't tell you how long to keep them, but consider the following situation:

- It's Wednesday. You're taking a full backup of your database every night and running in archive log mode.
- After the backup is complete, you delete all the archive logs created prior to that backup.
- At noon, you have a catastrophic disk failure and must restore backups from the previous night (Tuesday).
- You discover that the backup tape from the previous night had coffee spilled on it (tsk-tsk) and is no longer good.

See where we're going with this?

- You have to go back to the backup tape from two nights ago (Monday).
- You restore that backup and find that you can't roll forward to the time that your disk failed today because you trashed all the archive logs after each nightly backup.

Again, we recommend not only keeping archive logs for some time, but including them as part of your backup.

It seems that with no other requirements, we tend to keep archive logs for at least 30 days. This should give plenty of time to go back in the event that daily or even weekly backups incur some sort of unfortunate mishap.

Look at it this way: If you back up archive logs, you can remove them from the system to conserve space. Another reason to keep archive log backups: It allows you to restore your database to periods from long ago.

Take this instance: We have a client who, in June, wanted a copy of their database restored to December 31 at 11:59:59 PM of the prior year. We knew, from client conversations, that these operations were possible. Therefore, we keep all backups and all archive logs on tape and offsite indefinitely. We requested the files (from querying the recovery catalog) and retrieved them from long-term storage. We ended up restoring the database to a new server to avoid interfering with their current production database. Everyone lived happily ever after.

Enabling archiving

If you haven't already done so, enabling archiving is a simple process. However, keep these things in mind:

- You have to shut down and restart the database.
- You must have enough space to store your archive logs.

Before you turn on archiving, decide where to store the archive log files. Use the Flash Recovery Area (briefly mentioned in Chapter 4). We show you how to do it here from the command line.

Chapter 4's database-creation steps give you the option to enable archiving. If you haven't read Chapter 4 or recently created a database, we go through it here. Furthermore, in Chapter 4, we were using the GUI *Database Configuration Assistant (DBCA)*. Here, we do it from the command line.

Enabling the Flash Recovery Area

Follow along to enable the Flash Recovery Area:

1. **Open a command prompt to your operating system.**
2. **Log into SQ*Plus as SYSDBA:**

```
<sqlplus / as sysdba>
```

3. **Configure how much space you want to dedicate to your Flash Recovery Area:**

```
< alter system set db_recovery_file_dest_size = 100G;>
```

This example dedicates 100GB. You should see this:

```
System altered.
```

4. **Choose the destination:**

```
< alter system set db_recovery_file_dest=
'/u01/app/oracle/flash_recovery_area';>
```

You should see this:

```
System altered.
```

Now Oracle automatically creates your archive logs under the flash recovery area. It creates a folder for your database and the subfolder for the date the archives were created. It organizes them very nicely.

If you want to see how much of your flash recovery area is used, log into Enterprise Manager Database Control and click Availability➪Recovery Settings. If you scroll down, you see a screen similar to Figure 8-2.

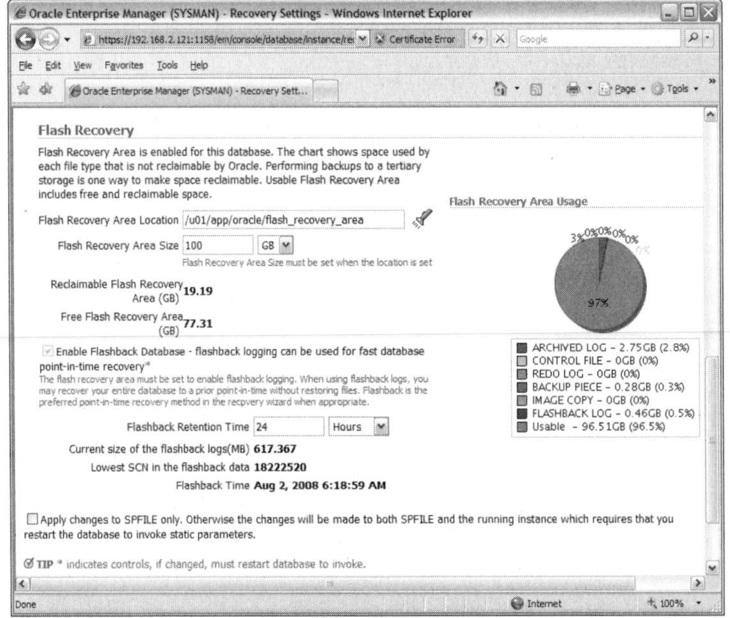

Figure 8-2: Flash Recovery screen.

After determining where you want to keep the archive logs, you can turn on archiving. The steps walk you through the process:

1. **Open a command prompt to your operating system.**
2. **Log in to SQL*Plus as SYSDBA:**

```
<sqlplus / as sysdba>
```

3. **Shut down the database:**

```
<shutdown immediate>
```

   You see this:

```
Database closed.
Database dismounted.
ORACLE instance shut down.
```

4. **Start the database in mount mode:**

```
<startup mount>
```

   You see something like this:

```
ORACLE instance started.
Total System Global Area 789172224 bytes
Fixed Size 2148552 bytes
Variable Size 578815800 bytes
Database Buffers 201326592 bytes
Redo Buffers 6881280 bytes
Database mounted.
```

5. **Issue the command to enable archive mode:**

```
<alter database archivelog;>
```

   You should see this:

```
Database altered.
```

6. **Open the database:**

```
<alter database open;>
```

   You should see this:

```
Database altered.
```

   Now your database is in archive log mode and archive log files should show up in your flash recovery area.

If you are impatient and want to see them now, type the following:

```
<alter system archive log current;>
```

You see this:

```
System altered.
```

If you navigate to your flash recovery area, you should see one of your archive logs under a subdirectory with today's date.

Backup File Types with RMAN

You can take backups with RMAN two ways. Table 8-1 lists some key points of both.

- *Backup sets* are a special type of RMAN file.
- *Copies* are block-for-block replicas of the files you're backing up. While they're made within RMAN via the COPY command, the end result is the same as if you copied it with an OS command.

Table 8-1 Backup Sets versus Copies

Backup Sets	*Copies*
Must be restored with RMAN before use	Block-for-block exact images of source file
Can be any part of an incremental strategy	Do not have to be restored to be used
Can be compressed during the backup	Cannot be compressed during the backup
Can be streamed to multiple devices for parallelism (including tape)	Can be rolled forward by applying incremental backups of source files
Can be into multiple, more manageable pieces	Cannot be split into multiple pieces
Can contain more than one data file	Can only be the first level (0) of an incremental strategy
Can be encrypted	Cannot be streamed directly to tape or to multiple devices

We tend to go with backup sets. Being able to compress and stream directly to tape while at the same time encrypting are very good qualities. However, using copies can significantly reduce recovery time since they do not have to be restored. They can be used from disk in place. All you have to do is roll them forward with whatever archive log files were generated between when the copy was made and when the failure occurred.

Backing up with backup sets

RMAN makes backing up your database a breeze. The examples in this section are hot backups to the flash recovery area.

A *hot backup* is simply a backup while the database is running. You can do it any time, but you usually pick a time when there is less activity. That way, it won't compete for resources.

Of course, figuring out what needs to be backed up is one of the first steps. You need to know what files are out there and whether they have been backed up.

1. **Launch RMAN as described in the section "Getting Oracle Recovery Manager."**

   These examples don't use a recovery catalog since it is discussed earlier in this chapter. Just remember to connect to it if you choose to use one. After you connect, the commands to do all the various types of backups remain the same whether you're connected to a catalog or not.

2. **Set your database to automatically back up the control file and spfile:**

   ```
   RMAN> show CONTROLFILE AUTOBACKUP;
   ```

3. **If you see something like this, skip to Step 6:**

   ```
   RMAN configuration parameters for database with db_unique_name DEV11G are:
   CONFIGURE CONTROLFILE AUTOBACKUP ON;
   ```

4. **If your response reads as follows, go to Step 5.**

   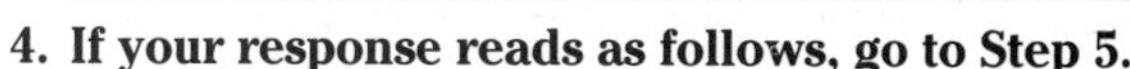

   ```
   CONFIGURE CONTROLFILE AUTOBACKUP OFF;
   ```

5. **Type this:**

   ```
   CONFIGURE CONTROLFILE AUTOBACKUP ON;
   ```

   You should see this:

   ```
   old RMAN configuration parameters:
   CONFIGURE CONTROLFILE AUTOBACKUP OFF;
   new RMAN configuration parameters:
   CONFIGURE CONTROLFILE AUTOBACKUP ON;
   new RMAN configuration parameters are successfully stored
   ```

6. **Get a list of the data files in your database:**

   ```
   <report schema;>
   ```

   You should see something like Figure 8-3.

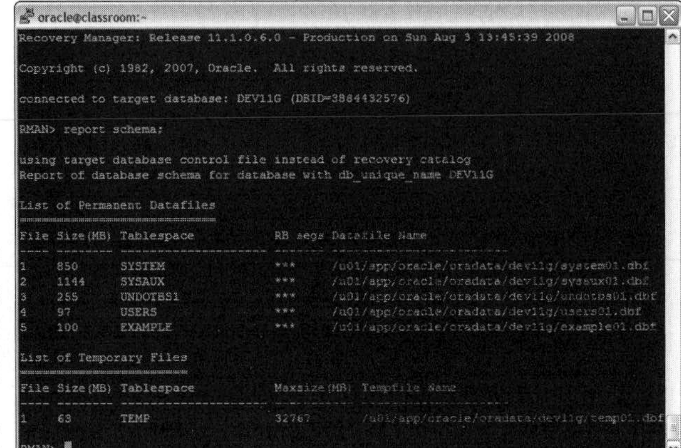

Figure 8-3: Running the RMAN REPORT command.

Backing up the database or tablespaces

You can back up these files several ways:

- Back up the whole database
- Back up one or more tablespaces
- Back up one or more data files

Back up the whole database with this:

```
<backup database;>
```

The output should look something like this:

```
Starting backup at 03-AUG-08
using target database control file instead of recovery catalog
allocated channel: ORA_DISK_1
channel ORA_DISK_1: SID=112 device type=DISK
channel ORA_DISK_1: starting full datafile backup set
channel ORA_DISK_1: specifying datafile(s) in backup set
input datafile file number=00002 name=/u01/app/oracle/oradata/dev11g/sysaux01.
               dbf
input datafile file number=00001 name=/u01/app/oracle/oradata/dev11g/system01.
               dbf
input datafile file number=00003
               name=/u01/app/oracle/oradata/dev11g/undotbs01.dbf
input datafile file number=00005
               name=/u01/app/oracle/oradata/dev11g/example01.dbf
input datafile file number=00004 name=/u01/app/oracle/oradata/dev11g/users01.dbf
channel ORA_DISK_1: starting piece 1 at 03-AUG-08
channel ORA_DISK_1: finished piece 1 at 03-AUG-08
piece handle=
```

```
/u01/app/oracle/flash_recovery_area/DEV11G/
     backupset/2008_08_03/o1_mf_nnndf_TAG20080803T134837_49cvvt1k_.bkptag=
                    TAG20080803T134837 comment=NONE
channel ORA_DISK_1: backup set complete, elapsed time: 00:02:18
Finished backup at 03-AUG-08
Recovery Manager complete.
```

You can back up just one tablespace:

```
<backup tablespace users;>
```

Or back up two tablespaces at the same time:

```
<backup tablespace system, users;>
```

Naming your backups

You can give your backup a name. It's called a *tag*. We name backups because it is easy to see which is which when looking at a list. A tag can be an alphanumeric string up to 30 characters.

Type the following to back up your database and give it a name (database_full_backup in this case):

```
<backup database tag=database_full_backup;>
```

Compressing your backups

As of Oracle 10g, you can compress your backups as they run. Compression usually shows a significant reduction in space usage.

In Oracle 11g you can change your compression algorithm (discussed earlier in the chapter) to help tune backup compression. This can save time or resources.

Our experience shows that any kind of compression can make the backup take two to three times as long. To find out what works best for you, try different compressions and note the times.

Take a compressed backup of your entire database with this code:

```
<backup as compressed backupset database tag=compressed_full_bak;>
```

Incremental backups

You may want to consider an *incremental backup,* which only copies some of the blocks based on when the last incremental was done and what blocks have changed. Incremental backups come in two levels (0 and 1) published in Oracle 11g.

Not only do incremental backups come in two levels, but they come in two types:

- **Differential** only copies blocks that have changed since the last incremental backup of any type. For example, if you do a level-1 differential on Monday and a level-1 differential on Tuesday, the Tuesday backup only gets the blocks changed since the level 1 on Monday.
- **Cumulative** gets all blocks that were changed since the last level-0 backup, even if several level-1 differentials were taken since then.

Incremental backups conserve time and space when designing a backup strategy. You might consider an incremental strategy if your database is extremely large and takes hours to do a full backup.

Since backups incur overhead on the system, if at all possible don't run them when users are trying to access data. If your database is getting large and the backup has run for five hours and is cutting into core business hours, look at an incremental approach to your backups.

These are typical solutions that use incremental backups:

- Sunday at 3:00 a.m. you schedule your full weekly backup. This will take five hours to complete during the least amount of user activity on the system. Your database is 400GB and even though you compress the backup, it still takes 50GB of space.
- Daily at 3:00 a.m., Monday through Saturday, you schedule a differential level-1 backup. This backup only takes 15 minutes and is 2GB in size after compression.

If your database is small, if it doesn't take long to back up, and the backup doesn't interfere with your operations, consider doing full backups every day to reduce the complexity of your backup strategy. Keep things simple when you can.

Block change tracking

Block change tracking just tracks what blocks have changed; when it comes time to do an incremental backup, you can get the blocks that you need instead of reading every single one. This speeds up incrementals tremendously.

Enable block change tracking on your database:

```
< alter database enable block change tracking
 Using file <specify a file name here>;>
```

Put the file with the rest of your data files and name it something like block_change_tracking.dbf. This feature has little overhead. The block change tracking file is, on average, $^{1}/_{30,000}$ the size of the data blocks to be tracked. You can have a very large database before worrying about this file taking up much space.

To do the weekly level-0 backup on Sunday, type the following:

```
<backup incremental level 0 as compressed backupset database tag=weekly_
            level_0;>
```

To do the daily level-1 backup, type the following:

```
<backup incremental level 1 as compressed backupset database tag=weekly_
            level_1;>
```

Do the daily backup every day besides Sunday if you are doing a weekly level 0 on Sunday. If you're doing a monthly level 0 (for example, on the first of the month), then run the daily level 1 *every other day* of the month. Basically, if you're doing a level 0 on a given day, there's no need to do a level 1.

To make sure you start your incremental backup strategy correctly, specify a level 0. If you do not, RMAN will do a *full* backup, which won't record the necessary information to do incrementals from there forward.

Making copies

If you want to incorporate copies into your backup strategy, the commands are slightly different than with backup sets.

Copies are block or block images of the files in your database. Their main advantage is that they don't have to be restored and can immediately be ready for action (making for quick database failure recovery). However, don't forget that they come at the cost of speed and space.

Make a copy of your entire database:

```
<backup as copy database;>
```

Many commands discussed in the backup sets sections are also available with copies.

Make a copy of just one tablespace:

```
<backup as copy tablespace users;>
```

Take a backup of your tablespace users and give it a tag (users_copy in this example):

```
<backup as copy tablespace users tag=users_copy;>
```

You can use copies as the level 0 of an incremental strategy. However, copies can only be for the level-0 portion of the incremental strategy.

To make a level-0 copy for the first stage of an incremental backup strategy, type this:

```
<backup incremental level 0 as copy database tag=level0_copy;>
```

Maintaining the Archives

Archive logs are a fundamental part of your backup and recovery strategy. However, they can take up a lot of space and need to be backed up. Luckily, backing up your archive logs is no more difficult than backing up anything else in your database. Furthermore, RMAN has some features to help you reclaim that space the archives occupy.

Make a backup of all your archive logs with this:

```
<backup archivelog all;>
```

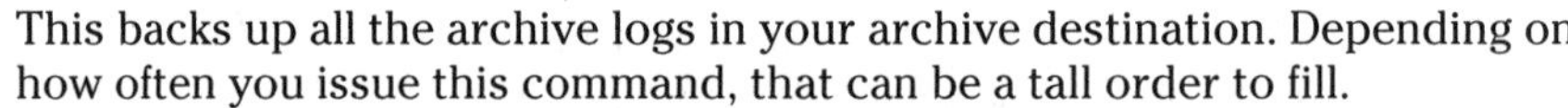

This backs up all the archive logs in your archive destination. Depending on how often you issue this command, that can be a tall order to fill.

Back up your archive logs at least once per day. Keep your archive logs up to 30 days.

Instead of backing up all archive logs every time, you might try backing up only the ones created in the last 24 hours. To do so, type this:

```
< backup archivelog from time 'sysdate - 1';>
```

You could issue that command every day as part of your backup strategy. You could even do it several time a day just to be sure you get all of your archive logs backed up as often as possible. Once the archive logs are backed up, you may not want them in the archive destination; they take up space after all.

RMAN offers a convenient command to clean up any successfully backed-up archives. If you want to back up all your archive logs and then delete the files that were backed up, type this:

```
< backup archivelog all delete input tag=archive_bak;>
```

We favor the `< backup archivelog all delete input tag=archive_bak;>` command as part of a backup strategy:

- It allows you to back up any archive logs that exist in your archive destination while at the same time freeing up space.
- RMAN only deletes the archive logs if the backup was successful.
- You don't have to worry about coming up with a time formula that will back up the archives every so often. Since it deletes the ones it successfully backs up, you can specify "all" every time ensuring that none are missed.

Run an archive log backup command every time you do any database backup. That way, you have everything you need to recover if there's a failure.

Viewing Backup Information

Use the LIST command to see what backups you have stored. You can LIST the following:

- All your backups
- Backups for certain tablespaces
- Backups of certain data files as well as archive logs and copies

There are different outputs to choose from:

- See a short listing called a summary
- See a fully detailed listing with the VERBOSE option

The LIST command is very powerful. Use it to show small bits of information about your backups, or all the information stored about your backups. Try some of the following examples to get a feel for how the command works:

- To see a summary list of the backups that contain the tablespace users, type this:

  ```
  <list backup summary of tablespace users;>
  ```

- To see a summary of all your backups, type this:

```
<list backup summary;>
```

- To see a verbose list of all your backups with the tag database_full_backup, type:

```
< list backup tag=database_full_backup;>
```

The LIST command is a little different if you want to see copies: You use the COPY keyword.

- To see copies of your database, type this:

```
<list copy of database;>
```

- To see what data files copies you have for tablespace users, type this:

```
< list copy of tablespace users;>
```

You will find a lot of information in a VERBOSE listing. Figure 8-4 shows what the output may look like.

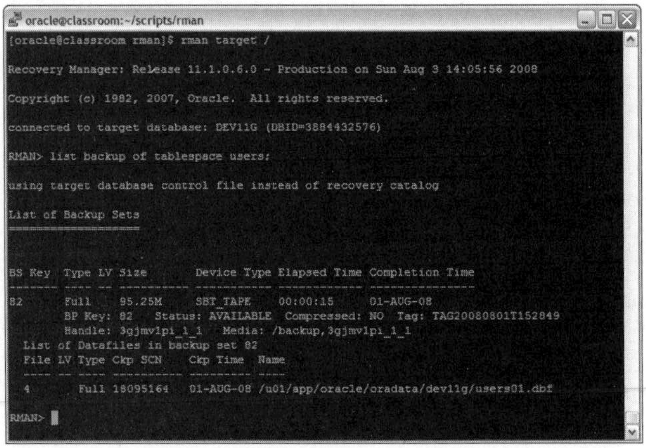

```
oracle@classroom:~/scripts/rman
[oracle@classroom rman]$ rman target /

Recovery Manager: Release 11.1.0.6.0 - Production on Sun Aug 3 14:05:56 2008

Copyright (c) 1982, 2007, Oracle.  All rights reserved.

connected to target database: DEV11G (DBID=3884432576)

RMAN> list backup of tablespace users;

using target database control file instead of recovery catalog

List of Backup Sets
===================


BS Key  Type LV Size       Device Type Elapsed Time Completion Time
------- ---- -- ---------- ----------- ------------ ---------------
82      Full    95.25M     SBT_TAPE    00:00:15     01-AUG-08
        BP Key: 82   Status: AVAILABLE  Compressed: NO  Tag: TAG20080801T152849
        Handle: 3gjmv1pi_1_1   Media: /backup,3gjmv1pi_1_1
  List of Datafiles in backup set 82
  File LV Type Ckp SCN    Ckp Time  Name
  ---- -- ---- ---------- --------- ----
  4       Full 18095164   01-AUG-08 /u01/app/oracle/oradata/dev11g/users01.dbf

RMAN>
```

Figure 8-4: List backup sets of the USERS tablespace with the VERBOSE option.

Take a closer look at Figure 8-4.

- **BS Key** is a backup set key. Every backup must have a backup set key, and ever-increasing unique identifier for each backup.
- **Type** tells you more about what type of backup was taken, such as a full or incremental backup.
- **LV** is short for *level.* When doing incremental backups, they can have multiple levels.

- **Size** is the size for that particular backup.
- **Device Type** indicates disk or tape for each backup set.
- **Elapsed Time** is how long the backup set took to run.
- **Completion Time** pretty much explains itself.
- **BP Key** is the backup piece key. If you break the backup into multiple pieces, each piece gets a unique identifier.
- **Status:** A backup is available if it is on the device that you backed it up to. You can make a backup unavailable if you remove it (for example, if you take the tape out of the drive and put in storage).
- **Compressed** tells if it was compressed or not.
- **Tag** is your backup's name.
- **Piece Name** is the actual file that is created to store the backup.

Recovering Your Oracle Database

Many types of failures can befall your database. Oracle Recovery Manager is a tool that can help you get back on your feet for many of these failures. Sometimes it is the only option; sometimes it is the best approach of several and sometimes it is not. This section focuses on the times RMAN shines and helps you bring a dead or damaged database back to life.

There are two types of failures where RMAN can really help:

- **Media failure:** Loss of files
- **User error:** Mistakes that lead to damaged databases

Whether RMAN can always help you when it comes to user error depends on what type of problem has been created. For example, if a user accidentally removes a file or a tablespace, RMAN can help very easily. However, if a user accidentally drops a table or corrupts data, RMAN *can* help, but it might not be the quickest or most efficient approach. If a user drops a table, it might be quicker to retrieve it from the database recycle bin or flashback database.

However, if the user has purged the recycle bin or the flashback database isn't configured, Recovery Manager is your only choice.

RMAN can do two types of recoveries:

- **Complete:** All files are brought back to the time the database failed. No data is lost.

- **Incomplete:** The database is recovered but stopped short of a full recovery. There may be data loss. Sometimes this is what you want. For example, if a user drops a table at 10:13 a.m. sharp, you do an *incomplete* recovery to 10:12 a.m. to get the database back before the drop occurs.

Complete recovery is what usually happens. However, be prepared for anything.

Verifying the problem

Finding out what went wrong with your database isn't always an easy task. Sometimes you get lucky (if you want to use the term *lucky* in the face of broken database). For example, maybe you just "know" what happened:

- System administrator told you a disk croaked
- User told you they dropped a table
- You, yourself, caused the error and you know what happened and why

These might not be the problem. Sometimes you're presented with sneaky problems. This is where you take on the role of a detective. Chapter 12 helps you investigate further.

What if you start the database or access data while the database is still open and get an error similar to this one:

```
ORA-01157: cannot identify/lock data file 4 - see DBWR trace file
ORA-01110: data file 4: '/u01/app/oracle/oradata/dev11g/users01.dbf'
```

You look for the file in the location that it gives. Lo and behold, it is gone (or maybe the whole disk is gone). You had more than one file on that disk. Why is Oracle only telling you that it can't find one of your files? Because when you start the database, Oracle reads the data file list in the control file. As soon as it can't find one in the list, it stops opening and presents the error. Or, if the database is already open, Oracle only tells you about the error that you are experiencing as a result of your specific action. Unfortunately, this is a little misleading; you might restore and recover the file only to find another error just like it for a different data file.

There are a couple things you can do when you see the error:

- Query the dynamic performance view V$RECOVER_FILE to see a list of all files that Oracle is having trouble with, the error, and the file number(s) in question. Take that file number and plug it into the view V$DATAFILE to get a list of the file names that need recovery.

- Oracle 11g has a fancy tool called the Data Recovery Advisor. This won't work in all situations. It will work when you have missing media, such as loss of files.

Complete recovery

Complete recovery (as opposed to incomplete recovery) is always what you want to shoot for. It means you recover every block and every transaction that was ever committed into the database. You let Oracle take over and do the recovery until the end of all the backup files and archive logs; don't manually intervene and stop it somewhere before it is finished.

Complete recovery: One or more data files

If you are get the "unable to identify/lock datafile" error, you need to do a couple things:

- Know the extent of the damage. This helps so you only have to do one recovery instead of two.

- Determine if the lost file is required for the instance to run (or if it is an application data file). Required data files are SYSTEM, SYSAUX, and UNDO. This is important for reducing your overall *mean time to recovery (MTTR)*. Oracle only crashes if you lose a required data file.

If you determine that the lost files are not important to basic operation, you can open the database (if it even went down) before you begin recovery. That allows at least partial data access to some users. You may prefer that users remain out of the system until you are done.

What's the first thing to do if Oracle 11g crashes? Go to the Data Recovery Advisor (DRA). For the DRA to work, the database has to be in NOMOUNT state. It can't be completely shut down.

1. **Log into your target with RMAN.**
2. **Type this:**

```
<list failure;>
```

   You see something like this:

```
using target database control file instead of recovery catalog
List of Database Failures
=========================
Failure ID Priority Status Time Detected Summary
---------- -------- --------- ------------- -------
1562 HIGH OPEN 11-JUL-08 One or more non-system datafiles are missing
```

   A non-system (critical) file is missing. What to do?

3. **Ask the DRA what to do:**

```
<advise failure;>
```

You see something like this:

```
List of Database Failures
=========================
Failure ID Priority Status Time Detected Summary
---------- -------- --------- ------------- -------
1562 HIGH OPEN 11-JUL-08 One or more non-system datafiles are missing
analyzing automatic repair options; this may take some time
allocated channel: ORA_DISK_1
channel ORA_DISK_1: SID=155 device type=DISK
analyzing automatic repair options complete
Mandatory Manual Actions
========================
no manual actions available
Optional Manual Actions
=======================
1. If file /u01/app/oracle/oradata/dev11g/users01.dbf was unintentionally
           renamed or moved, restore it
2. If file /u01/app/oracle/oradata/dev11g/example01.dbf was unintentionally
           renamed or moved, restore it
Automated Repair Options
========================
Option Repair Description
------ ------------------
1 Restore and recover datafile 4; Restore and recover datafile 5
 Strategy: The repair includes complete media recovery with no data loss
 Repair script:
/u01/app/oracle/diag/rdbms/dev11g/dev11g/hm/reco_727637560.hm
```

Get a load of that! Not only does the DRA tell you exactly what you need to do, it provides a script so you don't have to write a single line of code. If you open that script, it looks something like this:

```
 # restore and recover datafile
 restore datafile 4, 5;
 recover datafile 4, 5;
```

4. **Type the following to have the DRA fix the problem:**

```
<repair failure;>
```

You see something like this:

```
Strategy: The repair includes complete media recovery with no data loss
Repair script:
/u01/app/oracle/diag/rdbms/dev11g/dev11g/hm/reco_2784523833.hm
contents of repair script:
 # restore and recover datafile
 restore datafile 4, 5;
 recover datafile 4, 5;
Do you really want to execute the above repair (enter YES or NO)? yes
executing repair script
```

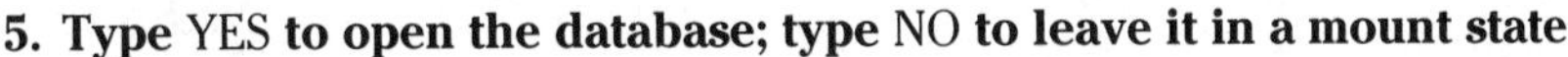

At the very end, if the database was closed, it asks if you want to open the database.

5. **Type** YES **to open the database; type** NO **to leave it in a mount state.**

Most of the time you will choose YES. You might choose NO if you want to spend more time going over what happened before you release the database back to the users.

If I had to nitpick about the DRA, here is what I'd say:

- It doesn't say you can offline those data files and then open the database for everyone else if the database is closed. It tells you that the files can be offline and recovered if the database is already open. At least it told you that they were non-system files.
- If you have to restore the files to a new location, the DRA can't take over and do the whole recovery for you. Say you lost a disk and it ain't coming back. The DRA isn't smart enough to choose a new location for you and incorporate that into a repair script. It tells you what is wrong and what it suggests doing, which may help get you going in the right direction, but it falls short after that.

But be realistic. How can you expect it to have every situation indexed for all types of systems and environments?

Have you upgraded to 11g yet? Are you making plans now?

Complete recovery: One or more control files

What if you manage to lose all your control files and your databases crashes?

Control files are critical system files.

DRA to the rescue:

1. **Log into RMAN.**
2. **List failure.**
3. **Advise failure.**
4. **Repair failure.**

(If you're lost just like the files, go to "Complete recovery: One or more data files" for the fully explained steps.) But wait a minute . . . Why didn't it open the database? Recovery from losing all your control files is a little more involved than standard data file recovery. (We suppose the DRA doesn't want to continue with the recovery without you getting a chance to check things out.)

Regardless, there are two things left for you to do manually:

1. **Re-sync all the data files with the recovered control files:**

```
<recover database;>
```

You see output similar to this:

```
Starting recover at 11-JUL-08
Starting implicit crosscheck backup at 11-JUL-08
allocated channel: ORA_DISK_1
channel ORA_DISK_1: SID=150 device type=DISK
Crosschecked 19 objects
Finished implicit crosscheck backup at 11-JUL-08
Starting implicit crosscheck copy at 11-JUL-08
using channel ORA_DISK_1
Crosschecked 16 objects
Finished implicit crosscheck copy at 11-JUL-08
searching for all files in the recovery area
cataloging files...
cataloging done
starting media recovery
media recovery complete, elapsed time: 00:00:00
Finished recover at 11-JUL-08
```

2. **Open the database yourself:**

```
<alter database open resetlogs;>
```

This is not an ordinary open because you're restoring a backup copy of the control file and having to re-sync control files with data files. Oracle wants to start fresh with its internal sequencing.

After any type of recovery, take a fresh, full backup immediately — just in case. We recommend it as a best practice — especially for a RESETLOGS recovery.

Complete recovery without the DRA

We don't want you to rest on your laurels too much so we're showing you a recovery without the DRA. The DRA won't help you in every situation. What if the file you need to restore has to go somewhere else? The DRA won't know where to put it.

Plus, it's good to understand how to recover without the DRA. You might find yourself in a non-11g database someday. The following method works all the way back to the dawn of Recovery Manager (as far as we know).

This example situation has you losing a data file but being unable to put it back in the same place. (By *you,* we mean *RMAN.*) You have to tell RMAN where to put the file; then RMAN will restore it to the proper location.

- You lost a disk with a data file on it.
- The disk will not be replaced and you have to restore the data file elsewhere.
- You tell RMAN where to put the data file.
- You tell RMAN to restore the data file.
- You tell RMAN to recover the data file.
- If the database was closed, you open it. If the database was open, you online the data file.

This example starts with the database closed; you open it and then fix the error.

Please give an intro sentence that tells readers what this example does (not specifics, but what tasks it accomplishes):

1. **Start the database and read this error:**

```
ORA-01157: cannot identify/lock data file 4 - see DBWR trace file
ORA-01110: data file 4: '/u01/app/oracle/oradata/dev11g/users01.dbf'
```

2. **See if that is the only missing file:**

```
<select * from v$recover_file;>
```

3. **Determine whether this is the only file affected and whether it is a critical file.**

   You also determine that it must be restored to a different disk.

4. **Launch RMAN and take the data file offline:**

```
<sql "alter database datafile 4 offline";>
```

   You see this:

```
sql statement: alter database datafile 4 offline
```

5. **Open the database:**

```
<alter database open;>
```

6. **Tell RMAN to restore to the correct location:**

```
<run {
set newname for datafile 4 to '/u02/app/oracle/oradata/dev11g/users01.dbf';
restore tablespace users;
switch datafile all;
recover tablespace users;
}>
```

In this case, it is disk u02, a different location. The output indicates that the file is being restored and recovered in the new location:

```
executing command: SET NEWNAME
Starting restore at 11-JUL-08
allocated channel: ORA_DISK_1
channel ORA_DISK_1: SID=131 device type=DISK
channel ORA_DISK_1: starting datafile backup set restore
channel ORA_DISK_1: specifying datafile(s) to restore from backup set
channel ORA_DISK_1: restoring datafile 00004 to /u02/app/oracle/oradata/
        dev11g/users01.dbf
Starting recover at 11-JUL-08
using channel ORA_DISK_1
starting media recovery
media recovery complete, elapsed time: 00:00:00
Finished recover at 11-JUL-08
```

7. **When the recovery finishes, alter the tablespace back online:**

```
<sql "alter tablespace users online";>
```

Quite a few more steps without the DRA, eh? Either way, it's not too difficult. If you haven't already, make sure you set up a test database and practice these and other scenarios. You'll be a recovery expert in no time at all.

Incomplete recovery

Incomplete recovery is usually a very unfortunate position to be in. Typically, it means you will be losing data (hence *incomplete*). Also, the DRA cannot help at all in this situation. In an incomplete recovery scenario, the database has not actually failed. Someone has done something to put the database in a state that requires you to go back in time.

Here is a situation where incomplete recovery may apply:

- It is Monday morning.
- You have taken a backup of your database last night.
- You are in archive log mode.
- At 10:00 a.m., Tammy tells you she accidentally dropped a major table out of the accounting schema around 9:45 a.m. Not only did she drop it, she purged it from the recycle bin because she knew it was the right one. It wasn't.
- Assuming you have no other way to retrieve the table from a logical backup or re-create it, you decide incomplete recovery is your only choice.

- You will take the database down to restore the backup from last night. Then you will roll the database forward to 9:44 a.m. and open it.
- Any transactions that occurred between 9:45 and 10:00 a.m. will be lost and have to be manually re-entered.

A key piece of information is that Tammy told you she dropped the table at 9:45 a.m.

Spend a few minutes doing some research to verify that the reported time is truthful. If you roll forward too far, the table will be dropped again during the recovery process and you will have to start over.

Here are the steps to incomplete recovery:

1. **Shut down the database.**
2. **Start up the database in mount mode.**
3. **Set the time for the restore to work off of.**
4. **Restore the database.**
5. **Recover the database.**
6. **Open the database with RESETLOGS.**

   The control files will not match the data files. You have to re-sync the control files with the data files.
7. **Open a prompt to your OS command line.**
8. **Log into your database with RMAN:**

   ```
   <rman target /
   ```
9. **Shut down your database:**

   ```
   <shutdown immediate>
   ```
10. **Use the following RMAN command to recover your database to the appropriate time (9:45 a.m. in this case):**

    ```
    RMAN> run {
    set until time =
    "to_date('11-JUL-2008:09:45:00','DD-MON-YYYY:HH24:MI:SS')";
    restore database;
    recover database;
    sql "alter database open resetlogs";
    }
    ```

Once the command completes, you should see something like this:

```
executing command: SET until clause
using target database control file instead of recovery catalog
Finished restore at 12-JUL-08
Starting recover at 12-JUL-08
using channel ORA_DISK_1
starting media recovery
…output snipped…
media recovery complete, elapsed time: 00:00:08
Finished recover at 12-JUL-08
sql statement: alter database open resetlogs
```

11. **Make sure the table you were trying to recover has indeed been recovered.**

There's nothing more embarrassing than telling everybody you fixed the problem only to have someone else discover that it still isn't there. If you discover it is not there, do the recovery again, going back a little further in time.

Recovering your database with copies

Copies allow for superfast recovery and fewer technical recoveries when you have lost a disk and the file has to go to a different location.

Some DBAs would argue a little that it's incorrect to use the copy in the place you backed it up. Good DBAs subscribe to the mantra, Everything has its place; everything in its place. However, times are changing a little. For example, the popularity of large *storage area networks (SAN),* where all your files go to the same place, is growing. DBAs don't have as much responsibility to organize, separate, stripe and label data; nor do they have as much time. The SAN does all the protection and striping for you. Furthermore, Oracle has even released, in essence, its own volume manager: *Automatic Storage Management (ASM).* Relax your regimented file and naming conventions a little bit. Use that time to make better use of the features that Oracle that helps protect and manage data.

You get a call from a user who is getting the following error:

```
SQL> select *
  2 from emp;
from emp
  *
ERROR at line 2:
ORA-01116: error in opening database file 4
ORA-01110: data file 4: '/u02/app/oracle/oradata/dev11g/users01.dbf'
ORA-27041: unable to open file
Linux-x86_64 Error: 2: No such file or directory
Additional information: 3
```

After some investigation, you see that someone has removed the data file from the USERS tablespace. This tablespace is critical and must be recovered immediately. You decide to recover with RMAN using a COPY of the data file.

1. **Log into your target with RMAN.**
2. **Make sure you have a copy of your USERS tablespace data file:**

```
<list copy of tablespace users;>
```

   You should see something like this:

```
List of Datafile Copies
=======================
Key File S Completion Time Ckp SCN Ckp Time
------- ---- - --------------- ---------- ---------------
45 4 A 12-JUL-08 14878139 12-JUL-08
 Name: /u01/app/oracle/flash_recovery_area/DEV11G/
datafile/o1_mf_users_47kn9j0z_.dbf
 Tag: FULL_DATABASE_COPY
```

3. **Take the tablespace offline (since the database is open):**

```
< sql "alter tablespace users offline";>
```

   You see this:

```
sql statement: alter tablespace users offline
```

4. **Switch to the copy:**

```
<switch tablespace users to copy;>
```

   You see something like this:

```
datafile 4 switched to datafile copy
"/u01/app/oracle/flash_recovery_area/DEV11G/
datafile/o1_mf_users_47kn9j0z_.dbf"
```

5. **Recover the copy, since it was taken earlier:**

```
< recover tablespace users;>
```

   You see something like this:

```
Starting recover at 12-JUL-08
using channel ORA_DISK_1
starting media recovery
media recovery complete, elapsed time: 00:00:04
Finished recover at 12-JUL-08
```

6. **Alter the tablespace back online:**

```
< sql "alter tablespace users online";>
```

   You see this:

```
sql statement: alter tablespace users online
```

All done! Do you see how quick that was without having to restore the file? Of course, you have to come to terms with it being in your flash recovery area.

- If that really bugs you, you can rename it and move it later, when you have a maintenance window.
- If that really bugs you, when you take the copy, you can copy it to an auxiliary area outside your flash recovery area (where you don't mind it being) in case you have to use it.

Chapter 9

Protecting Your Oracle Data

In This Chapter

- Getting user authentication
- Exploring roles and privileges
- Employing VPD
- Auditing a database
- Encrypting the work

Security is real concern. Especially in anything relating to computers and the Internet. As administrators of software applications like the Oracle database, we are concerned with security because we want to protect our data. Sometimes it's because we don't want people looking at our data. Another reason is to protect the data from being altered or corrupted. Being able to restrict and monitor the users in the system will help us provide a safe and secure operating environment for us and our customers or clients.

Authentication

Authentication is all about making sure your users are who they say they are. This process begins well before users even try to access the database. You need to set up a system that allows you to verify identity. You need a method for users to access the system that both identifies and restricts their privileges to their described needs. Finally, a security mechanism such as a password or operating system account is recommended so access isn't open to anyone who tries.

User authentication

Once you set up your databases, the next step is to allow users access to the data. You may have all sorts of users in your environment, from people who need full access to the data and database (like a DBA) to an application that runs on a machine for users connecting from the Internet.

User authentication, the first step to protecting your data, means verifying that a resource trying to connect to your database is authorized to do so.

You can establish the following by authenticating users:

- **Accountability:** Having an accountability system forces users to take responsibility for their actions. It helps track down the culprits when problems occur.
- **Trust:** A system of authentication allows you to operate within a realm of trust. Make sure a potential user is qualified before they're given data access. Qualifications can be as simple as a one-hour training class to a full-blown, government-sponsored background investigation.
- **Proper privileges:** You must restrict and grant access according to a resource's identity and qualifications. Different resources have different type of access to accomplish different jobs. This capability is in place through a system of varying roles and privileges.
- **Tracking mechanisms:** Many databases need a Big Brother. When something goes wrong, a tracking mechanism can help you hunt down and plug any security holes. It can also help you make sure resources in your environment aren't snooping.

Security past

In the past, Oracle has given us tools to implement very secure password authentication methods, but they have left the implementation up to us almost entirely. With each release of the database, Oracle has increased default security in the system. Oracle *has* been nonsecure in the past. However, administrators had to deal with access being nearly wide open when software was installed and a database was created. DBAs had to set and manage authentication. Unfortunately, not all database users knew what to configure and lock down. Many internal accounts were created with high levels of access with default passwords that were easily found anywhere on the Internet.

Password authentication

Password protection is the most common way to protect data in computer systems. This applies to bank ATMs, Internet web sites, and of course, your Oracle database. *Password protection* helps establish identity. Passing this verification is the first step in showing you're a trusted member of the club.

Nowadays when you create the database

- Default accounts are locked.
- SYS and SYSTEM passwords are chosen and set during database creation.
- Password security is enhanced by forcing complex passwords.

With these measures, the database is fairly secure as soon as it's created. Chapter 5 covers user creation; this chapter expands on password security options.

Enforcing password security with profiles

A *password profile* is a mechanism in the database that forces a user to follow guidelines when creating or changing passwords. The guidelines help provide stronger security in the system by not allowing weak passwords.

Are you guilty of the following?

- Making password the same as the username
- Making *password* your password
- Reusing the same password when the system asks you to change

Having to remember complex passwords is sometimes inconvenient, but accept it as part of your responsibility. If nothing else, how would you like to be blamed for someone guessing your password?

Nevertheless, password profiles are a DBA tool and they let you do the following:

- **Limit the number of times a password can be reused.** If you want to give your users a break, let them reuse the password twice — but that's it.
- **Limit the amount of time before a password can be reused.** Maybe you let them reuse the password, but they have to wait 90 days to do so.
- **Limit failed login attempts.** If this number is met, you can lock the account until a security administrator unlocks it or for a certain period of time.

- **Password lock time.** If a password is incorrectly entered the number of times based on the failed login attempts setting, you can force a waiting period before a user can try again. This can help against *brute force* attacks, where a machine bombards your database with a password cracker.
- **Give passwords a life time.** Once this threshold is met, ask the user to change his password.
- **Have a password grace time**. Once the life time is reached, the user is prompted with "You have *X* number of days to change your password."
- **Check password complexity.** A verification function
  - Makes sure the password and username are different
  - Makes sure the new password differs from the previous by three characters
  - Ensures the password is made up of alphabetical, numeric, and special characters.

You can create your own password verify function and attach it to a profile.

A *password verify function* is a program written in PL/SQL that examines passwords when they're chosen and accepts or rejects them based on criteria. If you have special password requirements, you can write your own password verify function and assign it to your password profile using the PASSWORD_VERIFY_FUNCTION attribute of the profile.

Oracle supplies a standard password verify function with the database. By default, it ensures the following:

- Password is not the same as the username (forward and backward)
- Password is more than seven characters
- Password is not the same as the server name
- Password is not a common poor choice such as welcome1, password, database, abcdefg

To use Oracle's provided password verify function, follow these steps:

1. **Log into SQL*Plus as SYS**
2. **Run the following:**

   ```
   $ORACLE_HOME/rdbms/admin/utlpwdmg.sql
   ```

   This creates the default password verify function and assigns it to the DEFAULT profile. If you're comfortable with PL/SQL, you can even take Oracle's example file and modify it to fit your needs.

Creating a password profile

To create a password profile follow these steps:

1. **Log into the database via SQL*Plus as SYSTEM.**
2. **Create the profile and limit the following: failed login attempts, password lock time, and password life time:**

```
<CREATE PROFILE report_writer LIMIT
FAILED_LOGIN_ATTEMPTS 3
PASSWORD_LOCK_TIME 1/96
PASSWORD_LIFE_TIME 90;>
```

   In this example failed login attempts are limited to three, password lock time is limited to 15 minutes, and password life time is limited to 90 days.

   You see this:

```
Profile created.
```

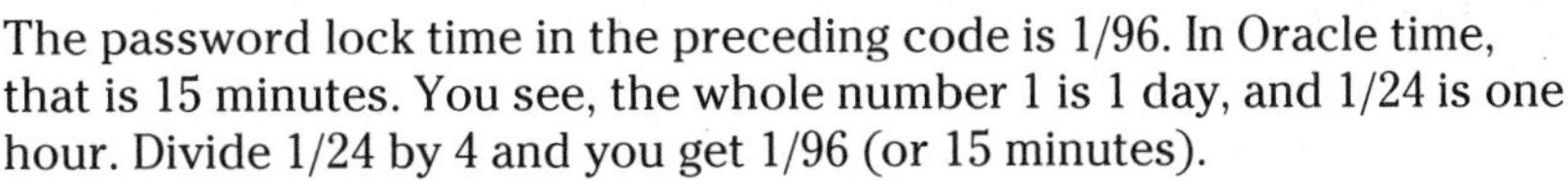

   The password lock time in the preceding code is 1/96. In Oracle time, that is 15 minutes. You see, the whole number 1 is 1 day, and 1/24 is one hour. Divide 1/24 by 4 and you get 1/96 (or 15 minutes).

3. **Assign the report writer user profile to a user:**

```
<alter user HR profile report_writer;>
```

   This example assigns the new profile to the HR user. You see this in return:

```
User altered.
```

DEFAULT profile

What if you don't give your users a profile? In that case, all users have the DEFAULT profile.

By default in Oracle 11g, the DEFAULT profile limits the following:

- FAILED_LOGIN_ATTEMPT = 10
- PASSWORD_GRACE_TIME 7 (DAYS)
- PASSWORD_LIFE_TIME 180 (DAYS)
- PASSWORD_LOCK_TIME 1 (DAY)
- PASSWORD_REUSE_MAX UNLIMITED
- PASSWORD_REUSE_TIME UNLIMITED

You can edit your profile or the DEFAULT profile. For example, to change the failed login attempts setting to 3 on the DEFAULT profile, type the following:

```
<alter profile default limit
  Failed_login_attempts 3;>
```

You see this:

```
Profile altered.
```

Operating system authentication

You may not always want to require a user password. In those cases operating system authentication can be useful and, if set up properly, offer some security advantage over using a password. Use operating system authentication with caution though.

Operating system authentication recognizes a user as logged into the OS and waives the password requirement. Operating system authentication can be especially useful when you have an application that requires a log in to the database to run a program. Say a job runs every night to generate reports and deposit them into a directory.

How will the user inside your batch job connect ? You could embed a password in the program, but that is not secure. Instead, you create an account in the database that links to the OS user and configure it with OS authentication. That way, you protect the OS user's password, and avoid a traditional username/password combination for the user to log in to run the reports.

You're safe as long as only authorized personnel know the OS user password.

Type this code to create an OS-authenticated user in Oracle for someone named REPORTS:

```
<create user OPS$REPORTS identified externally;>
```

You see this:

```
User created.
```

Notice how the OS user is called REPORTS and the Oracle user is called OPS$REPORTS.

The user prefix OPS$ must precede the OS username for the username to be identified externally.

External identification means that instead of the user requiring a password in the database, Oracle looks to the OS and matches the username (minus the OPS$) to a user on the operating system. Oracle assumes that since the user is logged into the OS, it must be authenticated. You can change that prefix, OPS$, by revising the Oracle parameter OS_AUTHEN_PREFIX.

After setting up all the necessary privileges for that user (detailed later in this chapter), the user can log in from the OS command line without a password:

```
<sqlplus />
```

Granting the Privileged Few

Once you create a user, you have to decide what types of things the user can do in the database. This includes the following:

- Logging in
- What data they can access
- Starting and stopping the database
- Whether they can create tables, indexes, and views
- Delete data
- Do backups

Decide what a user can do via *privileges.* The database has two types of privileges:

- *System privileges* control what a user can do in the database. For example, can they create tables, create users, drop tablespaces? These privileges apply mainly to adding or changing structures in the database.
- *Object privileges* control how a user can access the actual data in the database. For example, what data can they see, change, or delete? These privileges apply primarily to rows in a table or view.

Manage all privileges with the GRANT and REVOKE commands. It's pretty clear which one gives, and which one taketh away. However, you form the commands depending on the type of privilege.

System privileges

System privileges are the first privileges any user needs. There are literally hundreds of system privileges. This chapter lists the common ones that include about 90 percent of what users will need.

The CREATE SESSION privilege gives users access to the database.

Follow these steps to grant CREATE SESSION privileges to the OPS$REPORTS user:

1. **Log in to the database as the user SYSTEM.**
2. **Type the following:**

   ```
   <grant create session to ops$reports;>
   ```

   You see the following, which means OPS$REPORTS can connect to the database:

   ```
   Grant succeeded.
   ```

What if the password for the OS user REPORTS has been compromised? A quick way to make sure that user can no longer access the database, externally or not, is to revoke the CREATE SESSION privilege from that user.

Revoke the CREATE SESSION from OPS$REPORTS with these steps:

1. **Log in to the database as SYSTEM.**
2. **Type the following:**

   ```
   <revoke create session from ops$reports;>
   ```

   You see this:

   ```
   Revoke succeeded.
   ```

   When that user tries to connect he sees this:

   ```
   ERROR:
   ORA-01045: user OPS$REPORTS lacks CREATE SESSION privilege; logon denied
   ```

3. **Address the security breach.**
4. **Re-grant the privilege.**

   Processing will continue as normal.

A user might also have these system privileges that allow them to create objects in the database:

- RESUMABLE allows jobs to be suspended and resumed when space restrictions are met.
- FLASHBACK ARCHIVE allows users to retrieve data from the past. See Chapter 14 for more about flashback archiving.
- CREATE JOB allows users to create jobs that can be run in the Oracle Scheduler.
- CREATE SYNONYM allows users to be able to create alias for objects for easier access.

These apply commonly to developers:

- CREATE TABLE
- CREATE VIEW
- CREATE SEQUENCE
- CREATE PROCEDURE
- CREATE TRIGGER

DBAs commonly have these privileges:

- CREATE ANY TABLE creates tables in any user's schema.
- DROP ANY TABLE drops tables from any user's schema.
- CREATE TABLESPACE creates tablespace storage areas.
- ALTER USER changes user characteristics.
- DROP USER . . . uh, drops a user.
- ALTER SYSTEM changes system operation parameters.
- GRANT ANY OBJECT allows grantee to manage any object privilege against any object in the database. Very powerful!

WITH ADMIN OPTION is another feature with system privileges. You can grant this system privilege as part of a system privilege to allow the user to grant the privilege to someone else. For example, say you've hired a new DBA with the username RPLEW. You want RPLEW to connect to the database with the CREATE SESSION privilege, but you also want him to be able to grant that privilege to someone else.

To grant a system privilege WITH ADMIN OPTION

1. **Log into SQL*Plus as SYSTEM.**
2. **Type the following:**

```
<grant create session to RPLEW with admin option;>
```

You see this:

```
Grant succeeded.
```

Now RPLEW can administer CREATE SESSION as well.

If WITH ADMIN OPTION is revoked, all users given that privilege by that person will retain the privileges. Act accordingly.

Object privileges

Object privileges control data access and modification.

Understanding object privileges

You can grant only eight object privileges:

- **SELECT** lets the recipient select rows from tables. More on tables in Chapter 7.
- **INSERT** lets the recipient insert rows into tables.
- **UPDATE** lets the recipient change existing rows in tables.
- **DELETE** lets the recipient remove existing rows from tables.
- **REFERENCES** lets a user create a view on, or a foreign key to, another user's table. More on foreign keys in Chapter 7.
- **INDEX** lets one user create an index on another user's table. More on indexes in Chapter 7.
- **ALTER** lets one user change or add to the structure of another user's table.
- **EXECUTE** lets the recipient run procedures owned by another user.

Keep these privilege tidbits in mind:

- When you own an object, you automatically have all the privileges on that object. In other words, you don't have to be granted SELECT on your own table.
- Object privileges cannot be revoked from the owner of an object.

- Whatever schema owns the object ultimately controls that object's privileges.
- Without express permission, no one else can manage the object privileges of said object — well, no one except a user who might have the system privilege GRANT ANY OBJECT (usually reserved for DBAs).
- Object privilege cannot be revoked by anyone but the person who granted it except for someone with the GRANT ANY OBJECT privilege. Not even the owner can revoke a privilege on her own object unless she was the grantor.

Granting object privileges

In the following steps, the users MAGGIE, JASON, and MATT work in a database that contains recipes. This example uses object privileges to allow them to view and add more recipes.

1. **Log in.**
2. **Type the following:**

   ```
   <grant SELECT on VEGETARIAN_RECIPES to JASON;>
   ```

   This lets user MAGGIE allow JASON to select from her VEGETARIAN_RECIPES table. She sees this:

   ```
   Grant succeeded.
   ```

Similar to WITH ADMIN OPTION of system privileges, object privileges have something called WITH GRANT OPTION.

- MAGGIE can allow JASON to be able to INSERT into her table and allow JASON to pass on that privilege:

  ```
  <grant SELECT on VEGETARIAN_RECIPES to JASON WITH GRANT OPTION;>
  ```

- JASON can pass on that INSERT privilege to MATT:

  ```
  <grant SELECT on MAGGIE.VEGETARIAN_RECIPES to MATT;>
  ```

- MAGGIE cannot revoke the INSERT privilege from MATT. She has to ask JASON to do so.
- If JASON refuses to revoke INSERT privileges for MATT, MAGGIE can revoke the privilege from JASON and, in turn, revoke it from MATT. It's called a *cascading revoke.* Note that this is different from system privileges.
- MAGGIE can revoke the INSERT privilege from JASON and in the meantime automatically revoke them from MATT:

  ```
  <revoke INSERT on VEGETARIAN_RECIPES from JASON;>
  ```

  She sees this:

  ```
  Revoke succeeded.
  ```

If a user wants to see what object privilege they have given out, they can query the view USER_TAB_PRIVS.

For example, MAGGIE can see what privileges JASON has left on her objects:

```
<SELECT * FROM USER_TAB_PRIVS
WHERE GRANTEE = 'JASON';>
```

She sees something like this:

```
GRANTEE    OWNER      TABLE_NAME         GRANTOR    PRIVILEGE
---------- ---------- ------------------ ---------- ----------
JASON      MAGGIE     VEGETARIAN_RECIPES MAGGIE     SELECT
```

Role Playing

You can group privileges with database roles for ease of management. Instead of an object owner individually granting privileges to one or more users with similar job descriptions, the object owner can create a role and grant the role instead.

For example, say you're a DBA for a major retailer. Every day, new store clerks are hired. The application allows them to do dozens of requirements, including

- INSERT into the SALES table
- UPDATE the INVENTORY table
- DELETE from the ORDERS table

Follow these steps to use a role to grant privileges:

1. **Create a role.**
2. **Log into SQL*Plus.**
3. **Type the following:**

   ```
   <create role SALES_CLERK;>
   ```

   This role is called SALES_CLERK and you see this:

   ```
   Role created.
   ```

4. **Grant system and object privileges to the role:**

   ```
   <grant INSERT on SALES to SALES_CLERK;>
   <grant UPDATE on INVENTORY to SALES_CLERK;>
   <grant DELETE on ORDERS to SALES_CLERK;>
   ```

   And so on.

5. **Grant the role to the employees:**

```
<grant SALES_CLERK to RYAN, NANCY, LEIGH;>
```

Here the role is granted to new clerks RYAN, NANCY, and LEIGH. You see this:

```
Grant Succeeded.
```

Another nice thing about roles — *dynamic privilege management* — which is the concept that adding and removing privileges from a role immediately affect all users who have the role.

All users need special access during a certain time (a few months, for example), to be able to SELECT from the INVENTORY table. Instead of granting it to possibly hundreds of clerks, grant the role and they will automatically have it. It makes managing privileges much easier.

Oracle-supplied roles

Some roles come already created and set up by the database, making it easier to manage certain tasks.

Here are some of the many roles supplied by Oracle when the database is installed:

- **CONNECT** includes the privileges needed to connect to the database.
- **RESOURCE** includes many of the roles a developer might use to create and manage an application, such as creating and altering many types of objects including tables, view, and sequences.
- **EXP_FULL_DATABASE/IMP_FULL_DATABASE** allows the grantee to do logical backups of the database.
- **RECOVERY_CATALOG_OWNER** allows grantee to administer Oracle Recovery Manager catalog.
- **SCHEDULER_ADMIN** allows the grantee to manage the Oracle job scheduler.

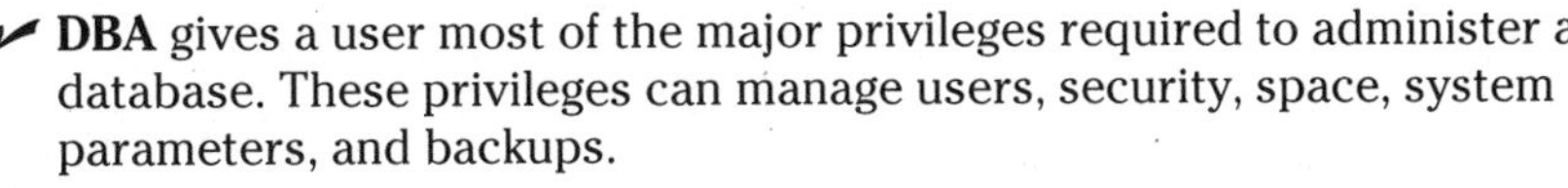

- **DBA** gives a user most of the major privileges required to administer a database. These privileges can manage users, security, space, system parameters, and backups.

The SYSDBA role

SYSDBA is the top dog of all roles. Anyone with this role can do anything they want in the database. Obviously you want to be careful with some of these. For example, be very particular whom, if anyone, you give the SYSDBA role. Those users should be fully trained, qualified Oracle administrators. If they are not, they could irreparably damage your database. Also, if too many people have this role, it destroys the chain of accountability in the database.

Oracle-supplied roles are managed just like the roles you create.

Virtual Private Database Concept

Some application environments need to support many users with access to the same base tables but with restricted row viewing.

Row-level security is also known as *Virtual Private Database (VPD).* Row restriction is entirely transparent and managed behind the scenes. A table may have 1,000 rows, but even if a user selects all the rows, he can only see those he's approved to see (without using a WHERE clause).

Row-level security creates policies against your objects. In essence, these policies are the WHERE clauses that the user needs in order to enter. Whenever a table is accessed, the policy is invoked. Based on the policy definition, the SQL statement is rewritten in the background and then executed. Finally, the restricted row set is returned to the caller. Also, these policies don't just apply to SELECT, but all INSERT, UPDATE, and DELETE statements against the table.

Auditing Oracle's Big Brother

Just when you thought it was safe to do whatever you wanted in the database, along comes auditing. No, really . . . being able to audit what happens in the database is like having police on the streets.

- It can help protect you from people with prying eyes or malicious intentions.
- It can also help you track down who's responsible for certain actions in the database.
- It can help analyze access data.

You can choose from many auditing options:

- **Users:** Auditing can be turned on for everything a user does, from logging in to what SQL statements they are running.
- **Objects:** Every action against an object can be audited.
- **System privileges:** Specific SQL statements like ALTER, DROP, CONNECT, and CREATE can be audited.
- **Combination:** Most likely, you will choose a combination of users, objects, and system privileges to accomplish your auditing needs.

You will rarely audit everything in the database. There is some overhead involved. It can cost you in terms of the following:

- **CPU:** Audit operations execute inside the database with each SQL statement or connection you run. The more you audit, the more work there is in the background for Oracle to do.
- **Storage:** Oracle audits generate an *audit trail* for you to look at later. Again, the more data being audited, the more information is generated.
- **Personnel:** Viewing and analyzing the auditing information could be a job in and of itself if you have a very large database with lots of users and lots of auditing. Someone has to interpret the audit trail and determine how the data will be used. The audit trail itself has to be managed. How long are you going to keep the info? Where will it go for long-term storage? Who will clean it up when it is no longer needed?

Find out what your auditing requirements are. Sometimes companies are bound by corporate guidelines. Or, you may be under the gun for industry certifications like Sarbanes-Oxley, which require a fair amount of auditing.

While Oracle auditing can cover a lot of the bases, it may not meet all your requirements. Make sure you can equate each one of your auditing requirements with Oracle auditing capability. In most cases, the database will have you covered.

Getting ready to audit

Oracle 11g changes the amount of auditing turned on by default. All the following database actions are automatically audited by default in 11g:

CREATE EXTERNAL JOB	EXEMPT ACCESS POLICY
CREATE ANY JOB	CREATE ANY LIBRARY
GRANT ANY OBJECT PRIVILEGE	GRANT ANY PRIVILEGE

DROP PROFILE

ALTER PROFILE

DROP ANY PROCEDURE

ALTER ANY PROCEDURE

CREATE ANY PROCEDURE

ALTER DATABASE

GRANT ANY ROLE

CREATE PUBLIC DATABASE LINK

DROP ANY TABLE

ALTER ANY TABLE

CREATE ANY TABLE

DROP USER

ALTER USER

CREATE USER

CREATE SESSION

AUDIT SYSTEM

ALTER SYSTEM

SYSTEM AUDIT

ROLE

Furthermore, the database parameter AUDIT_TRAIL is also set to DB. This is a significant change over previous versions. Before, it was set to NONE, meaning auditing was not turned on. To turn it on requires restarting the database, which can be a tall order in a production system. It's convenient that the default parameter is set to DB in case you forget when you create the database.

Since the AUDIT_TRAIL parameter is set to DB, all your audit entries go into the table SYS.AUD$. Keep an eye on this internal table. Depending on your level of auditing, it can grow very quickly. Consider creating a maintenance plan that has directives for either purging the table or moving the audit rows to more permanent long-term storage (depending on your organization).

If you set AUDIT_TRAIL to OS, a file is generated on the operating system (instead of audit entries being written to the SYS.AUD$ table). The files are written to the audit_file_dest parameter location.

Which option — DB or OS — is up to you. How do you want to access and manage the audit trail?

- Do you like managing it with SQL inside the database? Then choose DB.
- If you prefer using files and editors like Notepad or vi to work with your audit entries, then choose OS.

Some actions are always audited, whether you like it or not. All connections to the database with the SYSDBA privilege are logged into audit files that live in the location configured by the database parameter, audit_file_dest. You might want to know this so you can manage the audit trail and clean it up/ archive the data occasionally.

To see what your database parameter audit_file_dest is set to, follow these steps:

1. **Log into SQL*Plus.**
2. **Type the following:**

```
<show parameter audit_file_dest>
```

You should see something like this:

```
NAME                                 TYPE        VALUE
------------------------------------ ----------- ------------------------------
audit_file_dest                      string      /u01/app/oracle/admin/dev11g/adump
```

Many files in the audit_file_dest directory have an .aud extension. Monitor and clean up this location occasionally. Depending on your auditing and retention requirements, you can either delete them or move them to a more permanent residence.

Lastly, if your audit_file_dest parameter is not set, the audit files go to the directory under which you installed Oracle in the rdbms/audit folder.

The files in the audit_file_dest are named something like ora_20682.aud. The number (20682 in this case) is the OS process ID that generated the audit. The contents of the file will look something like this:

```
Audit file /u01/app/oracle/admin/dev11g/adump/ora_20682.aud
Oracle Database 11g Enterprise Edition Release 11.1.0.6.0 - 64bit Production
With the Partitioning, OLAP, Data Mining and Real Application Testing options
ORACLE_HOME = /u01/app/oracle/product/11.1.0/db_1
System name:    Linux
Node name:      classroom.perptech.local
Release:        2.6.18-53.1.14.el5
Version:        #1 SMP Wed Mar 5 11:37:38 EST 2008
Machine:        x86_64
Instance name: dev11g
Redo thread mounted by this instance: 1
Oracle process number: 21
Unix process pid: 20682, image: oracle@classroom.perptech.local (TNS V1-V3)

Wed Jul 16 12:29:06 2008
ACTION : 'CONNECT'
DATABASE USER: '/'
PRIVILEGE : SYSDBA
CLIENT USER: oracle
CLIENT TERMINAL: pts/1
STATUS: 0
```

As you can see, it contains a lot of information about the time, date, and machine. This audit file shows that a user named oracle on the OS connected as SYSDBA from the terminal pts/1.

Enabling and disabling audits

Turn auditing on and off with the AUDIT or NOAUDIT command.

You can do all the setup you want, but nothing is audited (except for defaults) until you choose to do so. This benefits you because you can set up and create and configure your application and objects before you have to manage an audit trail.

Because Oracle 11g does a fair amount of default auditing, consider turning off some of that before setting up your application. Then you can enable all the auditing you want right before your application goes to production. Make that decision based on your own business needs.

Auditing system privileges

With security being so important, Oracle 11g ships with some auditing turned on automatically. Furthermore, it's not always users' actions you want to audit, but what they are *trying* to do. An audit can be generated even when someone tries to do something they aren't allowed to do.

Auditing defaults

Default, preconfigured audits in 11g include the system privilege or statement audits, including commands and actions like CONNECT, ALTER, DROP, CREATE, and so on.

You can turn on auditing for any CREATE TABLE statement. You might want to track how often and who is creating tables in the database. Auditing CREATE TABLE this way means an audit entry is generated every time someone creates a table, whether or not they succeed:

```
<audit create table;>
```

You see this:

```
Audit succeeded.
```

Turn off auditing for CREATE TABLE statements:

```
<noaudit create table;>
```

You see this:

```
Noaudit succeeded.
```

You can issue this statement for particular users. To audit the CREATE TABLE statement for only the user MARSHALL, type this:

```
<audit create table by MARSHALL;>
```

You see this:

```
Audit succeeded.
```

To turn it off, type this:

```
<noaudit create table by MARSHALL;>
```

Auditing successful and unsuccessful attempts

The default is to audit both successful and unsuccessful attempts. You can audit the statement if the user successfully executes the command; the audit doesn't happen it the command fails. This can be useful two ways:

- If you audit only successful commands, you don't have to sift through a bunch of audit entries that show a user trying to get the correct syntax.
- If you audit specifically the unsuccessful commands, you can catch users trying to do things that they aren't supposed to. For example, let's say users are forbidden to drop tables which they do not own. First, you can make sure they don't by not giving them the DROP ANY TABLE system privilege. Secondly, if they try to do it anyway, it will generate an error and audit the unsuccessful attempt.

This statement audits the DROP TABLE command for the user FSAEED whenever it fails:

```
<audit drop any table by FSAEED whenever not successful;>
```

You see this:

```
Audit succeeded.
```

To audit only successful attempts, execute the following:

```
<audit drop any table by FSAEED whenever successful;>
```

Auditing objects

Consider object auditing if you want to audit statements like SELECT, INSERT, UPDATE, and DELETE.

- Actions against specific objects
- Privileges on all or specific tables

Sifting through an audit trail of a database with thousands of audited objects can be daunting. It's also likely that some objects simply do not need auditing. If so, restrict your auditing to specific objects.

Furthermore, you can audit objects with these parameters:

- When the operation was successful or when it isn't
- Just once per session or every time it is executed

If you audit an object just once per session, it is audited the first time the user issues the statement. Every time after that, it is ignored. This cuts down your audit trail, but also keeps you from being 100 percent sure if said user is responsible for later operations against a specific object in a session.

For example, if a user deletes a row from EMPLOYEES, the statement is audited. If the user goes back later and deletes another row within the same session, it will not be audited. You know what they say though, where there's smoke, there's fire!

Here's an audit on SELECT against the HR.EMPLOYEES table each time SELECT is executed in the session, whether successful or not:

```
<audit select on hr.employees by access;>
```

You see this:

```
Audit succeeded.
```

Here's an audit once per session:

```
<audit select on hr.employees by session;>
```

You see this:

```
Audit succeeded.
```

If you are a glutton for punishment (or you want to get back at the person responsible for managing the audit trail) you can audit all selects against any table in the database. Unless business rules require this, your system will take a performance hit and the audit trail will quickly grow large.

```
<audit select table;>
```

You see this:

```
Audit succeeded.
```

Verifying an audit

Once you turn on auditing in the database, keep track of what you do.

Luckily, Oracle provides a couple of views in the database to help you keep track:

- To verify what system privileges you configured for auditing, use the view DBA_STMT_AUDIT_OPTS.
- To see what privileges are being audited, type this:

  ```
  <select *
  From DBA_PRIV_AUDIT_OPTS;>
  ```

  You see something like this:

  ```
  USER_NAME  AUDIT_OPTION                SUCCESS    FAILURE
  ---------- --------------------------- ---------- ----------
             SYSTEM AUDIT                BY ACCESS  BY ACCESS
             CREATE SESSION              BY ACCESS  BY ACCESS
             CREATE USER                 BY ACCESS  BY ACCESS
             ALTER USER                  BY ACCESS  BY ACCESS
             DROP USER                   BY ACCESS  BY ACCESS
             ROLE                        BY ACCESS  BY ACCESS
  HR         CREATE TABLE                BY ACCESS  BY ACCESS
  HR         CREATE ANY TABLE            BY ACCESS  BY ACCESS
  ```

  You can interpret the output this way:

- USER_NAME tells you whether this privilege is being monitored for everyone or specific users. Columns without a username mean the privilege is being audited for everyone.

- AUDIT_OPTION is the privilege being audited.
- SUCCESS is whether the privilege is for success.
- FAILURE is whether the privilege is for failure.

Even if the view says BY ACCESS, you can't audit a system privilege by session.

To see the audits for objects, query the DBA_OBJ_AUDIT_OPTS view.

For example, view the audits turned on for objects owned by HR for the SELECT, INSERT, UPDATE, and DELETE privileges:

```
<select OWNER, OBJECT_NAME, OBJECT_TYPE, SEL, INS, UPD, DEL
from DBA_OBJ_AUDIT_OPTS
where owner = 'HR';>
```

You see something like this:

```
OWNER OBJECT_NAME OBJECT_TYPE SEL INS UPD DEL
----- ----------- ----------- --- --- --- ---
HR    EMPLOYEES   TABLE       S/- -/- -/- -/-
```

The following commands interpret this output:

- OWNER shows the owner of the table.
- OBJECT_NAME is the object name for the audit.
- OBJECT_TYPE names the object type for the audit.
- SEL is SELECT privilege.
- INS is INSERT privilege.
- UPD is UPDATE privilege.
- DEL is DELETE privilege.

The data shown under the privileges (- / -) is interpreted as a two-value field. The - before the slash can be an A for audited by access or an S for audited by session. If there is no S or A, that privilege is not audited. In the preceding example, only the SELECT privilege is audited by session.

The DBA_OBJ_AUDIT_OPTS view is best queried by limiting the rows by owner or actual object name. With most containing thousands of objects, it is easier to view the output by doing so.

Viewing audit information

After configuring for and turning on auditing, see what audit data is being collected. Again, Oracle provides views for you to get this information. Some of them follow:

- **DBA_AUDIT_TRAIL** shows all audit entries in the system.
- **DBA_AUDIT_OBJECT** shows all audit entries in the system for objects.
- **DBA_AUDIT_STATEMENT** shows audit entries for the statements GRANT, REVOKE, AUDIT, NOAUDIT, and ALTER SYSTEM.
- **DBA_AUDIT_SESSION** shows audit entries for the CONNECT and DISCONNECT actions.

To see all the audits captured for the HR.EMPLOYEES table by access, type:

```
<select os_username, username, owner, obj_name, action_name
from dba_audit_object
where owner = 'HR';>
```

You might see something like this:

```
OS_USERNAM USERNAME   OWNER OBJ_NAME             ACTION_NAME
---------- ---------- ----- -------------------- ---------------
oracle     OE         HR    DEPARTMENTS          SELECT
oracle     OE         HR    DEPARTMENTS          INSERT
```

Again, specific columns are selected. There is so much information in this table, that there is no way to fit it into this chapter. This output shows that the OE user selected from departments and inserted into departments. Try your own queries to see what kind of information you can get.

Turning off audits

Turning off auditing is as easy at turning it on. You may have to use the audit options to help remember what you have turned on.

Once you identify the audits you no longer need, use the NOAUDIT command to turn off the audits.

Say you are auditing all selects in the entire database and decide this is way too much information. Turn off this audit:

```
<noaudit select table;>
```

You see this:

```
Noaudit succeeded.
```

When you turn off an audit, you have to be very specific to reverse the exact syntax of the original audit command. For instance, NOAUDIT SELECT TABLE `noaudit select table` won't turn off an audit that was defined as AUDIT SELECT TABLE BY OE. The difference is "BY OE". You would have to say NOAUDIT SELECT TABLE BY OE.

Type this to turn off audits on alter system:

```
<noaudit alter system;>
```

You see this:

```
Noaudit succeeded.
```

If you want to turn off auditing for the table HR.DEPARTMENTS for SELECT by ACCESS, type this:

```
<noaudit select on hr.departments by access;>
```

You see this:

```
Noaudit succeeded.
```

Encrypting a Database

Just because someone can't get into your database doesn't mean she doesn't have access to your data. A clever hacker who gains access to your Oracle database's raw files can extract plain text data from these files.

Raw files include the following:

- Data files (see Chapter 2)
- Recovery Manager backup files (see Chapter 8)
- Data Pump export files (see Chapter 10)

Using Oracle's Advanced Security Option can help scramble, or *encrypt,* the data in these files so someone who gets ahold of them can't extract the data. As of this writing, the Advanced Security Option in the database is a separately licensed feature.

Encrypt these file by using Oracle Wallet and an Encryption Key. Depending on the strength of an encryption key, you can make these files virtually indecipherable to anyone.

We are not discouraging anyone from using encryption, but it comes at a cost:

- There is most certainly CPU overhead to view or work with encrypted files. Depending on the encryption strength, this can be significant.
- There is a fair amount of management overhead involved in an environment that requires encryption. You have to maintain proper access to Oracle Wallets and passwords. You typically have to have a dedicated authority to pass out the encryption keys and password access. There are also expirations on many of these items and encrypted data must be managed in a way that an expired key won't invalidate access to your data.

Some would argue that data security is priceless. However, not all real-world data needs security at the highest of levels. Sometimes your database might house strictly public information. You might want to restrict access to it with usernames, passwords, and privileges to prevent tampering or destruction; that may be enough.

Chapter 10

Keeping the Database Running

In This Chapter

- Performing daily common tasks
- Automating Jobs via the Database Scheduler
- Using Oracle Data Pump

In most instances, managing an Oracle database is a full-time job. That's why some people have the job title Oracle *database administrator (DBA).* A DBA must keep on top of a plethora of activities to make sure your database runs smoothly and doesn't let you down when you most need it.

The 11g Oracle database needs less attention in areas that were traditionally very hands-on. However, each release has new features that require the coddling and care that older features no longer need. Besides basic care and feeding, you might be asked to do some things on a regular basis: for example, loading data or scheduling jobs.

In this chapter we investigate some of the daily maintenance tasks you will find yourself doing, how to use the Oracle scheduler, and load and unload data using Oracle Data Pump.

Doing Your Chores

This section identifies some of the common actives you as DBA might perform. All databases are different. Each DBA has unique tasks and common management responsibilities. You might discover that not all the common tasks in this section apply to you. However, we think most of them do.

On the other hand, you might do something every day that's unique to your environment (and maybe everyone else's too). We apologize for that, but think this chapter's guidelines get you started toward a well-maintained, reliable database.

Making way, checking space

A lot of areas in the database require you to check on space for growth and shrinkage. Most people need to watch out for growth. In our experience, most databases grow over time — not shrink.

Some environments are severely restricted regarding how much space is available. In that case, identifying database resources that allow you to reclaim space can be equally valuable. Lastly, not having extraneous, empty blocks of storage in the database can also help performance.

Chapter 7 explains that when you create a brand-new tablespace, you choose a file for that tablespace to store its data. A *tablespace* is just a logical pointer to a file or files on the operating system. The *file* is the physical component of storage in Oracle. Everything is ultimately stored in a file.

Say you create a tablespace called MY_DATA by typing this:

```
<create tablespace my_data
datafile '/u01/app/oracle/oradata/dev11g/my_data01.dbf'
size 10M;>
```

When this tablespace is created, Oracle allocates 10MB of space from the operating system. The OS sees this space as used. However, if you look in the database, this space is free. Essentially the space "disappears" from the OS and "appears" in the database.

Again, when you create a tablespace, the system administrator sees that the space on the system has shrunk; to the DBA, the database has grown. We're beating this to death because this distinction is important.

Imagine that you have 100GB of space available on the OS and you create a 99GB tablespace. Someone looking on the OS side would start sounding alarms: New space must be purchased! But the DBA can calm any fears by saying, "Don't worry. That 99GB is still free, but Oracle owns it now. The OS can't see it."

Before you jump into adding space, how much space is actually unused in your database? Too often people add space to a system that has plenty of free space available.

You can monitor available real estate in a tablespace a couple different ways:

- Use Enterprise Manager database control.
- Query the data dictionary.

Since not everyone has the Enterprise Manager tool, we show you both ways.

Enterprise Manager

Enterprise Manager offers a couple ways to check space depending on what you want to see.

1. **Log into Enterprise Manager as a DBA user.**
2. **Go to the home page.**
3. **Click the Server tab.**
4. **Click the Tablespaces link in the Storage section.**

   You see a screen like Figure 10-1.

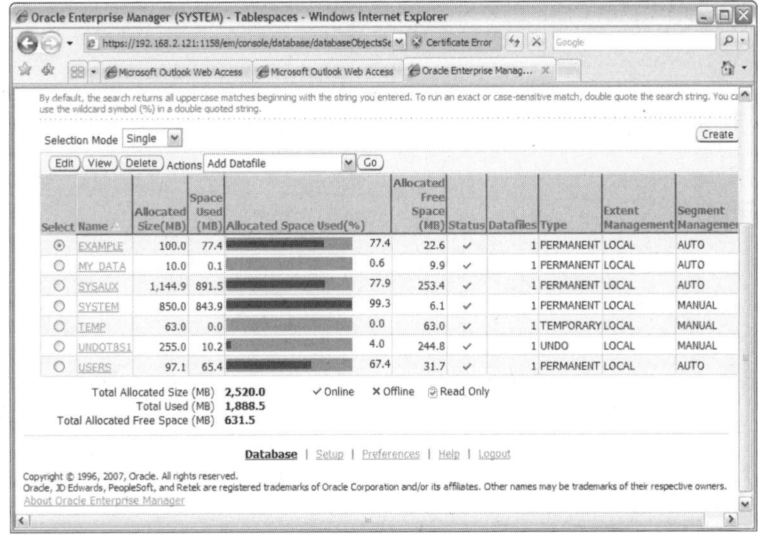

Figure 10-1: Tablespace usage screen in Enterprise Manager looks like this.

If you look closely a lot of information is available here:

- **Tablespace Name:** By row, which tablespace contains information/data.
- **Allocated Size (MB):** The amount of space that the tablespace currently has access to on the file system. It doesn't mean that much space is unused. It's the total amount of used *and* free space in megabytes (MB).
- **Space Used (MB):** The amount of space, in megabytes, you've used creating objects and inserting/loading data.

- **Allocated Space Used (%):** A graphical representation of how much space is used. Nice for reports and showing to people who prefer pictures.
- **Allocated Free Space (MB):** The amount of space, in megabytes, left for creating objects and loading data.
- **Data files:** How many data files are part of the tablespace. If you have more than one data file, click the Tablespace Name link to see all of them.

SQL

If Enterprise Manager isn't available in your environment, a couple of SQL queries can get you the same information.

1. **Log into SQL*Plus.**
2. **Type the following code:**

```
< select tablespace_name, file_name, bytes
from dba_data_files;>
```

With this code you get the tablespace name, its associated data files, and their sizes. You see something like this:

```
TABLESPACE_NAME              BYTES
--------------- --------------
UNDOTBS1               267,386,880
SYSAUX               1,200,553,984
USERS                  101,777,408
SYSTEM                 891,289,600
EXAMPLE                104,857,600
MY_DATA                 10,485,760
```

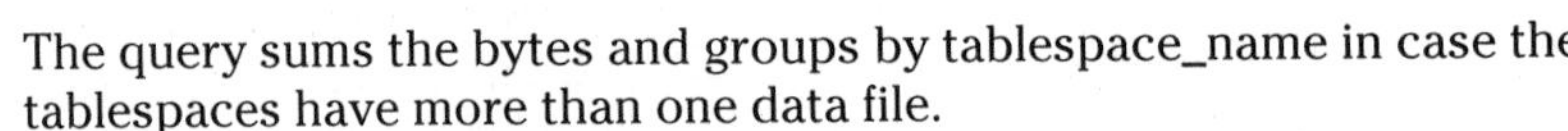

The query sums the bytes and groups by tablespace_name in case the tablespaces have more than one data file.

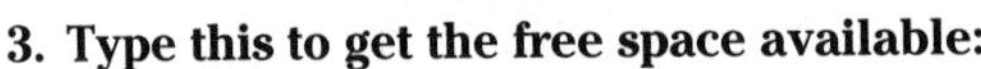

3. **Type this to get the free space available:**

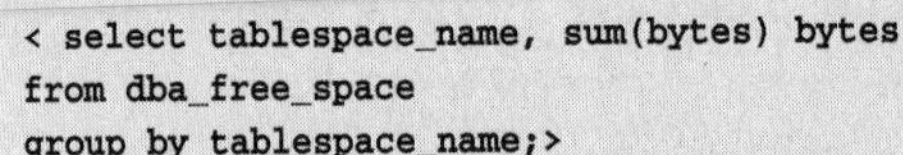

```
< select tablespace_name, sum(bytes) bytes
from dba_free_space
group by tablespace_name;>
```

You see something like this:

```
TABLESPACE_NAME              BYTES
--------------- --------------
SYSAUX                 264,503,296
UNDOTBS1               255,524,864
USERS                   33,226,752
SYSTEM                   6,422,528
EXAMPLE                 23,724,032
MY_DATA                 10,420,224
```

This represents what's left over in your tablespaces that you can use for creating objects and loading data.

4. **Take those numbers and calculate your percentages.**

   If you're clever with SQL, you can do it all in one query. You can see where Enterprise Manager makes things very easy here.

We'd love to say it's as simple as that. Alas, more goes into it whether you use Enterprise Manager or SQL. You see, the preceding sets of steps give you a rough estimate. It's a pretty good estimate, but it's not exact. Will it get you through the night knowing you have enough space for batch jobs to run? Yes, probably.

Beware the false numbers caused by

- **When you create a tablespace, the space is taken away so the OS can't see it. Similar things can happen within the database.**

  For example, when you create table, by default it creates an extent 64k big. That 64k is reserved for rows so it no longer shows up in your free space allocation table. What if you took a 10MB tablespace and created 150 new tables with 64k initial extents? No data, just empty tables. Your free space view would tell you that only 0.1MB of that 10MB is left, yet you haven't put any data into the table. Enterprise Manager would tell you the same thing. Later in the chapter we talk about how you can see how much space is used within a table for more accurate space readings.

- **Autoextensible data files (described in Chapter 7).** A data file might say it's 10MB, but if it reaches that, it automatically grows up to the maximum size specified in the autoextend clause.

For a query that shows your tablespace sizes more accurately, type this:

```
< select tablespace_name, file_name, bytes, autoextensible, maxbytes
from dba_data_files;>
```

You see something like this:

```
TABLESPACE_NAME          BYTES AUT        MAXBYTES
--------------- -------------- --- ---------------
USERS              101,777,408 YES  34,359,721,984
UNDOTBS1           267,386,880 YES  34,359,721,984
SYSAUX           1,200,553,984 YES  34,359,721,984
SYSTEM             891,289,600 YES  34,359,721,984
EXAMPLE            104,857,600 YES  34,359,721,984
MY_DATA             10,485,760 NO                0
```

In this example, the AUT column stands for autoextensible. If it shows `YES`, the MAXBYTES column tells you how big the data file can automatically grow. This detail is important when you're deciding whether to add space.

If you look back at Figure 10-1 and compare it to the output of the preceding query, you see that Enterprise Manager doesn't take a data file's autoextensibility size into account.

Follow these steps to see the information in Enterprise Manager:

1. **Go to the Tablespaces page.**
2. **Choose Datafile from the Object Type drop-down menu.**

   The screen lists data files instead of tablespaces.
3. **Click the radio button next to the data file to want to learn more about.**
4. **Click the View button above the data file listing.**

   You see more details, including autoextensible and maximum file size.

Monitoring space in your segments

Segments are objects that take up space in the database. Segments are objects that, when created, allocated one or more extents from the free space in your tablespaces. The two most common databases segments follow:

- Tables
- Indexes

Before putting in any data in a table, Oracle goes to the tablespace where it lives and allocates an extent. You can call this a *used extent* because it belongs to an object. The remaining space in the tablespace is free extents you can use when objects grow or new objects are created.

As you start putting data into that table, the extent that was allocated upon creation begins to fill up. Once it reaches capacity, the table goes out to the tablespace and grabs another extent. It continues until either you stop adding data or the tablespace runs out of free space.

To have a better idea of how objects grow, consider these guidelines:

- When you first create an object, the default extent size is 64k.
- The object continues to grow on 64k extents until it has 16 extents.
- The 17th extent is 1MB.
- It continues to grow in 1MB extents for the next 63 extents (total of 64, including the first 1MB extent).
- The 81st extent is 8MB.
- After 8MB extents, the last size Oracle uses is 64MB extents.

Knowing how your segments grow can help you predict space requirements. This is an important skill to have when monitoring storage.

If you constantly insert data into your table, you got it covered. However, that isn't always the case. Some tables grow and shrink. To be specific, they grow, but the shrinking, if necessary, is up to you.

First of all, it comes in handy to understand how the objects in your application are used. Consider these examples:

- What tables grow?
- What tables, if any, shrink over time?
- What tables receive inserts and are never added to again except for reads?
- What tables are under constant manipulation (INSERT, UPDATE, DELETE)?

Tables that stay the same are easy. You don't have to worry much about those unless you want to tune them for performance. We already covered how to monitor a table's growth, so any tables that grow without getting any rows deleted are covered…unless, again, you want to tune them for performance (but that's another topic).

The tough ones

- Tables that shrink and grow
- Tables that only shrink

Growing and shrinking: Tricky tables

A table that fits this category might be loaded every night, then deleted from throughout the day, like a batch processing table — for example, an ORDERS table that's batch loaded at night from all the orders that were taken from a web site; as the orders are processed the next day, rows are deleted one by one. At the end of the day, all the rows are gone. What do you need to monitor for this table?

You should be most concerned with how big the table gets each day after the batch load. Businesses want orders to increase. What about the deletes? Should you shrink the table at the end of the day before the next batch load to free up space? Absolutely not. Although it's small, the growth of an object is overhead on the system processing. By leaving it the same size day to day, you know the space will be constantly reused. It's kind of like recycling. You mainly want to monitor this type of object for growth.

What about a table that gets mostly inserted into, but also gets deletes? Say for every 1 million rows inserted in a week, 30 percent are deleted. This table can present an interesting challenge.

Take a quick look at how rows are inserted to better understand how objects grow and use space:

- You have a new table with one 64k extent.
- Your block size is 4k so that extent is 16 blocks.
- You start inserting data; 100 rows fit in a block.
- By default Oracle fills blocks 90 percent full and then stops (so you can update the row later and have it grow). For example, some fields are left null until a later date, then you fill them in. You don't want the block to get filled too easily by an update; otherwise Oracle has to move the row to a new block that fits it. This *rows migration* degrades performance.
- When all the blocks are filled in the free extents, the table allocates a new extent and the process starts over.

What if you start deleting rows at the same time you're inserting? Will Oracle reuse the space where you deleted the row? It depends. Again, Oracle has a built-in feature that sacrifices space in favor of performance. Oracle inserts a row into a block that was once full, but only if deletes bring the block to 40 percent full.

Oracle doesn't want to manage a block that teeters between full, not full, full, not full, and so on. Although Oracle has reduced the performance overhead that comes with managing blocks and which ones you can insert into, managing block storage still has a cost associated with it. Imagine you have a table with 10,000 blocks and are constantly inserting and deleting from that table. Oracle could spend all the CPU cycles managing what blocks can have inserts and which can't if there were only a one-row difference between full and not-full blocks.

That's why Oracle uses the 40-percent rule. A block takes all the inserts it can until it's 90 percent full, but the block can't get back in line until it's been reduced to 40 percent full.

Again, what if you insert 1 million rows a week and delete 30 percent of them? What if the 30 percent that you delete are randomly selected and spread evenly across the blocks? Over time, those blocks never get down to 40 percent full. After a year, you may have a table that is 10GB with 3GB of it empty row space that won't be reused.

As with many other operations, you have a couple of ways to determine whether you can release an object's space. You must do that after evaluating the object's usage pattern. Apply the following methods only to objects whose space you feel isn't getting reused. Else, you waste your time and untold CPU and IO resources.

- Enterprise Manager
- Math

Enterprise Manager

Enterprise Manager is the easy way. A built-in tool called the Segment Advisor goes to the segment blocks and determines if an unused row space can be de-allocated. It's relatively easy to use.

1. **Log into Enterprise Manager as a DBA user.**
2. **From the home page, scroll to the bottom to the Related Links section.**

   The three columns are shown in Figure 10-2.
3. **Click the Advisor Central link in the middle column.**

   At the top of the next page, you see three more columns of links.

Figure 10-2: Related Links section of Enterprise Manager home page.

4. **Click Segment Advisor.**

   Figure 10-3 shows the Segment Advisor: Scope page. You can configure the segment advisor to run against tablespaces or specific schema objects. It points out that the database automatically determines what objects are work candidates. If your objects aren't new to the system (the automatic job runs daily), see if they're already identified.
5. **Choose the Schema Objects radio button and click Next to check a specific object.**

   Next you have to add the object or objects you want to analyze.

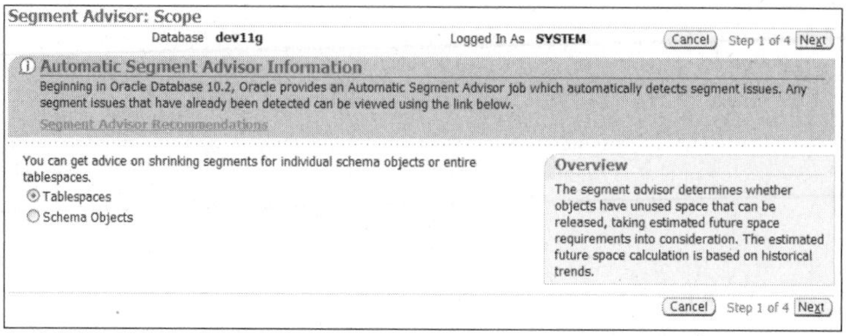

Figure 10-3: The Segment Advisor: Scope page lets you choose between analyzing segments or tablespaces.

6. **Click the Add button.**

   The segment search screen appears.

7. **Enter your information.**

   Figure 10-4 shows a search for objects named like emp in the schema hr of type Table.

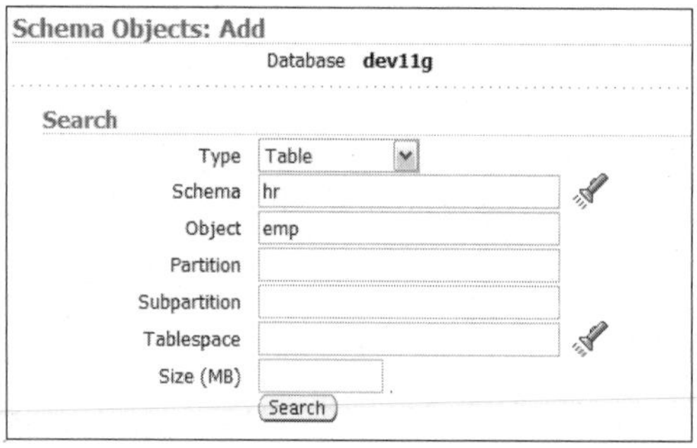

Figure 10-4: Use the segment search screen to select objects for analysis.

8. **Click Search, select your object by checking the box, and click OK.**

9. **When finished adding objects, click Next.**

10. **Indicate when you want to run the analysis.**

    On a large object that's gigabytes in size, consider doing this off-hours or over the weekend; it can strain the system.

11. **Click Next.**

    The final screen reviews your job.

12. **When you're satisfied, click Submit.**

    We chose a relatively small table call emp, which is engineered to recommend space shrinkage. Once your job runs, you can click the link identified by your job name to get results and recommendations by tablespace.

13. **Click the Recommendation Details button.**

    Figure 10-5 shows the EMP table is recommended for space reclamation.

Recommendation Details for Tablespace: USERS

The following table contains the reclaimable space information for the evaluated segments in the selected tablespace. Based on growth trends, the advisor takes into consideration estimated future space requirements. Oracle recommends shrinking or reorganizing these segments to release wasted space. Select the segment to implement the recommendation.

Task Name **SEGMENTADV_6915433**
Status **COMPLETED**
Running Time (seconds) **0**
Started **Aug 8, 2008 6:50:55 PM EDT**
Ended **Aug 8, 2008 6:50:55 PM EDT**
Time Limit (mins) **UNLIMITED**

Schema Segment Partition Minimum Reclaimable Space (MB) (Search)

(Implement)

Select All | Select None

Select	Schema	Segment	Recommendation	Reclaimable Space (MB)	Allocated Space (MB)	Used Space (MB)	Segment Type
☐	HR	EMP.	(Shrink)	11.49	36.00	24.51	TABLE

Figure 10-5: You can reduce the EMP table by 11MB.

14. **Click Shrink.**

    If you did multiple objects, check the boxes next to those tables you want to fix; then click the Implement button.

It asks if you just want to compact the rows in the block and leave the space out there (a good idea if you're going to keep inserting) or if you want to release the space.

Lastly, it sets up a job that you can run immediately or put into the scheduler to run at a later date. Remember, depending on the size of the object, this can cause significant overhead and time.

Plain old arithmetic

It takes a little math to determine whether you can release an object's space (the same operation Enterprise Manager does in the preceding section).

Before you can decide whether to make room in a table, analyze the table to gather statistics. When we say analyze, we mean *analyze.* The ANALYZE command gets the necessary statistics to do this computation; DBMS_STATS doesn't get those stats.

This example uses the emp table. Do the following to analyze the table appropriately:

1. **Log into SQL*Plus and type the following:**

```
< analyze table emp compute statistics;>
```

   You see this:

```
Table analyzed.
```

2. **Run a query against the USER_TABLES view by typing this:**

```
<select table_name, avg_space, blocks
from user_tables
where table_name = 'EMP'>
```

   You see something like this:

```
TABLE_NAME                     AVG_SPACE     BLOCKS
------------------------------ ---------- ----------
EMP                                  3264       4528
```

   The AVG_SPACE column shows the average amount of free space per block.

3. **Use the following formula to calculate the amount of empty space in the emp table:**

   (AVG_SPACE - (DB_BLOCK_SIZE × FREE_SPACE)) × TAB_BLOCKS

   For this example, the formula looks like this: (3623 - (8192 × .10)) × 4528 = 11066432 (approximately 11MB)

   This math may not be the same Enterprise Manager uses, but you can see it's very close.

4. **Decide whether there's enough space to make it worthwhile to shrink the object.**

5. **Issue this SQL command to enable Oracle to move rows around in the table type:**

```
Alter table emp enable row movement;
```

   You see this:

```
Table altered.
```

6. **Issue this SQL command to do the shrink:**

```
<alter table emp shrink space;>
```

   You see this:

```
Table altered.
```

7. **Re-analyze the table and re-execute the query to check the statistics.**

```
<select table_name, avg_space, blocks
from user_tables
where table_name = 'EMP'>
```

   You should see something like this:

```
TABLE_NAME                      AVG_SPACE     BLOCKS
------------------------------ ---------- ----------
EMP                                   933       2979
```

   As you can see, the AVG_SPACE is about 10 percent of the block size. This is normal for default block space organization.

Check things like the Flash Recovery area. Any day that produces a lot of archive logs or large backup files can quickly overcome the allocated space. If you don't have something like Enterprise Manager watching this, you can encounter problems like a hung database or failing backups. These situations can have dire consequences on your database system.

Checking users

Perhaps it's maintenance. Perhaps it's a regular security sweep. Either way, occasionally logging in to the database and checking on the connected sessions is beneficial.

You can find things like this if you check on a regular basis:

- Stale sessions
- Login abuse such as people sharing accounts
- Abnormally long running jobs
- Unauthorized logins

Finding stale sessions

Stale sessions have been logged in to the system for a long time and no one's done anything with them. Getting rid of stale sessions can help control resource usage.

Everyone's system is different so you have to rely on some of your own knowledge to decide whether the absence of activity is abnormal. To get a list of logged-in users and the last time they issued a command, connect to the database as a DBA user and type the following:

```
<select sid, serial#, username, last_call_et
from v$session
where username is not null;>
```

You might see something like this :

```
SID SERIAL# USERNAME         LAST_CALL_ET
--- ------- ---------------- ------------
 12    9853 SYSMAN                      3
 14    6552 HR                          0
 56      42 DBSNMP                      6
112   59271 SYSTEM                    160
 65   23451 MPYLE                  743160
 98    8752 CRM                         1
 32    4551 CRM                         3
 45   16554 HR                         36
119    9812 KHANR                   36522
```

MPYLE and KHANR are the two potentially bothersome accounts in this example. The LAST_CALL_ET column output data has the number of seconds since there was any activity. MPYLE has been inactive for over eight days! KHANR is a little less alarming at about 10 hours, but nonetheless, that would most likely require some explanation.

Note that the command uses the WHERE clause USERNAME is NOT NULL. Oracle internal processes show up in this list as unnamed users and we don't want those getting in the way of evaluation. Also, this example includes identification columns SID and SERIAL#. Together, these two columns uniquely identify a session within the database.

If you see a session you want to get rid of, type the following:

```
<alter system kill session '65,23451';>
```

You should see this:

```
System altered.
```

Releasing the bug

We had a client system that had regularly over 3,000 connected sessions. While evaluating the sessions, we discovered that 1,200 sessions had never issued a single command after logging in and setting a date format. It turned out to be an application bug that created multiple sessions for each application operation — one of them a session to set the date format. Of course, it did no good to set a session date format and log into another session to do the work. Regardless, the client fixed the bug. It released nearly 6GB of memory from the OS!

Before you go killing sessions that have long periods of inactivity, check with application folks to make sure something isn't part of a connection pool that just hasn't been used for a while. Usually, removal is safe if it isn't an application ID or you can identify the user. Do your research!

Policing for login abuse

People everywhere are abusing their login privileges. Unfortunately, it's usually people higher up in the application chain of command. These people tend to have more privileges. We sometimes find them giving out their login ID to subordinates to help with work.

Track this abuse down by comparing the database login ID with the OS login ID. Oracle tracks both. Type the following to see all the users connected with both IDs:

```
<select sid, serial#, username, osuser, program
from v$session
where username is not null;>
```

You might see something like this:

```
       SID    SERIAL# USERNAME   OSUSER     PROGRAM
---------- ---------- ---------- ---------- -----------------
       112       3741 MPYLE      MPYLE      sqlplusw.exe
       122       3763 MPYLE      RKHAN      sqlplusw.exe
       115       9853 SYSMAN     oracle     OMS
       122      35878 HR         HRAPP      sqlplus@classroom
       124          4 DBSNMP     oracle     emagent@classroom
```

MPYLE has given his login ID to RKHAN (or at least the evidence suggests that). Evaluate this information; appropriate measures can be taken if it's in violation of company policy.

Checking on the backup

Checking your backups should be a regular part of your daily routine. Checking backups includes these things:

- The database. From an Oracle DBA's standpoint, you need to make sure the entire backup process is logged.
- Occasional follow up with appropriate personal about OS backups.
- Regular checkup to ensure the sys admin is moving the database backup from disk to tape.

Too many environments put system backups on the back burner because they were scheduled jobs; no alerting was in place. If you subscribe to this methodology, you could be signing up for a heap of trouble.

Keep these backup tips in mind:

- **Oracle Recovery Manager has a LOG command that you can pass in with your backup script.** This details every step of the backup as it runs. This shell script example logs the output of your RMAN backup on Linux/UNIX:

```
#/usr/bin/ksh

# Environment Settings
export ORACLE_BASE=/u01/app/oracle
export ORACLE_HOME=$ORACLE_BASE/product/11.1.0/db_1
export ORACLE_SID=dev11g
export BAK_DATE=`date '+%d%b%Y_%H_%M'`
export PATH=$ORACLE_HOME/bin:$PATH

# Run Backup
rman target / cmdfile=full_hot_backup.rmn
log=full_hot_backup_${ORACLE_SID}_${BAK_DATE}.log

# Check Error Code
Export ECODE=$?

if [ $ECODE -gt 0 ]; then
        mailx -s "RMAN BACKUP FAILED!" dba@perptech.com
else echo "RMAN BACKUP SUCCESSFUL"
fi
```

  The simple script, which you might schedule in cron, runs a backup script of your choice (called full_hot_backup.rmn) and logs the output to a file with the database name and date attached.

After the backup completes, the script checks whether RMAN exited cleanly. It does this by checking a mechanism called an *error code.* Well-written programs have this mechanism. If the environment variable $? has a value of non-zero, something failed.

In this case, I have an if-then section that sends an email if that backup failed. Of course, if there's a failure, you have to find out why and fix it. Either way, implementing a notification similar to the example helps you tighten your backup and recovery planning.

- **Make sure the backup is usable.** This is important for all backups, but is especially important if you store any backups to tape. Make sure those backups can be restored from tape and then actively recovered to a database. For obvious reasons you don't necessarily have to do this with your production database. You can do the restore to a different database. It might be a good way to test your backup while "refreshing" a test database at the same time. Either way, as reliable as you would like to think tapes can be, you need to test them. What if one of the tape heads is going bad and writing out corrupt blocks? Doing this will also help you to practice your recovery strategies.
- **At the very least, date and save this log in a directory on the system.** If you want to go one step further, have it emailed to you every day when the backup completes.
- **Look at the backup log for errors.** Imagine how you'd feel if you experienced a failure and had to tell your boss that you can't recover because the backup's been failing for six months. It's surprising how often we run into situations like this while helping clients with their backup and recovery strategies.

Checking batch jobs

Almost all companies we have worked for have some sort of nightly batch jobs that run against the database. They range from loading data, generating reports, to some sort of data processing. They might be scheduled by you or someone else. Either way, we find it common that the DBA is the one responsible for their monitoring and success. If you think about it, they are on your turf with you being in charge of the database and all.

Whether you or someone else developed the scripts, they, like RMAN, should have some sort of logging and notification system in place. This will make it easier for you to identify a problem when it occurs. By having status emails generated and sent out, it all but forces you to keep up with the results. If your email program allows filtering, you can send the notifications to separate folders for each batch job. Just remember to check them. Again, we're trying to help you cover all the bases that an Oracle DBA might commonly have on his or her plate.

Audit records

What's the use of auditing in the database if you aren't doing anything with the information? You should develop some ideas on what types of information you are looking for. In addition, regularly back up and purge the audit logs (whether they are in the database or the OS). This way, they aren't taking up space and they are easier to search when looking for potential problems.

System logs

Oracle generates all kinds of system logs. Depending on what features you enabled in the database, there may be more or less. Some logs (alert and listener, for example) should be regularly

- Checked
- Renamed
- Backed up

If certain logs grow too large, it can cause problems in the database.

Besides size, these logs contain valuable information sometimes that can help identify problems. In addition to Oracle's logs, don't hesitate to look at items like Windows Event view or the message logs on Linux/UNIX systems. They also contain valuable information.

Automating Jobs with the Oracle Scheduler

With the addition of the Oracle Scheduler, you can run almost any type of program with a robust resource-management and scheduling system.

The scheduler can run these programs:

- PL/SQL Stored Procedures
- PL/SQL Anonymous Blocks
- Java Stored Programs
- Local and remote external programs such as shell scripts and executables

You can schedule jobs that are

- **Timed-based:** A job can run simply from wall-clock time. It can repeat on a schedule based on hours, days, months, and so on.
- **Event-based:** The results of certain conditions or events in the environment can cause a job to run. This trigger is useful when you have to wait for other processes to finish before a job is run.
- **Dependency-based:** You can set up dependency such as success or failure. Depending on the outcome of one job, one or more dependant scenarios can be executed.

Scheduler objects

The scheduler can use a number of objects to run jobs. Not all of them are mandatory. These objects specify job parameters, timing, execution windows, and resource limits.

- **Programs:** Programs are the actual code that the scheduler will runs. They identify the execution code, arguments, and job type.
- **Schedules:** The job schedules are just want you think. They contain parameters such as when and how often. A schedule can be created and then shared for many jobs.
- **Jobs:** When a job object is created it contains the executable and the schedule required to run the job. You can the enable the job for it to begin the task based on the parameters. Jobs are categorized as:
    - **Database** runs out of the database from PL/SQL commands.
    - **External** runs off the operating system from external executables.
    - **Chain (Dependency)** runs based on status of other jobs.
    - **Detached** runs to simply kick off another job in a new process.
    - **Lightweight** are simple jobs that only exists for their immediate execution. They are not stored as schema objects. Used for quick, low-overhead applications.
- **Windows:** Helps schedule jobs for certain times which can help control resource usage. When a window becomes active, certain resource directives are enabled that might restrict a job from overwhelming the system.

Creating your first scheduler job

This Oracle Scheduler example creates a simple job that runs a stored PL/SQL procedure. The procedure selects a count of the number of users on the system and inserts that number into a table with a timestamp. It runs every five minutes.

Follow these steps to schedule a job for the first time:

1. **Log into SQL*Plus as the SYS user.**
2. **Give the intended job creator the ability to create jobs:**

   ```
   <grant create job to hr;>
   ```

   You should see this:

   ```
   Grant succeeded.
   ```

   This example job is created and run by HR.
3. **Let HR see the V$SESSION table:**

   ```
   <grant select on v_$session to hr;>
   ```

   You should see this:

   ```
   Grant succeeded.
   ```

   The _ in V_$SESSION isn't a typo! V$SESSION is a synonym for V_$SESSION. For the grant to work, you have to give the view name.
4. **Log into SQL*Plus as the job creator and make a table to hold the data:**

   ```
   < create table user_count (
   number_of_users NUMBER(4),
   time_of_day     TIMESTAMP
   )
   TABLESPACE users;>
   ```

   You see this:

   ```
   Table created.
   ```
5. **Create a stored procedure:**

   ```
   < CREATE OR REPLACE PROCEDURE insert_user_count AS
      v_user_count NUMBER(4);
   BEGIN
     SELECT count(*)
             INTO v_user_count
        FROM v$session
        WHERE username IS NOT NULL;
   ```

```
   INSERT INTO user_count
      VALUES (v_user_count, systimestamp);
   commit;

END insert_user_count;
/ >
```

The stored procedure gathers the number of users and inserts them into the table with a timestamp. You should see this:

```
Procedure created.
```

6. **Create a program for the job:**

```
< BEGIN
DBMS_SCHEDULER.CREATE_PROGRAM (
   program_name           => 'PROG_INSERT_USER_COUNT',
program_action          => 'INSERT_USER_COUNT',
program_type            => 'STORED_PROCEDURE');
END;
/>
```

You see this:

```
PL/SQL procedure successfully completed.
```

7. **Enable the program:**

```
<exec dbms_scheduler.enable('PROG_INSERT_USER_COUNT')>
```

You see this:

```
PL/SQL procedure successfully completed.
```

8. **Create a schedule for the job to run:**

```
< BEGIN
DBMS_SCHEDULER.CREATE_SCHEDULE (
  schedule_name     => 'my_weekend_5min_schedule',
  start_date        => SYSTIMESTAMP,
  repeat_interval   => 'FREQ=MINUTELY; INTERVAL=5; BYDAY=SAT,SUN',
  end_date          => SYSTIMESTAMP + INTERVAL '30' day,
  comments          => 'Every 5 minutes');
END;
/>
```

This example job runs every five minutes. You see this:

```
PL/SQL procedure successfully completed.
```

9. **Create your job with the program and schedule you defined:**

```
< BEGIN
DBMS_SCHEDULER.CREATE_JOB (
   job_name          =>  'my_user_count_job',
   program_name      =>  'prog_insert_user_count',
   schedule_name     =>  'my_weekend_5min_schedule');
END;
/>
```

You see this:

```
PL/SQL procedure successfully completed.
```

10. **Enable your job so it runs within the defined schedule:**

```
< exec dbms_scheduler.enable('my_user_count_job')>
```

You see this:

```
PL/SQL procedure successfully completed.
```

The job runs at the specified start time (at SYSTIMESTAMP). If you choose a calendar date in the future, it doesn't start until then.

11. **After the job's been running for 17 minutes, type the following to see your USER_COUNT table:**

```
< select *
from user_count;>
```

You see this:

```
NUMBER_OF_USERS TIME_OF_DAY
--------------- --------------------------------
             14 09-AUG-08 02.15.14.118495 PM
             14 09-AUG-08 02.00.14.137300 PM
             13 09-AUG-08 02.05.14.120116 PM
             13 09-AUG-08 02.10.14.120680 PM
```

Once you have the job running, you can get details about the success or failure by querying the following views:

```
USER_SCHEDULER_JOB_RUN_DETAILS
USER_SCHEDULER_JOB_LOG
```

These views show information only about your jobs. To get information on the recent runs of our job, log in as the job creator and type this:

```
< select job_name, status, run_duration, cpu_used
from USER_SCHEDULER_JOB_RUN_DETAILS
where job_name = 'MY_USER_COUNT_JOB';>
```

You see this:

```
JOB_NAME             STATUS     RUN_DURATION     CPU_USED
-------------------- ---------- --------------- -------------------
MY_USER_COUNT_JOB    SUCCEEDED  +000 00:00:00   +000 00:00:00.01
MY_USER_COUNT_JOB    SUCCEEDED  +000 00:00:00   +000 00:00:00.01
MY_USER_COUNT_JOB    SUCCEEDED  +000 00:00:00   +000 00:00:00.00
MY_USER_COUNT_JOB    SUCCEEDED  +000 00:00:00   +000 00:00:00.01
```

Once your job is no longer needed, you have a couple of choices.

Disabling a job

You can easily re-enable it later. To disable your job, type the following:

```
<exec dbms_scheduler.disable('my_user_count_job')>
```

You should see this:

```
PL/SQL procedure successfully completed.
```

Removing the job

Remove just the job and leave the program out there, or remove both. Same goes for the schedule you created.

If you no longer need this particular job, you can remove it:

```
<exec dbms_scheduler.drop_job('my_user_count_job')>
```

You should see this:

```
PL/SQL procedure successfully completed.
```

If you no longer need your program, you can remove it:

```
<exec dbms_scheduler.drop_program('prog_insert_user_count')>
```

You should see this:

```
PL/SQL procedure successfully completed.
```

If you no longer need a particular schedule, you can remove it:

```
<exec dbms_scheduler.drop_schedule('my_weekend_5min_schedule')>
```

You should see this:

```
PL/SQL procedure successfully completed.
```

The job schedule you created can be used for multiple jobs; be careful when removing your schedule.

Using Oracle Data Pump

Oracle Data Pump is one tool we use constantly.

Data Pump is modeled after Oracle's Export/Import tools that were available prior to Oracle 10g. Export/Import is still available but Data Pump has taken the tasks traditionally done by Export/Import and added a lot more options and flexibility.

Data Pump is useful for some of these things:

- Moving data from one schema to another
- Moving data from one version of Oracle to another
- Moving data from one OS to another
- Creating Logical Backups

Like the older Export/Import utilities, you must run Data Pump from the command line. That makes it easy to script and schedule automated jobs. Data Pump is controlled by a series of parameters and files.

You should be familiar with these files:

- **Dump file:** This file is created during a Data Pump Export. It's the import file when you do a Data Pump Import. It's binary so you can't open it to see anything useful.
- **Parfile:** This optional file lists the parameters that control the Data Pump Import or Export. You create this text-based file yourself.
- **Log file:** This output is for all Data Pump Import and Export jobs unless you specify otherwise. You can name it yourself or let it have a default name. It's useful for getting jobs statistics and for troubleshooting.

You can interactively do these things with Data Pump jobs:

- Start
- Stop
- Pause
- Restart
- Kill

This means you can start a job from the command line, detach from it to do something else (while it's still running), and re-attach later to check progress or make changes. When a Data Pump job runs into a problem, it automatically suspends itself; that way you have a chance to fix the problem before the job fails altogether. This can be a real time-saver. Prior to Data Pump, if an Export/Import job ran into a problem, it would fail immediately, sometimes wasting hours of time.

In our experience, Data Pump Export is significantly faster than traditional exports on large jobs. If you have a small job, like one or two small tables or a small schema, it doesn't really seem to make a difference. But on large jobs, the difference is phenomenal.

In one example a job took around 12 hours to dump out about 200GB with the old Export tool. When we upgraded from 9i to 11g and converted to Data Pump, it took only 45 minutes. Part of the reason is that Data Pump can be easily parallelized. *Parallelizing* Data Pump means starting multiple processes that run simultaneously to split up the job. The only way to parallelize traditional exports is to manually split the workload into multiple jobs. That was tedious and time consuming.

Data Pump Export

The command line-program expdb launches Data Pump Export. All Data Pump Export jobs are "estimated" at the beginning so you see the estimate before it runs the actual export.

From the OS command line, launch Data Pump Export and have it show a list of the parameter:

```
<expdp>
```

You see something like this:

```
Export: Release 11.1.0.6.0 - Production on Sunday, 10 August, 2008 14:30:01

Copyright (c) 2003, 2007, Oracle. All rights reserved.


The Data Pump export utility provides a mechanism for transferring data objects
between Oracle databases. The utility is invoked with the following command:

   Example: expdp scott/tiger DIRECTORY=dmpdir DUMPFILE=scott.dmp

You can control how Export runs by entering the 'expdp' command followed
by various parameters. To specify parameters, you use keywords:

   Format:  expdp KEYWORD=value or KEYWORD=(value1,value2,...,valueN)
```

```
   Example: expdp scott/tiger DUMPFILE=scott.dmp DIRECTORY=dmpdir SCHEMAS=scott
               or TABLES=(T1:P1,T1:P2), if T1 is partitioned table

...output snipped...
```

You can see that Data Pump lists all the parameters you have to choose from and gives a brief explanation of each.

You can specify parameters two ways:

- On the command line
- In a parameter file

Go over some of the more useful parameters in detail:

- **COMPRESSION:** Modified in 11g, this parameter allows you to compress the output of Data Pump while the job is running. This is handy when space is at a premium. This parameter degrades the performance of the export but that's to be expected.

  Prior to 11g, we had to compress after the job. That doesn't do a lot of good when you don't have the space to export the data before compression. Also, while this parameter was available in 10g, it only compressed the metadata in the export. If you ask us, that's practically useless. Now this parameter is one of the better ones available.

- **CONTENT:** This specifies what type of data you want to get. Do you want just object definitions? Do you want just the data? Both?
- **DIRECTORY:** This specifies the directory where you want the dump file to go. This is an Oracle Object directory, not a simple path on the OS. We show you how to create a directory later in this chapter.
- **DUMPFILE:** This parameter names the dump file to be output. You can also have Data Pump number the files if you like. This is handy when you use parallelism or have Data Pump break the job into multiple files of manageable size. To have Data Pump number the files, use the %U argument:

  ```
  DUMPFILE=my_dp_exp_%U.dmp
  ```

  Data Pump starts with 1 and numbers the files to 99. What if you need more than 99 files? Try something like this:

  ```
  DUMPFILE= my_dp_exp_seta_%U.dmp, my_dp_exp_set_b_%U.dmp
  ```

You can have it dump to multiple files. This is especially useful when you're parallelizing the output.

- **ESTIMATE:** This parameter estimates your job size but won't run it. Very handy when space is at a premium. This parameter stops the job after estimating.
- **EXCLUDE:** You can exclude certain objects from the export. For example, say you want everything but the HR and OE schemas as well as all views and functions. EXCLUDE can have multiple entries. You can say this:

```
EXCLUDE=SCHEMAS:"'HR','OE'"
EXCLUDE=VIEW,FUNCTION
```

- **INCLUDE:** Mutually exclusive with EXCLUDE, use this parameter if you want to get a specific type of object. When the list is small, this can be very useful:

```
INCLUDE=VIEWS, TRIGGERS
```

- **FILESIZE:** You can break your Data Pump Export into multiple files, which aids file management. For example, if you have a 200GB export to do, you might not want a 200GB dump file to manage afterward. Instead, use this parameter to break it into 4GB chunks or something similar.
- **FLASHBACK_TIME:** If you want to dump the data from a time other than the present, you can use this parameter to specify a date and time. As long as your database still has the old data in its undo retention space, this can be very useful.
- **NETWORK_LINK:** You can connect from one database to export to another by setting up a database link and specifying it with this parameter.
- **PARALLEL:** To help speed up your dump, you can parallelize it. Try different values to find the most efficient number of processes across different systems. At the very least, you should be able to parallelize by the number of CPUs you have while recalling the capabilities of the storage media to which you're writing.
- **SCHEMAS:** Gives a list of schemas to Data Pump and tells it what to get. By default, Data Pump exports the schema that's logging in to do the job.
- **TABLES:** Restricts the export to a list of tables.
- **TABLESPACES:** Restricts the export to a list of tablespaces only.

Data Pump Import

The command-line program impdb launches Data Pump Import. From the OS command line, launch Data Pump Import and have it show a list of the parameters:

```
<impdp help=y>
```

You see something like this:

```
Import: Release 11.1.0.6.0 - Production on Sunday, 10 August, 2008 15:15:49

Copyright (c) 2003, 2007, Oracle. All rights reserved.


The Data Pump Import utility provides a mechanism for transferring data objects
between Oracle databases. The utility is invoked with the following command:

     Example: impdp scott/tiger DIRECTORY=dmpdir DUMPFILE=scott.dmp

You can control how Import runs by entering the 'impdp' command followed
by various parameters. To specify parameters, you use keywords:

     Format:  impdp KEYWORD=value or KEYWORD=(value1,value2,...,valueN)
     Example: impdp scott/tiger DIRECTORY=dmpdir DUMPFILE=scott.dmp
…output snipped…
```

Like Data Pump Export, Import lists the parameters that can be used with the import portion of Data Pump. Many of these parameters behave the same way they do when you're using Data Pump Export.

Take a closer look at some the Data Pump Import parameters:

- **CONTENT:** If you have a full content export file, you can choose to only import the metadata. For example, you might want to create all the tables with no rows. Obviously, if you didn't include the rows in the export dump file, you can't tell Data Pump Import to put them in!
- **ESTIMATE:** Estimates the size of the Data Pump Import.
- **DIRECTORY:** Tells Data Pump Import where it can find the dump file. It doesn't have to be the same place it was dumped, but you must move the file to the new location. This might be useful when moving the file to another machine or OS.
- **DUMPFILE:** A complete listing of all the files created by Data Pump Export.

- **EXCLUDE:** Works much like Data Pump Export, but tells Data Pump Import what to leave from the dump file.
- **INCLUDE:** Another way of controlling what objects are put into the target database.
- **FLASHBACK_SCN, FLASHBACK_TIME:** Use with the Data Pump Import tool only when connecting through a NETWORK_LINK. Data Pump Import can connect directly to a remote database across a database link and write the data directly into the target system. Use these parameters to pull data from the past.
- **NETWORK_LINK:** You can connect from one database and import into another by setting up a database link and specifying it with this parameter. No files are created when this method is used. Very handy for logical recovery and cloning.
- **PARALLEL:** Help speed up your import.
- **REMAP_SCHEMA:** This parameter is handy for copying the objects/data from one schema to another.
- **REMAP_TABLESPACE:** Moves the objects into a new tablespace. By default, they go into the same tablespace they came from. This parameter is useful when used in conjunction with remap_schema and while moving data from one database to another.
- **SCHEMAS:** Gives a list of schemas to Data Pump to tell it what to import. By default, Data Pump imports everything in the file. In essence, you can have a full export, but then pick and choose what you want to import.
- **TABLES:** Like SCHEMAS, you can choose from your dump file what to import.
- **TABLESPACES:** You can choose what tablespaces you want import from the dump file.

Creating Oracle Directories

As mentioned, an Oracle directory is required for Data Pump. A *directory* is basically a portal to a location on the operating system.

Directories are controlled by both system and object privileges. You need a system privilege, CREATE DIRECTORY, to create one. If your user doesn't own the directory, you need READ and/or WRITE object privileges on the directory to use it.

To create a directory, log on to the database as a user with appropriate privileges and type the following:

```
create directory my_data_pump_dir as '/u01/app/oracle/dumpfiles';
```

You should see this:

```
Directory created.
```

Using Data Pump with a Parameter File

A *parameter file* is a text file listing the parameters for the Data Pump Export or Import and setting the chosen values. Data Pump Export and Import parameter files are constructed the same way.

Follow these steps to run a Data Pump Export with this parameter file:

1. **Type the parameter file into a text editor and save it to a directory.**

   This example is a parameter file that exports the DEPARTMENTS and EMPLOYEES tables of the HR schema:

   ```
   # File: /u01/app/oracle/scripts/datapump/my_data_pump_parfile.par
   DIRECTORY=my_data_pump_dir
   DUMPFILE=my_data_pump_dumpfile.dmp
   LOGFILE=my_data_pump_logfile.log
   SCHEMAS=HR
   TABLES=EMPLOYEES, DEPARTMENTS
   COMPRESSION=ALL
   ```

2. **Open a command-line prompt and go to the directory where your parameter file is saved.**
3. **Launch Data Pump Export with your parameter file:**

   ```
   <expdp parfile=my_data_pump_parfile.par>
   ```

   You should see this:

   ```
   Export: Release 11.1.0.6.0 - Production on Sunday, 10 August, 2008 16:53:33

   Copyright (c) 2003, 2007, Oracle. All rights reserved.

   Username:
   ```

4. **Type in the username and give the password for the user you want to export with.**

   You should see something like this:

```
Connected to: Oracle Database 11g Enterprise Edition Release 11.1.0.6.0 -
          Production
With the Partitioning, OLAP, Data Mining and Real Application Testing
          options
Starting "SYS"."SYS_EXPORT_SCHEMA_01":  /******** AS SYSDBA parfile=my_
          data_pump_parfile.par
Estimate in progress using BLOCKS method...
Processing object type SCHEMA_EXPORT/TABLE/TABLE_DATA
Total estimation using BLOCKS method: 128 KB
…output snipped…
. . exported "HR"."DEPARTMENTS"                          5.437 KB      27
          rows
. . exported "HR"."EMPLOYEES"                            8.726 KB     107
          rows
Master table "SYS"."SYS_EXPORT_SCHEMA_01" successfully loaded/unloaded
************************************************************************
          ****
Dump file set for SYS.SYS_EXPORT_SCHEMA_01 is:
  /u01/app/oracle/dumpfiles/MY_DATA_PUMP_FILE.DMP
Job "SYS"."SYS_EXPORT_SCHEMA_01" successfully completed at 16:49:25
```

5. **Create the user and the tablespace.**

   Make sure both users have the same privileges.

6. **Create a parameter file that imports the data into a new user in its own tablespace.**

   In this example HR2 is imported to its own tablespace, HR2_DATA.

   Since this is also only a partial piece of the HR data model, you exclude constraints and triggers; they have dependent objects that aren't in the export dump file. You don't have to exclude them, but you get an error in the log file as Data Pump tries to create them.

   Such a parameter file might look like this:

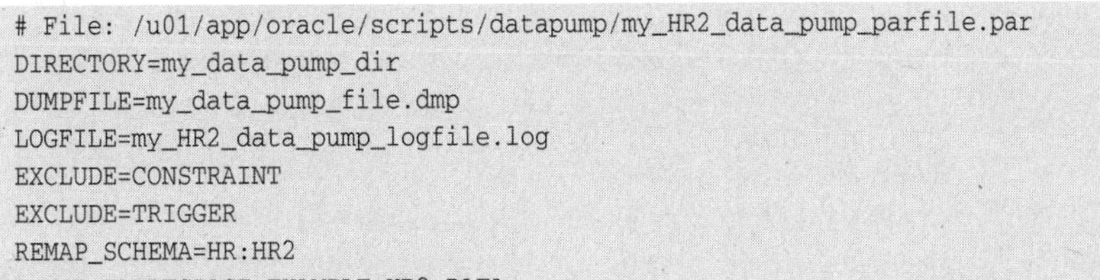

```
# File: /u01/app/oracle/scripts/datapump/my_HR2_data_pump_parfile.par
DIRECTORY=my_data_pump_dir
DUMPFILE=my_data_pump_file.dmp
LOGFILE=my_HR2_data_pump_logfile.log
EXCLUDE=CONSTRAINT
EXCLUDE=TRIGGER
REMAP_SCHEMA=HR:HR2
REMAP_TABLESPACE=EXAMPLE:HR2_DATA
```

7. Run the import:

```
<impdp parfile=my_hr2_data_pump_parfile.par>
```

You should see something like this:

```
Import: Release 11.1.0.6.0 - Production on Sunday, 10 August, 2008 17:39:35

Copyright (c) 2003, 2007, Oracle. All rights reserved.

Username: / as sysdba

Connected to: Oracle Database 11g Enterprise Edition Release 11.1.0.6.0 -
        Production
With the Partitioning, OLAP, Data Mining and Real Application Testing
        options
Master table "SYS"."SYS_IMPORT_FULL_01" successfully loaded/unloaded
Starting "SYS"."SYS_IMPORT_FULL_01":  /******** AS SYSDBA parfile=my_hr2_
        data_pump_parfile.par
Processing object type SCHEMA_EXPORT/USER
Processing object type SCHEMA_EXPORT/TABLE/TABLE
Processing object type SCHEMA_EXPORT/TABLE/TABLE_DATA
. . imported "HR2"."DEPARTMENTS"                        5.437 KB      27
        rows
. . imported "HR2"."EMPLOYEES"                          8.726 KB     107
        rows
…output snipped…
Job "SYS"."SYS_IMPORT_FULL_01" successfully completed at 17:39:53
```

If the user is someone other than the schema you're exporting, you need one of these two things:

- DBA privileges
- The DATAPUMP_EXP_FULL_DATABASE role

If you're going to import into a user other than the one you're running the job with, you need one of these two things:

- DBA privileges
- The DATAPUMP_IMP_FULL_DATABASE role

By default, the log file is created in the same directory as your dump file. The logfile is a text file that any text editor can read.

Chapter 11

Tuning an Oracle Database

In This Chapter

- Nailing tuning basics
- Gathering with Automatic Workload Repository (AWR)
- Using utomatic Database Diagnostic Monitor (ADDM)
- Tuning into SQL
- Understanding 10046 trace event with TKPROF

Oracle performance tuners have an indistinguishable systematic approach that compares to any real-world tuning effort, Oracle or other. Regardless of the method used to tune Oracle, base your goals on the needs of the business or purpose of the application.

In this chapter we cover the methods, concepts, and tools necessary for Oracle 11g performance tuning. We show you the commonly used methods to diagnose and alleviate Oracle 11g performance issues. You also discover how to apply this knowledge to proactive tuning principles.

Evaluating Tuning Problems

Tuning problems are usually related to poorly designed applications. Hardware upgrades aren't normally the all-saving remedy. Although hardware architecture does have a place in a basic tuning discussion, it's not necessarily the remedy.

As a novice to Oracle or a decision maker, exhaust all affordable options before giving in to the "You need more hardware" or the generic Oracle support comment, "You need to upgrade."

Although system hardware — the components all working toward the same goal in supporting the business — can be an area of focus for Oracle tuning, it can indirectly become a piece of the problem. These expensive hardware components, shown in Figure 11-1, include the following but are not limited to:

- Servers, such as hosts, nodes, and boxes
- Network routers and data switches
- Disk storage (Storage Area Networks [SAN]) or Network Attached Storage (NAS) and less-expensive storage arrays

Hopefully, these hardware components have been optimized to support the applications that use them.

Hardware performance can be attributed to the use of CPU, I/O, memory, and network. Generally speaking, as hardware usage increases, performance degrades aggregately, meaning that as you get closer to 100 percent usage thresholds, the worse the hardware will perform. Because hardware components are somewhat dependent on each other, they can affect the host's overall performance. Operating specific utilities and DB Console can help you determine how a host is performing during peak activity.

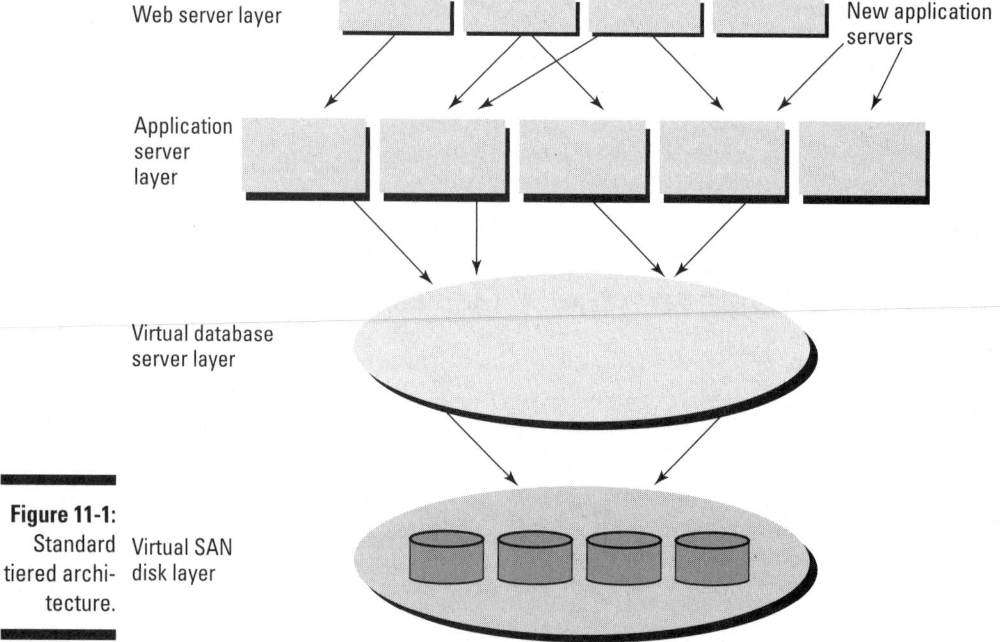

Figure 11-1: Standard tiered architecture.

The 11g reactive tuning basics are actually straightforward:

1. **Identify the issue(s) based on your business's process requirements.**

   Front-line users send you emails saying that things are running slowly. The billing manager calls complaining that the billing cycle took three hours longer than normal. The real determining factor to investigate a perceivable performance issue is a business decision. What is most important to the business? The billing cycle finishing in a specified period or that front-line users have priority during the most active periods? The answer is usually both.

   Always be truthful, and be sure to inform senior management if you are going to do something questionable, such as scheduling a backup or building an index during important processing hours. Don't lose your credibility by not being forthcoming. Adversely, don't be a cowboy in production.

2. **Establish the tuning goal.**

   Ensure that your tuning goals are focused toward the issue(s). If it's not broken, then don't try to fix it. Concentrate your efforts on determining the root cause.

3. **Determine the best method to resolution.**

   Form the plan by documenting your reasoning of the root cause and how you plan to resolve it. Share the plan with your counterparts and management. Include any special circumstances or risks. Be prepared to articulate your reasoning. A strong contingency plan is helpful in keeping people out of your cubicle.

4. **Test your plan.**

   Your plan might be a simple tweak, or it may involve a combination of adjustments that will hopefully make you a superstar. Most test plans aren't capable of performing an apples-to-apples test, so you need to feel confident with your plan. Keep in mind that your plan may involve multiple, time-consuming tests and retests.

   A new 11g feature, Database Replay, can help you with testing. We cover Database Replay in detail in Chapter 14.

5. **Execute your plan.**

   Stop holding your breath. You did your research and hopefully tested adequately. You need to document your results and compare them to the expected baseline or service level. This documentation is useful when quantifying your positive impact to the organization.

Tuning Your Database

A performance-minded DBA focuses on IO throughput (contention relief), memory, and CPU usage. Oracle 11g captures OS and database statistical information so that you can find most performance-based issues by accessing *Automatic Workload Repository (AWR)* with *Automatic Database Diagnostic Monitor (ADDM),* SQL Tuning Sets, V$ views plus the hosts CPU, I/O, and memory usage. Tuning techniques for 11g are driven toward utilizing AWR. In addition, you can examine other performance items at the database system level, such as init.ora parameters that the Oracle kernel controls.

Oracle init.ora performance-tuning parameters can have a major impact on how Oracle thinks. Before making any init.ora changes for performance, do your homework and test your theory because simple changes can negatively affect an 11g database. Certain parameter changes can greatly influence how queries are executed in the database via the *Cost-Based Optimizer (CBO).* The good news is that Oracle 11g can manage some memory structures automatically to help reduce the pressure on the DBA. In addition, some init.ora parameters are derived from the OS and are most likely accurate and don't require adjusting.

11g's Automatic Memory Management allows Oracle to manage all the database memory. It can allocate and deallocate memory between the *System Global Area (SGA)* and the *Program Global Area (PGA)* according to the database activity. This memory management configuration is recommended by Oracle and was also discussed in Chapter 2.

To turn on Oracle's Automatic Memory Management, set the following init parameters in the database init.ora or spfile.ora initialization file and then restart the database instance:

- **MEMORY_MAX_TARGET=nM:** Maximum amount memory for Oracle to use in megabytes.
- **MEMORY_TARGET=nM:** Initial memory to use in megabytes but can't exceed the value of MEMORY_MAX_TARGET. It should include the combined size of the SGA and the PGA.
  - SGA_TARGET=0
  - PGA_AGGREGATE_TARGET=
- **DB_BLOCK_SIZE:** Sets the size of how the Oracle blocks are stored and scanned for reads in the database. Typical size is 8192 or 8k. Warehouses databases can jump to a 32k block size. This parameter can drastically affect performance.

- **SGA_TARGET:** Sets the total memory size for these things:
  - *Buffer cache* (Data blocks in memory)
  - *Java pool* (Java in memory)
  - *Large pool* (Large PL*SQL statements)
  - *Share pool* (Parsed SQL statements in general)

  If you're using Automatic Memory Management, then you would set SGA_TARGET=0 and then set MEMORY_TARGET=*n*M – where *n* is a value of the SGA and PGA combined in megabytes.
- **OPTIMIZER_INDEX_COST_ADJ:** Sets the amount of effort Oracle will use to look for an index to help resolve a query. Setting the value too high can kill performance. It ranges from 1 to 1000; the default is 100.
- **DB_FILE_MULTIBLOCK_READ_COUNT:** Sets the number of blocks that are read in a single I/O. If you set this number to a higher value, Oracle may think that a full table scan is quicker than an index lookup scan. Default is 8, but most systems are set to 32. Consider storage system stripe sizes with this parameter.
- **PGA_AGGREGATE_TARGET:** Sets automatic controls on the amount of memory used for sorting large queries. Sorting to disk is very costly compared to memory. Finding a balance between large and small sorts can be challenging. PGA_AGGREGATE_TARGET isn't set if using Automatic Memory Management.
- **LOG_BUFFER:** Sets the amount of memory Oracle uses to buffer redo entries before writing them to the redo log files. This is often an I/O contention problem that you can resolve by increasing the value. Default is this formula: 512KB or 128KB × Number of CPUs on the Server (whichever is greater).

Gathering Performance Information with Automatic Workload Repository

Automatic Workload Repository (AWR) is a combination of performance utilities used to gather performance information. It has built-in automated mechanisms to capture real-time statistics that are continually captured and written to the AWR tables once an hour by default. These statistics, called *snapshots,* accumulate into a series of performance snapshots you can comb through to evaluate database performance. By default, the snapshots are retained for 8 days, but you're encouraged to modify the retention period to at least 30 days if plenty of space is available in the sysaux tablespace. You can modify the interval period as well.

A typical size guesstimate for AWR data using an 8-day cycle and 1-hour interval snaps with moderate activity is 200MB to 400MB. Decreasing the interval period or increasing the retaining period will require more space. To be safe, ensure that you have plenty of space in the sysaux tablespace and that the data files are set to autoextend. Keep an eye on the growth so it doesn't become a problem.

Technically, AWR is licensed with the enterprise version of Oracle 11g. Verify your license agreements before using it.

You can change the AWR snapshots two ways:

- **SQL*Plus method:** Good for novices that use SQL*Plus on the server the database instance resides on
- **Database Control method:** The GUI web tool, which is fairly intuitive and best for those with no 11g experience

SQL*Plus method

Here's how to implement the SQL*Plus method.

1. **Connect to SQL*Plus with DBA privileges.**

   You must have DBA privileges to execute these commands, so log in as a user with DBA role or as SYSDBA.

2. **Execute the following to change the AWR snapshot increment from the 1-hour default to 30 minutes:**

```
BEGIN
  DBMS_WORKLOAD_REPOSITORY.modify_snapshot_settings(
    retention => 43200,        -- Minutes (= 30 Days)
    interval  => 30);          -- Minutes
END;
/
```

3. **To delete a previous set of snapshots, execute the following example in SQL*Plus listing the range to delete:**

```
BEGIN
  DBMS_WORKLOAD_REPOSITORY.DROP_SNAPSHOT_RANGE(1,2528);
END;
/
```

After you have snapshots to work with, you can run AWR reports manually by executing the following script in SQL*Plus. It's interactive and gives you a choice of which consecutive snapshots you'd like to include in the report, which format you'd like to see it in (HTML or text), and lastly, a choice of file name.

4. **To view the text or HTML-based AWR information manually, use the following example:**

```
SQL> @$ORACLE_HOME/rdbms/admin/awrrpt.sql

Current Instance
~~~~~~~~~~~~~~~~

   DB Id    DB Name      Inst Num Instance
----------- ------------ -------- ------------
 3881932609 DEV11G              1 dev11g


Specify the Report Type
~~~~~~~~~~~~~~~~~~~~~~~
Would you like an HTML report, or a plain text report?
Enter 'html' for an HTML report, or 'text' for plain text
Defaults to 'html'
Enter value for report_type: text



Instances in this Workload Repository schema
~~~~~~~~~~~~~~~~~~~~~~~~~~~~~~~~~~~~~~~~~~~~

   DB Id     Inst Num DB Name      Instance     Host
------------ -------- ------------ ------------ ------------
* 3881932609        1 DEV11G       dev11g       classroom

Using 3881932609 for database Id
Using          1 for instance number


Specify the number of days of snapshots to choose from
~~~~~~~~~~~~~~~~~~~~~~~~~~~~~~~~~~~~~~~~~~~~~~~~~~~~~~
Entering the number of days (n) will result in the most recent
(n) days of snapshots being listed.  Pressing <return> without
specifying a number lists all completed snapshots.


Enter value for num_days:
```

```
Listing all Completed Snapshots

                                                              Snap
Instance     DB Name         Snap Id    Snap Started  Level
------------ ------------ --------- ------------------ ---
dev11g       DEV11G             180 26 Mar 2008 01:00    1
                                181 26 Mar 2008 02:00    1
                                182 26 Mar 2008 03:00    1
                                377 03 Apr 2008 06:00    1
                                Ö
                                379 03 Apr 2008 08:00    1
                                380 03 Apr 2008 09:00    1
                                381 03 Apr 2008 10:00    1

Specify the Begin and End Snapshot Ids
~~~~~~~~~~~~~~~~~~~~~~~~~~~~~~~~~~~~~~
Enter value for begin_snap: 378
Begin Snapshot Id specified: 378
Enter value for end_snap: 380
End   Snapshot Id specified: 380
Specify the Report Name
~~~~~~~~~~~~~~~~~~~~~~~
The default report file name is awrrpt_1_378_380.txt.  To use this name,
press <return> to continue, otherwise enter an alternative.
Enter value for report_name: $HOME/awr7to9.txt
```

After entering the fully qualified report name, you see a large amount of data scroll by. You may now view the report, which contains most of the statistical information during the period of 7a.m. to 9 a.m. It contains CPU, IO, memory, and network usage. It also shows more detailed Oracle memory usage, wait events, and top-running SQL statements that are taking the most time and resources. This report is quite handy in pinpointing particular times that the database was sluggish.

Database Control method

You can also run an AWR report by running the awrrpti.sql script. To use the Database Control method, simply access the DB Control web site that was created when you installed the database:

1. **From the database home, click Server.**
2. **Under the Statistics Management area, click Automatic Workload Repository.**
3. **Click Run AWR Report.**

4. **Choose a beginning period and click OK.**
5. **Choose an ending period and click OK.**

   You see a racing clock and the words Creating Report. The screen refreshes shortly after with the AWR report. Figure 11-2 is snippet of the web-based AWR report created by using DB Control.

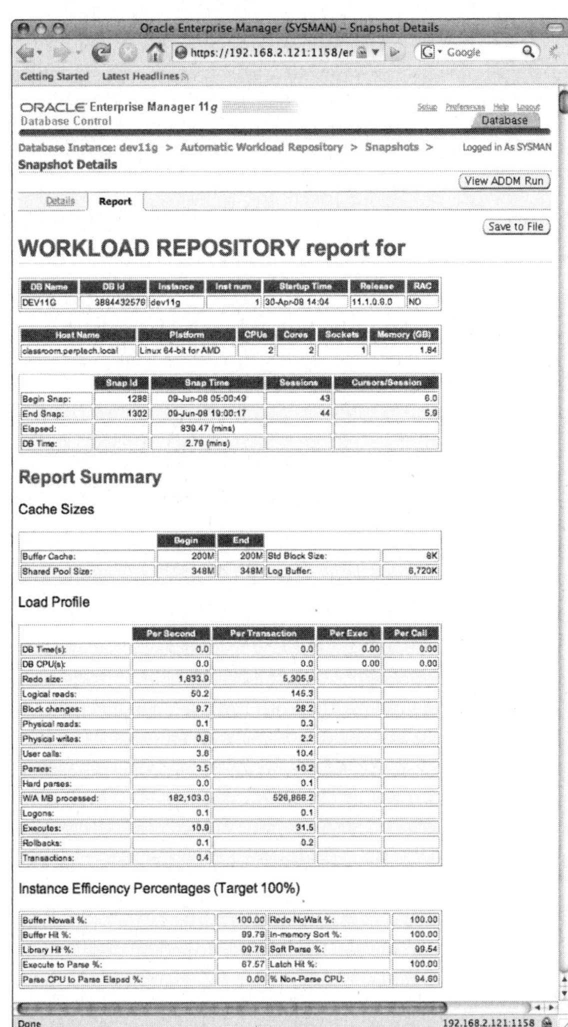

Figure 11-2: DB Console AWR report.

Using the Automatic Database Diagnostic Monitor (ADDM)

You can run the *Automatic Database Diagnostic Monitor (ADDM)* on your database's current performance or based on a specific set of AWR snapshots for previous performance analysis. To access ADDM information (technically, it's just AWR data that Oracle analyzes and then provides recommendations on), you must first create a report. You can create a report by simply using the Database Control web site or by running the addmrpt.sql or the addmrpti.sql script, which runs in similar fashion to the previous awrrpt.sql example.

The addmrpt.sql script creates an ADDM report based on the current AWR information where the addmrpti.sql script prompts you for a beginning and ending AWR snapshot and then analyzes the performance between them:

```
SQL> @$ORACLE_HOME/rdbms/admin/addmrpti.sql
```

The resulting report shows you areas of impact that you can further research for improvement.

To access or review ADDM through DB Console, follow these steps:

1. **From the database home using the DB Console web site, click Server.**
2. **In the Related Links area, click Advisor Central.**
3. **Under Advisors, click ADDM.**
4. **Choose Run ADDM to analyze past performance.**

   The current performance option creates a snapshot immediately and then runs ADDM against it.
5. **Choose the AWR snapshot beginning and ending time, which are listed.**

   The time to create the report depends on the activity within each snapshot period and the number of snapshots used in the set being analyzed.
6. **Click OK.**

7. **If Database Control asks whether you're sure you want to exit, click Yes.**

   The ADDM screen appears. You can now view specific and summarized information of your ADDM run. The basic analysis will be a few findings, recommendations for the findings, and actions for the recommendations. Figure 11-3 is an example of the ADDM results. Figure 11-4 is the actual ADDM report with recommendations.

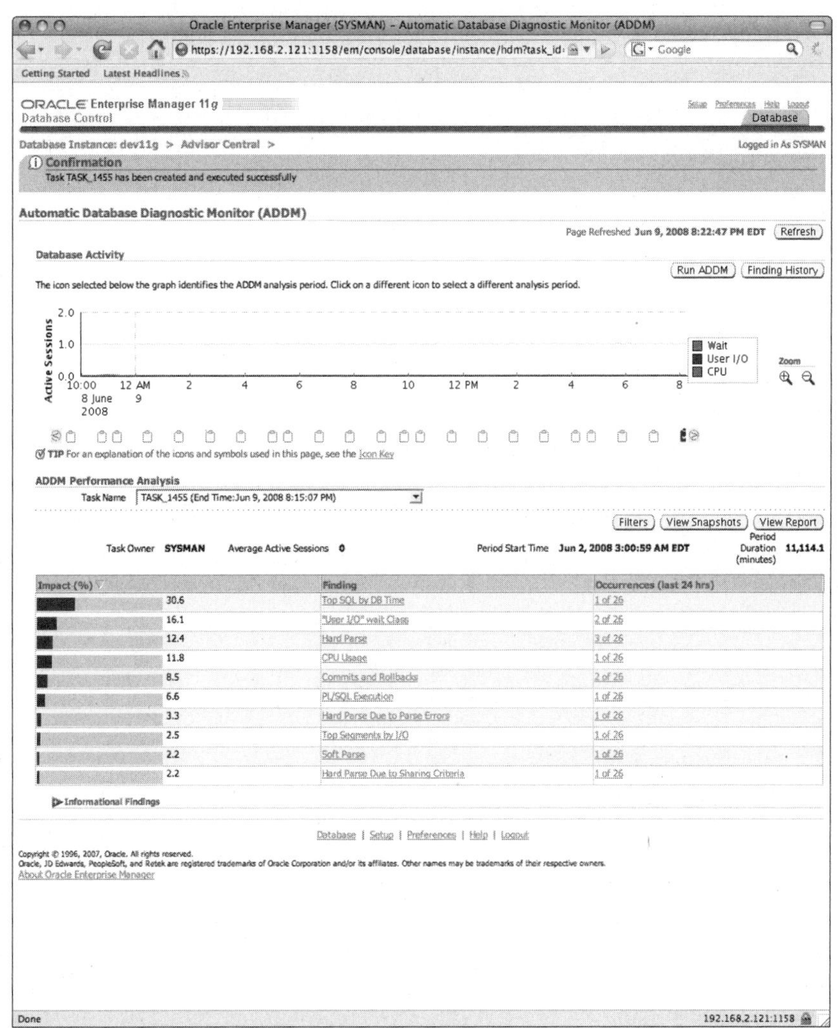

Figure 11-3: ADDM example.

```
ADDM Report for Task 'TASK_1455'
          -------------------------------

Analysis Period
---------------
AWR snapshot range from 1118 to 1304.
Time period starts at 02-JUN-08 03.00.59 AM
Time period ends at 09-JUN-08 08.15.07 PM

Analysis Target
---------------
Database 'DEV11G' with DB ID 3884432576.
Database version 11.1.0.6.0.
ADDM performed an analysis of instance dev11g, numbered 1 and hosted at
classroom.perptech.local.

Activity During the Analysis Period
-----------------------------------
Total database time was 5120 seconds.
The average number of active sessions was .01.

Summary of Findings
-------------------
    Description                        Active Sessions      Recommendations
                                       Percent of Activity
    ---------------------------------  -------------------  ---------------
1   Top SQL by DB Time                 0 | 30.61            5
2   "User I/O" wait Class              0 | 16.07            0
3   Hard Parse                         0 | 12.35            0
4   CPU Usage                          0 | 11.77            2
5   Commits and Rollbacks              0 | 8.52             2
6   PL/SQL Execution                   0 | 6.58             4
7   Hard Parse Due to Parse Errors     0 | 3.27             1
8   Top Segments by I/O                0 | 2.55             1
9   Soft Parse                         0 | 2.24             2
10  Hard Parse Due to Sharing Criteria 0 | 2.17             1


~~~~~~~~~~~~~~~~~~~~~~~~~~~~~~~~~~~~~~~~~~~~~~~~~~~~~~~~~~~~~~~~~~~~~~~~~~~~~~~
~~~~~~~~~~~~~~~~~~~~~~~~~~~~~~~~~~~~~~~~~~~~~~~~~~~~~~~~~~~~~~~~~~~~~~~~~~~~~~~


          Findings and Recommendations
          ----------------------------

Finding 1: Top SQL by DB Time
Impact is 0 active sessions, 30.61% of total activity.
-------------------------------------------------------
SQL statements consuming significant database time were found.

   Recommendation 1: SQL Tuning
   Estimated benefit is 0 active sessions, 17.1% of total activity.
   ----------------------------------------------------------------
   Action
      Investigate the SQL statement with SQL_ID "b6usrg82hwsa3" for possible
      performance improvements.
      Related Object
         SQL statement with SQL_ID b6usrg82hwsa3.
         call dbms_stats.gather_database_stats_job_proc (  )
   Rationale
      SQL statement with SQL_ID "b6usrg82hwsa3" was executed 15 times and had
      an average elapsed time of 58 seconds.
```

Figure 11-4: ADDM_ report.txt.

```
   Recommendation 2: SQL Tuning
   Estimated benefit is 0 active sessions, 5.5% of total activity.
   ---------------------------------------------------------------
   Action
      Tune the PL/SQL block with SQL_ID "6gvch1xu9ca3g". Refer to the "Tuning
etc.
etc.
etc.

Finding 10: Hard Parse Due to Sharing Criteria
Impact is 0 active sessions, 2.17% of total activity.
-----------------------------------------------------
SQL statements with the same text were not shared because of cursor
environment mismatch. This resulted in additional hard parses which were
consuming significant database time.
Common causes of environment mismatch are session NLS settings, SQL trace
settings and optimizer parameters.

   Recommendation 1: Application Analysis
   Estimated benefit is 0 active sessions, 2.17% of total activity.
   ----------------------------------------------------------------
   Action
      Look for top reason for cursor environment mismatch in
      V$SQL_SHARED_CURSOR.

   Symptoms That Led to the Finding:
   ---------------------------------
      Hard parsing of SQL statements was consuming significant database time.
      Impact is 0 active sessions, 12.35% of total activity.

~~~~~~~~~~~~~~~~~~~~~~~~~~~~~~~~~~~~~~~~~~~~~~~~~~~~~~~~~~~~~~~~~~~~~~~~~~~~~~~
~~~~~~~~~~~~~~~~~~~~~~~~~~~~~~~~~~~~~~~~~~~~~~~~~~~~~~~~~~~~~~~~~~~~~~~~~~~~~~~

          Additional Information
          ----------------------

Warnings
--------
The optimal memory target for the instance could not be determined because the
value of "memory_target" changed during the analysis period.

Miscellaneous Information
-------------------------
Wait class "Application" was not consuming significant database time.
Wait class "Concurrency" was not consuming significant database time.
Wait class "Configuration" was not consuming significant database time.
Wait class "Network" was not consuming significant database time.
Session connect and disconnect calls were not consuming significant database
time.

The database's maintenance windows were active during 32% of the analysis
period.
```

Improving Queries with SQL Tuning

Tuning methods use 11g utilities to identify and reduce the heavy workload of resource-intensive SQL statements. Oracle 11g uses an execution plan to resolve queries and is the driving decision maker behind the Oracle query optimizer. This engine uses the most efficient (least cost) way for the database to resolve a query. For example, it may be more efficient (cheaper) for Oracle to complete a full table scan than to do an index lookup followed by a partial table scan. The optimizer generates the execution plan before it runs the query for the first time. (For information on how the SQL plan management will store the plan, see the section "SQL Profiling and Plan Management," later in this chapter.)

Keep the business process in perspective. A report may take hours to complete and more time to tweak. The report may benefit from more tuning, but the business focus can be on concurrent user response time versus long-running reports. Concentrate on the business objective.

In addition to the AWR and ADDM reports described earlier in this chapter, several other good tools are available for 11g SQL tuning:

- Explain plan
- Active Session History (ASH)
- SQL Access Advisor
- SQL Tuning Advisor
- SQL Profiling and Plan Management

Explain plan

Oracle's explain plan is a simple tool used to view the execution plan that Oracle's query optimizer chooses in resolving a query. Oracle can make poor decisions on how best to resolve a query, and you need the ability to make adjustments that will allow the query to run more efficiently. The following steps create a table where the query execution results are stored. The table is then selected against to review the output. In addition, a simpler method called autotrace can be used and is illustrated here:

1. **Create the plan table by connecting to SQL*Plus with DBA privileges:**

```
SQL> CONNECT sys/password AS SYSDBA
   Connected
   SQL> @$ORACLE_HOME/rdbms/admin/utlxplan.sql
Table created.
```

2. **Grant privileges on the plan table to public (all):**

```
SQL> GRANT ALL ON sys.plan_table TO public;
Grant succeeded.
```

3. Create a public synonym for the table:

```
SQL> CREATE PUBLIC SYNONYM plan_table
     FOR sys.plan_table;
Synonym created.
```

Figure 11-5 shows a good example of an explain plan output. Notice the full table scans? An index or two may be in order.

```
SQL> set autotrace on
SQL> set line 132
SQL> set pages 5000
SQL> select e.employee_id, e.last_name, e.first_name, j.start_date,
d.department_name
  2  from hr.job_history j,
  3         hr.employees e,
  4         hr.departments d
  5  where e.job_id = j.job_id
  6    and d.department_id = e.department_id
  7    and rownum < 10
  8  /

EMPLOYEE_ID LAST_NAME                 FIRST_NAME           START_DAT
DEPARTMENT_NAME
----------- ------------------------- -------------------- --------- -----------
-------------------
        107 Lorentz                   Diana                13-JAN-93 IT
        106 Pataballa                 Valli                13-JAN-93 IT
        105 Austin                    David                13-JAN-93 IT
        104 Ernst                     Bruce                13-JAN-93 IT
        103 Hunold                    Alexander            13-JAN-93 IT
        206 Gietz                     William              21-SEP-89 Accounting
        205 Higgins                   Shelley              28-OCT-93 Accounting
        202 Fay                       Pat                  17-FEB-96 Marketing
        144 Vargas                    Peter                24-MAR-98 Shipping

9 rows selected.


Execution Plan
----------------------------------------------------------
Plan hash value: 3484349169

--------------------------------------------------------------------------------
----
| Id  | Operation            | Name        | Rows  | Bytes | Cost (%CPU)| Time     |

--------------------------------------------------------------------------------
----
|   0 | SELECT STATEMENT     |             |     9 |   873 |    10  (10)| 00:00:01 |

|*  1 |  COUNT STOPKEY       |             |       |       |            | 00:00:01 |

|*  2 |   HASH JOIN          |             |    10 |   970 |    10  (10)| 00:00:01 |

|   3 |    TABLE ACCESS FULL |EMPLOYEES    |   107 |  3317 |     3   (0)| 00:00:01 |

|   4 |     NESTED LOOPS     |             |     36|  1188 |     6   (0)| 00:00:01 |

|   5 |      TABLE ACCESS FULL |JOB_HISTORY |    10|   170 |     2   (0)| 00:00:01 |
```

Figure 11-5: Explain plan.

```
|   6 |  TABLE ACCESS FULL| DEPARTMENTS |     18 |   288 |      2   (0)| 00:00:01 |
---------------------------------------------------------------------------------
----

Predicate Information (identified by operation id):
---------------------------------------------------

   1 - filter(ROWNUM<10)
   2 - access("E"."JOB_ID"="J"."JOB_ID" AND
              "D"."DEPARTMENT_ID"="E"."DEPARTMENT_ID")

Statistics
----------------------------------------------------------
        355  recursive calls
          0  db block gets
        161  consistent gets
          0  physical reads
          0  redo size
       1149  bytes sent via SQL*Net to client
        524  bytes received via SQL*Net from client
          2  SQL*Net roundtrips to/from client
          6  sorts (memory)
          0  sorts (disk)
          9  rows processed

SQL> spool off
```

Active Session History (ASH)

Active sessions in the database with significant execution elapsed time are sampled every second and are stored with plan execution details in memory for a period of time. The amount of time depends on the activity in the database. They're then flushed to disk. You can find active information in the V$ACTIVE_SESSION_HISTORY view. Session information flushed to disk appears in the DBA_HIST_ACTIVE_SESS_HISTORY view.

This information allows you to examine session data and avoid additional time-consuming tracing steps as discussed in the section "SQL Profiling and Plan Management" later in this chapter. To run the ASH report, simply use the following script. It requests a beginning and ending time and then reports the activity in between.

```
SQL> @$ORACLE_HOME/rdbms/admin/ashrpt.sql
```

Follow along to access or review ASH through the DB Console:

1. **From the database home using the DB Console web site, click Performance.**
2. **Click Top Activity.**

3. **Click Run ASH Report.**
4. **Choose a beginning and ending time.**
5. **Click Generate Report.**

Think of ASH as your own private AWR reports. Instead of looking at all database load activity, you're only looking at your own.

SQL Access Advisor

SQL Access Advisor is a tuning tool that can assist you in determining whether indexes, partitions, or materialized views would improve performance. It's a cumbersome and time-consuming process, and we only want to bring to your attention how it works and that it's there for your downtime pleasure.

Setting up SQL Access Advisor to run effectively requires structural statistics. Gathering estimated statistics is normally a nightly scheduled task if the workload and the size of the database allow time for it. Statistics are very important for this tool to work effectively.

How does SQL Access Advisor work? You must create an Access task to define the advisory parameters to be used during a workload on the database. SQL Access Advisor analyzes the statistics and workload together to generate recommendations. You can then review these recommendations and implement them in the database.

To navigate to SQL Access Advisor through the DB Console:

1. **From Database Home using the DB Console web site, click Server.**
2. **Click Advisor Central.**
3. **Click SQL Advisors.**
4. **Click SQL Access Advisor.**

SQL Tuning Advisor

You can use SQL Tuning Advisor to find issues with one or many costly SQL statements that have already been identified as issues. SQL Tuning Advisor tasks are run nightly by default when you create or migrate a database with 11g. The task called sys_auto_sql_tuning_task runs every night to find heavy load SQL statements and tries to find ways to increase their performance. It can provide beneficial recommendations on one or more SQL statements with the automatic tuning advisor.

You must first create a tuning set when using multiple SQL statements. The recommendations are in the form of SQL text or a SQL profile (see the next section). You can then restructure or accept the SQL or the plan to implement the new changes.

Set the initialization parameter STATISTICS_LEVEL to TYPICAL (default) or ALL. Setting it to BASIC disables automatic SQL tuning. ADDM also requires the CONTROL_MANAGEMENT_PACK_ACCESS initialization parameter to be set to DIAGNOSTIC+TUNING (default), or it will be disabled.

To navigate to SQL Tuning Advisor through the DB Console:

1. **From Database Home using the DB Console web site, click Server.**
2. **Click Advisor Central.**
3. **Click SQL Advisors.**
4. **Click SQL Tuning Advisor.**

Figure 11-6 is a view of the main SQL Advisors page. You can click one of the following sources, which will take you to the location where you can use the SQL Tuning Advisor:

- Top Activity
- Historical SQL (AWR)
- SQL Tuning Sets
- Snapshots
- Preserved Snapshot Sets

SQL Profiling and Plan Management

The query optimizer can sometimes produce inaccurate execution plans due to missing, stale, or incomplete statistics and context information (stuff that helps form an execution plan). Traditionally, DBAs have corrected this problem by manually adding Oracle hints to the application code, which forces the optimizer to adjust its plan. Here is a common index hint:

```
select /*+ INDEX(emp_city idx_job_code) */ emp_name,
job_code from emp where job_code = 'D';
```

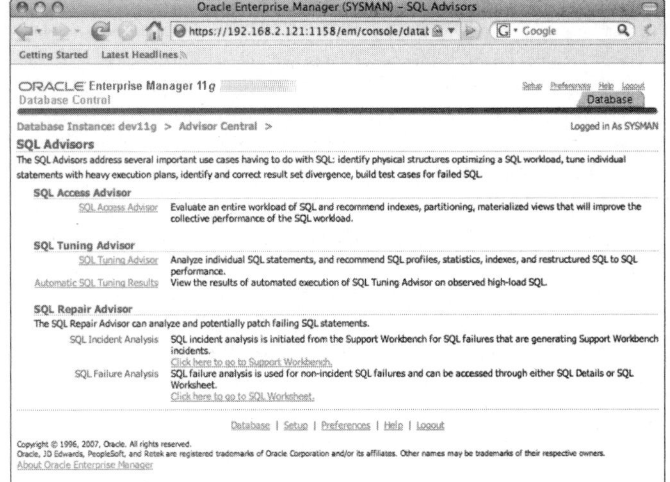

Figure 11-6: SQL Advisors page.

For Commercial, off-the-shelf (COTS) packaged applications, changing the application code violates support agreements. The only alternative available is to log a request with the application vendor, which may take weeks, or you can use SQL profiles and SQL Plan Management (SPM).

SQL profile generates stats and creates recommendations that are tested against the database during nightly maintenance windows. You can automatically implement these profiles by setting the advisory parameter to ACCEPT_SQL_PROFILES=TRUE. To set this parameter, you must use the DBMS_SQLTUNE package:

```
BEGIN
  DBMS_SQLTUNE.set_tuning_task_parameter(
    task_name => 'SYS_AUTO_SQL_TUNING_TASK',
    parameter => 'ACCEPT_SQL_PROFILES',
    value     => 'TRUE');
END;
/
```

With SPM, the optimizer manages the plans automatically and verifies that only accepted plans are used. New plans are accepted only if the current plan is outperformed by the newly generated one, which causes SQL plans to evolve over time. SQL plans can become outdated if the data changes drastically or if particular initialization parameters are adjusted.

Profiling and Plan Management help eliminate the manual processes used to manage SQL statements. The accepted plans can then be migrated to a test database for further testing using newer hardware or by using different init.ora parameters.

10046 trace event

Event 10046, a previously unpublished Oracle event, is a tracing mechanism used to find SQL performance issues. Oracle support and DBAs often need to pinpoint or know more about the database performance than the explain plan or sql_trace have to offer.

Event 10046 triggers Oracle to log the raw information about the decisions that the Oracle kernel and the optimizer are making to resolve or respond to a session's activities. These timing measurements and wait events are reflected in a trace file, which can help identify specific bottlenecks that may not have been identified using other performance-tuning means. The event information is written to a trace file under the 11g diagnostic destination (init parameter diagnostic_dest, which is '(volume_name)/diag/rdbms/(database_name)/(sid_name)/trace'). The information can also include the bind variable values.

You can set the 10046 event for a given session in several ways. You don't need to alter a session to set TIMED_STATISTICS=TRUE and set MAX_DUMP_FILE_SIZE=UNLIMITED if they were previously set in the init.ora startup file. You can also trace the database level with this event as opposed to the session level.

Tracing with event 10046 writes large amounts of content to the trace file. Be sure that the volume or disk that contains the diag directory has plenty of space available. We're talking about a monstrous size file. Be sure to turn it off when you're done with the trace.

The following example reflects a technique to start 10046 tracing:

```
SQL> alter session set events '10046 trace name context forever, level number';
```

The following mini table lists values for the levels that you can use for the 10046 event.

0	No statistics
1	Basic statistics and the same as setting sql_trace=true
4	Same as level 1 except adds BIND section
8	Same as level 1 except with wait events
12	Combines levels 1, 4, and 8

Here's how to turn on timing if it's not already set at the database level:

```
SQL> alter session set timed_statistics=true;
```

You also need to set tracing to unlimited, or you may get an incomplete trace file when dump file size limit is reached:

```
SQL> alter session set max_dump_file_size=unlimited;
```

Setting the TRACEFILE_IDENTIFIER is optional but recommended to help identify trace files when you go looking for them. You can use the TRACEFILE_IDENTIFIER before you start the tracing to later help identify your trace file in the trace directory.

```
SQL> alter session set tracefile_identifier='MYSESSION';
```

The following code sets extended SQL trace to level 8. (See the previous table, which describes the various trace levels.)

```
SQL> alter session set events '10046 trace name context forever, level 8';
```

Now that tracing is set up, you execute the SQL statements you want to review. During this SQL execution, the raw data to be analyzed by the tool is generated.

This command disables tracing:

```
SQL> alter session set events '10046 trace name context off';
```

To trace another user session, you need to find the SID and serial# of the session you want to trace. To find a session to trace, run the following SQL*Plus statement:

```
set linesize 200
select username, sid SID, serial#,
       osuser, program, status,
       to_char(logon_time,'MM/DD/YYYY hh24:mi')Logon_time
from v$session
where serial# <> '1'
and status = 'ACTIVE'
and username like upper('%&user%')
order by logon_time
/
```

Once you have the SID and serial number of the session you want to trace, you can use Oracle-supplied packages to start and stop the tracing. This example is the DBMS_SYSTEM package:

```
SQL> execute sys.dbms_system.set_bool_param_in_session (&&SID, &&SERIAL,'timed_
            statistics',true);
```

This statement turns timing on if it's not already set at the database level:

```
SQL> execute sys.dbms_system.set_int_param_in_session (&&SID, &&SERIAL,
              'max_dump_file_size',10000000);
```

This syntax sets tracing to a very large value of 10,000,000. Otherwise, you may get an incomplete trace file when dump file size limit is reached.

```
SQL> execute sys.dbms_system.set_ev(&&SID, &&SERIAL, 10046, 8, ' ');
```

This code sets extended SQL trace to level 8. See the previous table for information on all trace levels.

Execute the SQL statements you want to test. During this execution, the statements are being traced.

This statement disables tracing:

```
SQL> execute sys.dbms_system.set_ev(&&SID, &&SERIAL, 10046, 0, ' ');
```

The DBMS_SUPPORT package is preferred and fully supported by Oracle but the preceding DBMS_SYSTEM works just fine. You have to install the DBMS_SUPPORT package, but it isn't available on all platforms. To install, run the dbmssupp.sql script as sysdba located in $ORACLE_HOME/rdbms/admin directory. Examples of using DBMS_SUPPORT instead of DBMS_SYSTEM include:

```
SQL> execute sys.dbms_support.start_trace_in_session (&&SID, &&SERIAL,
             waits=>true, binds=>false);
```

The following statement is equivalent to setting SQL trace to level 8. Level 12 tracing can be established by setting binds=>true.

Execute your SQL statements you want to test. During this execution, the statements are being traced.

Once you execute all the SQL statements you want to trace, stop the tracing process:

```
SQL> execute sys.dbms_support.stop_trace_in_session(&&SID, &&SERIAL);
```

In some applications, it may be difficult to start tracing because of physical timing (catching the session before it starts running SQL) or because a session is using connection pooling, therefore; a logon trigger may help. Just enable it only for as long as needed because it can cause a performance problem in heavily used systems. The user that creates the trigger must be granted alter session explicitly.

Tweak the following example to ensure that you trace only the session you are trying to capture or tune:

```
CREATE OR REPLACE TRIGGER SYS.enable_10046_trace_trigger
AFTER LOGON ON DATABASE
--  10046 TRACELEVELS
-- 0  - Turn off tracing.
-- 1  - Basic SQL_TRACE.
-- 4  - Level 1 plus Bind Variables.
-- 8  - Level 1 plus wait events.
-- 12 - Level 1 plus Bind/Wait event information.
DECLARE
v_exe       v$session.program%TYPE;
v_sid       v$session.SID%TYPE;
v_osuser    v$session.osuser%TYPE;
v_machine   v$session.machine%TYPE;
v_ok        VARCHAR (10);
BEGIN
-- Get user SID information
SELECT SID
INTO v_sid
FROM v$mystat
WHERE ROWNUM < 2;
-- Get Program executable for this session
SELECT program
INTO v_exe
FROM v$session
WHERE SID = v_sid;
-- Get OSUSER Details
SELECT osuser
INTO v_osuser
FROM v$session
WHERE SID = v_sid;
-- Get Machine Details
SELECT machine
INTO v_machine
FROM v$session
WHERE SID = v_sid;
IF USER = 'ACCESS_USER' AND v_exe = 'access.exe' AND v_osuser = 'cartman' and
               v_machine='Win_Machine4'
THEN
EXECUTE IMMEDIATE 'alter session set timed_statistics=true';
EXECUTE IMMEDIATE 'alter session set max_dump_file_size=unlimited';
EXECUTE IMMEDIATE 'alter session set
               tracefile_identifier=''session_trace_trigger''';
EXECUTE IMMEDIATE 'alter session set events ''10046 trace name context forever,
               level 8'' ';
DBMS_SESSION.set_identifier ('SQL TRACE ENABLED VIA LOGIN TRIGGER');
END IF;
END;
```

Examining the trace file is a little less complex than interpreting the ancient Mayan language. Oracle offers a tool called TKPROF that you can use to format trace files into something a little more legible. It can sort trace information into more specific areas, such as CPU or I/O. Some experienced Oracle performance tuners prefer to read trace files in their raw formats because TKPROF can skew the raw data by bundling items into a non-time sequential format. But overall, TKPROF can reduce the time it takes to research the trace information.

To execute TKPROF, use the tkprof command-line utility. Execute the utility in the same directory your trace file lives. You specify the following things:

- The name of the trace file to analyze
- The name of the output file
- The database username and password that has a plan table

It is common to specify sys=no and waits=yes to suppress unnecessary system statements and to include database wait information.

Here's an example of how to run TKPROF and a partial view of what a TKPROF trace file looks like:

```
unix> tkprof dev11g_ora_18892.trc tk_trace.txt explain=system/Indy_500$$$ sys=no
             waits=yes

unix> more tk_trace.txt

TKPROF: Release 11.1.0.6.0 - Production on Wed Jun 11 21:51:37 2008

Copyright (c) 1982, 2007, Oracle.  All rights reserved.

Trace file: dev11g_ora_18892.trc
Sort options: default

********************************************************************************
count    = number of times OCI procedure was executed
cpu      = cpu time in seconds executing
elapsed  = elapsed time in seconds executing
disk     = number of physical reads of buffers from disk
query    = number of buffers gotten for consistent read
current  = number of buffers gotten in current mode (usually for update)
rows     = number of rows processed by the fetch or execute call
********************************************************************************
```

```
SQL ID : 1u7rv40zh44sz
select *
from
 hr.employees


call     count       cpu    elapsed       disk      query    current        rows
------- ------  -------- ---------- ---------- ---------- ----------  ----------
Parse        1      0.00       0.03          0          0          1           0
Execute      1      0.00       0.00          0          0          0           0
Fetch        9      0.00       0.01          6         15          0         107
------- ------  -------- ---------- ---------- ---------- ----------  ----------
total       11      0.00       0.04          6         15          1         107

Misses in library cache during parse: 1
Optimizer mode: ALL_ROWS
Parsing user id: 5  (SYSTEM)

Rows     Row Source Operation
-------  ---------------------------------------------------
    107  TABLE ACCESS FULL EMPLOYEES (cr=15 pr=6 pw=6 time=0 us cost=3 size=7276
               card=107)


Rows     Execution Plan
-------  ---------------------------------------------------
      0  SELECT STATEMENT   MODE: ALL_ROWS
    107   TABLE ACCESS   MODE: ANALYZED (FULL) OF 'EMPLOYEES' (TABLE)


Elapsed times include waiting on following events:
  Event waited on                             Times   Max. Wait  Total Waited
  ----------------------------------------   Waited  ----------  ------------
  SQL*Net message to client                      10        0.00          0.00
  SQL*Net message from client                    10       24.74         42.68
  db file sequential read                         1        0.01          0.01
  db file scattered read                          1        0.00          0.00
********************************************************************************
```

The resulting output file shows the following data in chronological order:

- Each SQL statement executed
- The corresponding SQL execution plan
- The performance metrics for each statement

You should review the TKPROF output file to find statements that aren't performing well and tune those individual statements. Once all the statements are tuned, execute and trace the statements again to verify they have been improved.

Chapter 12

Troubleshooting an Oracle Database

In This Chapter

- Using troubleshooting methodology
- Troubleshooting with Oracle database logs
- Employing other diagnostic utilities

No matter what the salespeople claim, any system made by mortal beings will have issues and sometimes even break; that's reality. Worse yet, those same salespeople who claimed their system was perfect aren't around to fix it when it does break; that's *your* job. Fortunately, this chapter provides the information you need.

Before jumping into database-specific diagnostic techniques, we give you a method for troubleshooting at the system level. Remember: Oracle exists as part of an overall information *system.* Here you explore the methods and tools you need to operate at system level.

Oracle provides a wealth of information, almost an overload, in its multiple log and trace files. Between the different files and tracing levels, odds are the information you need to solve the problem is there somewhere . . . if you know where to look for it. We provide that info.

Just when you thought you couldn't get any more information about your Oracle database, we do just that via Oracle diagnostic tools and scripts. We're not showing tools that provide pointless data; we explain tools that provide fast, actionable information.

Troubleshooting with System Methodology

If an Oracle crash hasn't happened to you yet, it will happen sometime. And when it does, it won't be at a convenient time.

The problem is that people assume that because they have an Oracle-based system, the problem must be with Oracle. It could be, but you don't know just yet. Oracle is simply a component of a larger system and the root cause and solution may not be Oracle based. Even if you get an Oracle database error message, the cause may be something outside of Oracle.

Don't react to a problem report on face level. Apply a structured, repeatable pattern when addressing problems. We can't stress this next statement enough: *Yours is a technical profession and you're paid to solve problems; not simply to react and hope for a quick fix.*

Everyone has a troubleshooting methodology tailored for their unique environment, but we suggest the following as a start:

1. **Identify the real problem.** Determine and confirm what is happening in the system.
2. **Perform basic system checks.** Check the server, operating environment, and connectivity for outright errors and performance degradation.
3. **Perform basic database checks.** Confirm the database is running and see if you can log in to it.
4. **Determine what your error messages mean.**
5. **Develop a solution and apply it.** Confirm that the fix works and that there aren't unintended consequences.

With experience and time you will modify the steps for your environment. Depending on the situation, you may process some steps very fast — but they're still processed, not skipped.

Identifying the real problem

Before doing anything to "fix" the perceived problem, you need to *know* what the *real* problem is. You can't guess or assume. It's far better to treat the real cause of a problem, not just the symptoms.

People reporting problems get excited, miss key details, make assumptions, and often inaccurately state the nature and severity of a problem; that's simply human nature. If you think otherwise, ask any cop or ER doctor about the quality of the initial witness reports they receive. This is exacerbated in computer work because many people who are reporting problems aren't technical and cannot articulate very well.

You need to determine what system component has the problem and what is specifically happening before you can develop and apply a fix. Ask the following questions:

- **What:** What specifically is happening? Have the user walk through what he's doing when the error occurs. Work directly with the person having problems and monitor in real time rather than getting second- or third-hand information. Get screen shots or the error messages themselves.
- **Who:** Who's being impacted? Is it one or two users or everyone? Is it a specific sub-classification of users or everyone? Also, is it your production, test, or development system? Never assume that because someone is excited, it must be production. Nothing is more embarrassing then trying to fix the wrong database.
- **Where:** Are affected users spread over a wide geographic location or are affected users in a specific city or building?
- **When:** How long has this been occurring and has it occurred before? Also, does it happen every time or just sometimes? If it only happens occasionally, drill down into what's being done prior to the error. If it only occurred since a recent system change (such as patch, upgrade, reboot), that can be a valuable clue. The question "What has recently changed in the system" is a *great* question to ask!
- **How bad:** Is this a total loss of service where the company is stopped or is it just an annoyance on a seldom-used development system?

After asking these questions you should know what's happening, who it's happening to, how bad it is, and when it started. You should also have a rough idea of what subsystem or components to start checking.

Keep a cool head when troubleshooting hot issues; be methodical and work in a logical manner until the problem is fixed (and confirmed to be fixed). Others may become excited, stressed, or unprofessional, but you need to keep your wits and professionalism as you work toward a solution. Don't let yourself be intimidated by irate users or management standing over your shoulder.

Performing basic system checks

You need to perform basic system checks to ensure the system is in a state that can support a database. If the network is down, server is overloaded, or disk system has ran out of space, your database may be impacted and display database errors, but the root problem is system related.

Investigate these key areas:

- **Network:** Can you connect to the server or application?
- **Server utilization:** What are the top processes on the server?
- **CPU utilization:** Is the CPU maxed out?
- **Memory:** How much memory is available?
- **Available disk space:** Is there disk space available?
- **System event logs:** Is anything being reported to the system?

You don't need to be a system administrator to perform these checks.

Network

If you can't connect to the database server, odds are neither can your users. You have two easy ways to check this:

- Ping to test server connectivity.
- Log in to the server as the Oracle user.

From the DOS or Linux command prompt, type **ping <*SERVER NAME*>** to see if the target server can be reached.

```
$ ping classroom.perptech.local
PING classroom.perptech.local (192.168.2.121) 56(84) bytes of data.
64 bytes from classroom.perptech.local (192.168.2.121): icmp_seq=1 ttl=64
          time=0.020 ms
64 bytes from classroom.perptech.local (192.168.2.121): icmp_seq=2 ttl=64
          time=0.007 ms
64 bytes from classroom.perptech.local (192.168.2.121): icmp_seq=3 ttl=64
          time=0.007 ms

--- classroom.perptech.local ping statistics ---
3 packets transmitted, 3 received, 0% packet loss, time 1999ms
rtt min/avg/max/mdev = 0.007/0.011/0.020/0.006 ms
```

In the preceding code three ping packets were sent and all three arrived successfully. Depending on the ping version, you get back slightly different output, but all specify if the server was reachable.

If the server comes back as unavailable, the problem is one of these things:

- The server is shut down.
- The network is down.
- You're prevented from pinging servers.

Sometimes security blocks ping, so check if it works before problems occur so you know the test is valid.

Once you confirm the server can be reached, try actually logging in as the owner of the Oracle software if possible. Note that on some systems you have to log in as yourself (for security-auditing purposes) and then switch users to the Oracle software owner. This confirms the server is not only running, but can support a login attempt.

Server utilization

If a program, process, or job is consuming all the resources on a server and has been doing so for a long enough time, a database can

- Slow down
- Be rendered unusable
- Be killed (in rare cases)

The processes themselves may be valid, or be a competing database (multiple databases can be on the same server), or an out-of-control, runaway process.

To determine the nature of the programs running, you first must identify them before you can determine if they're valid or hurting the system. There are several graphical tools to do this.

- On **Windows**, use Windows Task Manager to see which applications are running (under the Applications Tab). For more detail use the Processes tab shown in Figure 12-1.
- For **Linux/UNIX**, use the command top to display the top processes on a server, as shown in Figure 12-2. The output is text based and refreshed every few seconds. You can see the most active processes on the server and their *process ID (PID)*.

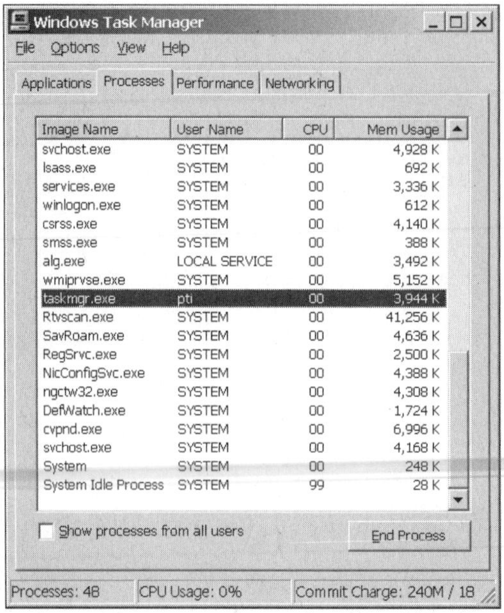

Windows Task Manager

File Options View Help

Applications | Processes | Performance | Networking

Image Name	User Name	CPU	Mem Usage
svchost.exe	SYSTEM	00	4,928 K
lsass.exe	SYSTEM	00	692 K
services.exe	SYSTEM	00	3,336 K
winlogon.exe	SYSTEM	00	612 K
csrss.exe	SYSTEM	00	4,140 K
smss.exe	SYSTEM	00	388 K
alg.exe	LOCAL SERVICE	00	3,492 K
wmiprvse.exe	SYSTEM	00	5,152 K
taskmgr.exe	pti	00	3,944 K
Rtvscan.exe	SYSTEM	00	41,256 K
SavRoam.exe	SYSTEM	00	4,636 K
RegSrvc.exe	SYSTEM	00	2,500 K
NicConfigSvc.exe	SYSTEM	00	4,388 K
ngctw32.exe	SYSTEM	00	4,308 K
DefWatch.exe	SYSTEM	00	1,724 K
cvpnd.exe	SYSTEM	00	6,996 K
svchost.exe	SYSTEM	00	4,168 K
System	SYSTEM	00	248 K
System Idle Process	SYSTEM	99	28 K

Show processes from all users   End Process

Processes: 48   CPU Usage: 0%   Commit Charge: 240M / 18

Figure 12-1: Windows Task Manager has multiple processes executing as multiple users via the Processes tab.

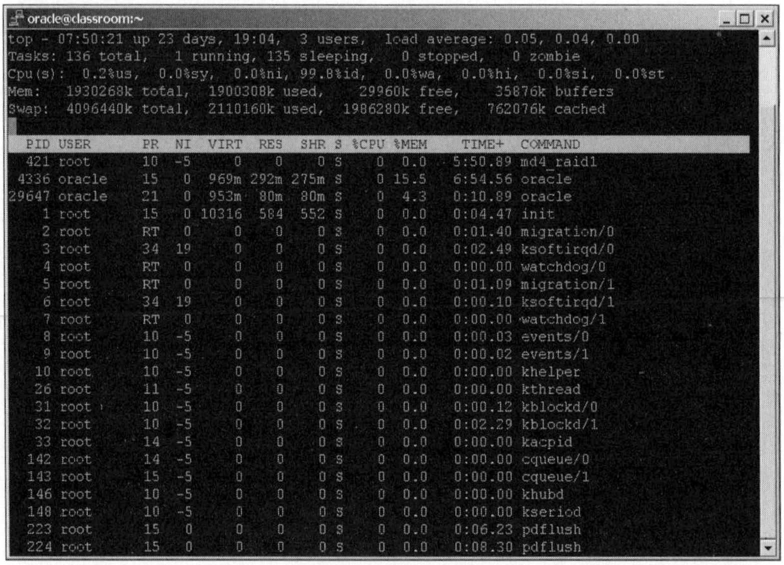

oracle@classroom:~

```
top - 07:50:21 up 23 days, 19:04,  3 users,  load average: 0.05, 0.04, 0.00
Tasks: 136 total,   1 running, 135 sleeping,   0 stopped,   0 zombie
Cpu(s):  0.2%us,  0.0%sy,  0.0%ni, 99.8%id,  0.0%wa,  0.0%hi,  0.0%si,  0.0%st
Mem:   1930268k total,  1900308k used,    29960k free,    35876k buffers
Swap:  4096440k total,  2110160k used,  1986280k free,   762076k cached

  PID USER      PR  NI  VIRT  RES  SHR S %CPU %MEM    TIME+  COMMAND
  421 root      10  -5     0    0    0 S    0  0.0   5:50.89 md4_raid1
 4336 oracle    15   0  969m 292m 275m S    0 15.5   6:54.56 oracle
29647 oracle    21   0  953m  80m  80m S    0  4.3   0:10.89 oracle
    1 root      15   0 10316  584  552 S    0  0.0   0:04.47 init
    2 root      RT   0     0    0    0 S    0  0.0   0:01.40 migration/0
    3 root      34  19     0    0    0 S    0  0.0   0:02.49 ksoftirqd/0
    4 root      RT   0     0    0    0 S    0  0.0   0:00.00 watchdog/0
    5 root      RT   0     0    0    0 S    0  0.0   0:01.09 migration/1
    6 root      34  19     0    0    0 S    0  0.0   0:00.10 ksoftirqd/1
    7 root      RT   0     0    0    0 S    0  0.0   0:00.00 watchdog/1
    8 root      10  -5     0    0    0 S    0  0.0   0:00.03 events/0
    9 root      10  -5     0    0    0 S    0  0.0   0:00.02 events/1
   10 root      10  -5     0    0    0 S    0  0.0   0:00.00 khelper
   26 root      11  -5     0    0    0 S    0  0.0   0:00.00 kthread
   31 root      10  -5     0    0    0 S    0  0.0   0:00.12 kblockd/0
   32 root      10  -5     0    0    0 S    0  0.0   0:02.29 kblockd/1
   33 root      14  -5     0    0    0 S    0  0.0   0:00.00 kacpid
  142 root      14  -5     0    0    0 S    0  0.0   0:00.00 cqueue/0
  143 root      15  -5     0    0    0 S    0  0.0   0:00.00 cqueue/1
  146 root      10  -5     0    0    0 S    0  0.0   0:00.00 khubd
  148 root      10  -5     0    0    0 S    0  0.0   0:00.00 kseriod
  223 root      15   0     0    0    0 S    0  0.0   0:06.23 pdflush
  224 root      15   0     0    0    0 S    0  0.0   0:08.30 pdflush
```

Figure 12-2: The top utility shows the top processes.

Additionally, at the top of the screen is the machine's *load average*. This derived value reflects relative load on the server.

  - Values up to 3 are light and shouldn't reflect performance problems.
  - Values in the teens reflect higher use of a busy system and performance may suffer.
  - Values above 20 indicate a busy system where performance is likely impacted.

- For **Linux/UNIX**, the uptime command helps you see system load:

```
$ uptime
 23:13:03 up 4 days, 10:27,  1 user,  load average: 0.00, 0.00, 0.00
```

System load values are the same as with top:

  - The leftmost value is the current load.
  - The middle value is the load 5 minutes previous.,
  - The rightmost value is the load 15 minutes prior.

The other useful value is the time since the last server restart. Obviously if users reported problems and you see the server recently rebooted a few minutes prior, the server reboot (or crash) is the likely culprit.

- On **UNIX Sun Solaris** systems, prstat is an alternative to top.
- On **HP-UX** systems, glance is extremely useful.

CPU utilization

Servers may have single or multiple CPUs. Regardless, there needs to be processing available for the server to process application requests.

If a machine has a very high or complete CPU use, performance issues will occur.

- On **Windows** the previously mentioned Windows Task Manager has a Performance tab. That tab displays CPU use as a percentage and as recent spikes, as you can see in Figure 12-3.
- For **Linux/UNIX** systems, the previously described top command displays CPU utilization at the top of the screen.

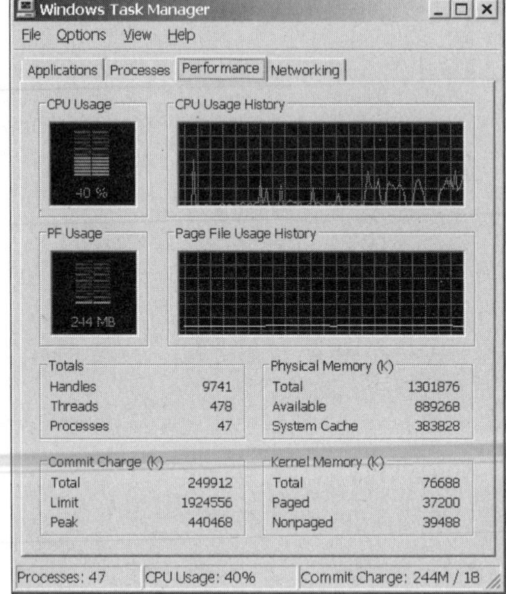

Figure 12-3: The Windows Task Manager Performance tab shows CPU use.

Memory

If the server is lacking memory, system performance suffers or even stands still. It isn't desirable to run a server with little or no memory available. If you find the server is consistently memory starved, either add more memory or reduce the amount of memory allocated for programs.

- To check memory on **Windows**, the Windows Task Manager Performance tab provides the total memory on the machine and amount available.
- **Linux/UNIX** systems have multiple tools to check memory, but the top utility provides this information rapidly.

Available disk space

Disk space is different than *disk utilization*. The frequency of reads and writes on a disk is utilization and can be a major performance factor. Running out of available disk space can bring your system to a halt and is the focus here because you, as the DBA, can do something about it.

However, poor disk utilization won't often bring your system to a complete standstill without warning. Measuring and accurately interpreting disk utilization, especially in large SAN environments, is outside the scope of this book. You should work with your storage engineers to address that topic.

What can happen when a disk fills up? It depends on what's writing to that disk. At minimum, log files can't be written to and tablespaces can't be expanded. At worst, archive log files can't be successfully written and the database hangs. With other software, processes can spin high amounts of CPU and Java Virtual Machines can crash — any of which is likely to generate a panicked call to your desk.

The quickest way to check for disk space is to see if any file systems are 100 percent full.

- For **Windows** systems, the fastest way is to go to My Computer and look at free space for each disk drive. Be sure to have Details selected under the View tab to get the full information.
- The df -m command helps **Linux** users:

```
$ df -m
Filesystem     1M-blocks    Used Available Use% Mounted on
/dev/md4          179203   21288    148665  13% /
/dev/md0             213      17       186   9% /boot
tmpfs                943       0       943   0% /dev/shm
/dev/md2           10653     503      9601   5% /tmp
/dev/md3           11626     819     10207   8% /var
```

  This code shows the file systems, their percentage used, percentage free (available), and the actual amounts in megabytes. The df -k command can show the same info but listed in kilobytes. This is useful because some versions of UNIX don't support the -m flag.
- On **HP-UX UNIX** systems, use bdf.

System event logs

If all else fails, listen to what the computer is telling you, so to speak! As a DBA, you should have at least read access to the system event logs on your server and hopefully all servers that are part of the application. System event logs record routine events on the server, but also may list special error events that could be the cause of your system problems. Sometimes it clearly lists hardware issues, or it could be file systems are full, or maybe listing that the machine just rebooted or crashed. All of these are good things to know when you're trying to track down a problem.

The location of the event logs can be varied and often additional logs are beyond the OS logs to review once you learn your system.

- On **Windows** systems go to Control Panel➪Administrative Tools➪Event Viewer to see the system and application logs.
- On **Linux/UNIX** systems, /var/adm/messages and /var/log/syslog are quite valuable. The dmesg command can see the end of the most recent system log file.

Much of this information may not make sense to a DBA who isn't OS savvy; however, seeing errors can be enough to seek the opinion of the system administrator.

Moonlighting

Ever notice the system time examples in many technical books are often late at night or very early in the morning, like the 11:13 p.m. example regarding the uptime command? Many, if not most, technical authors are primarily consultants or otherwise actively working in their field full time. Benefit to the reader is you get good, practical, and current information. Negative for the writers is they don't get a lot of sleep during these projects!

Performing basic database checks

If you've confirmed you can get to the server and that it should be able to support an application database, perform three basic database checks:

- Verify the database is running.
- Verify Oracle Net functionality.
- Perform a database connection.

Running database instance

See if it's actually running.

Oracle database instances execute with different mandatory processes such as PMON.

- On **Linux/UNIX** systems, simply check for the PMON process. Without PMON there's no Oracle database instance running.

  ```
  $ ps -ef|grep pmon
  oracle   13515   1  0 23:24 ?   00:00:00 ora_pmon_dev11g
  ```

  The PMON process is for dev11g, which is a running Oracle database. You could search for additional database processes, but if you know PMON is, you can safely assume the rest of the database instance is running too.

- On **Windows** systems check Control Panel⇨Administrative Tools⇨Services to see if the Oracle service has started. You can also look under Windows Task Manager to find similar information.

After you confirm a working basic network infrastructure and a connectable database server, you have to confirm the Oracle Net infrastructure is working so users can connect to the database.

Oracle NET functionality

Execute tnsping from the DOS or Linux command prompt. It uses the Oracle NET protocol to see if it can connect to the database.

```
$ tnsping dev11g

TNS Ping Utility for Linux: Version 11.1.0.6.0 -
Production on 17-SEP-2008 23:30:27

Copyright (c) 1997, 2007, Oracle.  All rights reserved.

Used parameter files:
/u01/app/oracle/product/11.1.0/db_1/network/admin/sqlnet.ora


Used TNSNAMES adapter to resolve the alias
Attempting to contact (DESCRIPTION_LIST = (DESCRIPTION= (ADDRESS_LIST= (ADDRESS=
             (PROTOCOL=tcp) (HOST= classroom.perptech.local) (PORT=1521)))))
OK (0 msec)
```

Note how it specifies the host, port, SID information for that database.

- If that doesn't match what you know to be correct, it is a clue.
- If it doesn't come back at all, it may be a network or server failure.
- Depending on the Oracle error returned, it may suggest an error with the database listener process.

Database connection

When you know the database is up and you can establish an Oracle Net communications handshake, log in to see if you can establish a database session.

1. **Identify the problem tier that users are reporting.**
    - In a client-server application, this is your workstation.
    - In a multi-tier architecture, this is likely the web application server.
2. **From that tier, try logging into the database via SQL*Plus, preferably as a typical user:**

```
$ sqlplus system@dev11g
SQL*Plus: Release 11.1.0.6.0
- Production on Sat Sep 20 12:59:03 2008
Copyright (c) 1982, 2007, Oracle.  All rights reserved.

Enter password:
```

```
Connected to:
Oracle Database 11g Enterprise Edition Release 11.1.0.6.0
- 64bit Production
With the Partitioning, OLAP, Data Mining and
Real Application Testing options
SQL> show user
USER is "SYSTEM"
```

The SQL*Plus attempt shows connecting to a remote database as an application user. You want to force the use of the Oracle Net infrastructure in this test. The @dev11g denotes that you'll use Oracle Net to connect to the remote database rather than directly logging in if you're already on the same server.

If you logged in, then you're done with your basic database checks; you confirmed a user can connect to the database. On the other hand, you may have encountered any of the following common errors:

- **Cannot archive log file:** If the archive dump destination is full, or for any other reason the archiver processes can't properly write the archive log file, your login attempt will fail. Oracle does this because even a login generates archive log information and Oracle guarantees it will track that information or it won't perform the action.

  Fix: Resolve that archiver problem.

  You can always log in on the server itself with / as sysdba to perform maintenance.

- **Database in restricted session:** The database may be running, but if in restricted session only users with RESTRICTED SESSION system privilege can login. Generally, the database is in the state because some form of database maintenance is occurring and the DBA doesn't want normal users in the system.

  Fix: Determine why the database is in restricted session mode and take it out of that mode if appropriate. Or you can grant RESTRICTED SESSION to the user(s), but that usually defeats the purpose of having restricted session.

- **Login simply hangs:** Sometimes the login attempt hangs and doesn't immediately generate an error message. These can be tough to diagnose because you're not getting any feedback.

  Fix: Try connecting from a different tier. Also try logging in from the database server itself; see if you can find where you can connect from and generate an actionable log message. Also revalidate your network, server, and system checks to confirm they are valid, and search for error messages.

Performing basic database checks is a way to confirm there's nothing obviously wrong with the database, such as it isn't running or you can't connect to it. Once you perform those checks, you can begin the more detailed problem and error log analysis.

Analyzing error messages

Ever hear the expression "hiding in plain sight"? That often happens when people see an Oracle error message. They see it, but they don't actually read it and think about what it is saying. As a result, the most valuable clue you have isn't being fully maximized.

Avoid falling into that trap. Make the most of your error messages:

- Slow down and read the error message — several times if necessary. Think about what it is saying. Don't just rattle off ORA-1234 and the description. Ask yourself what specific action is failing based on the context of the error message and what is going on at the time of the message.
- Pretend you're the application and ask what you're doing when the error occurred. Then apply the text of the message to see which piece or action is failing.
- Apply most of your focus on the *first* error message you receive. Often a series of error messages will occur related to one event, but typically that first message is the cause of the other messages.
- Know the different types of error messages and which components they relate to.

  - ORA denotes database or SQL errors.
  - TNS denotes database listener or Oracle Net communication issues.
  - HTTP is web related.
  - LDAP denotes details with your directory server, perhaps Oracle Internet Directory.

  The architecture of your system will determine what components may generate errors. Know what components exist within the system and the process flow so you can tell what part of the system is failing based on the type of message.
- Become familiar with normal messages versus extraordinary error messages. Many harmless informational messages crop up for events that aren't errors — particularly when working with log files. Know what your system logs look like during normal operations so that when real errors do occur, you can identify them easily in a myriad of informational messages.
- Plug the error message into Oracle Metalink and Internet search utilities to get more detailed descriptions and possible fixes. Expect lots of irrelevant information and false leads. But odds are your search will also include information that helps identify and fix the problem.

Knowing database and system anatomy

A firm understanding of Oracle database architecture and processes is key to your ability to understand error messages and diagnostic output. Think of it as database anatomy. Just as you would flee if your doctor said "I don't really understand that heart-stuff"; what kind of DBA is clueless about the SYSTEM tablespace? Even if you think you know it, a periodic review of Chapter 2 is time well spent for any DBA.

Where in the overall system does your database fit and what are the components? If people are reporting an HTTP-404 error, you probably want to get the web administrator involved as it may be a web server or content problem. But if your database generates the HTML content via mod_plsql Web Toolkit, it may actually be your database having issues. Not knowing that would result in the problem being routed to the wrong people, further delaying the fix. There simply is no substitute for knowing the specifics of how your system works and being able to apply that knowledge.

Error system example

Look at this example of a common message that confuses people. Upon analysis the cause is simple to identify.

```
ORA-01034: ORACLE not available.
```

ORA denotes a database message (versus TNS for a listener or HTTP for a web error). What does `Instance not available` mean in terms of databases? If you know database architecture, you know that an *instance* is the memory and background processes for a database. Thus, the database instance may not be running; you need to confirm that.

A quick ps –ef | grep pmon on the server shows no PMON process running, so now you have confirmed the database instance is down. A further check using the uptime command shows the server was restarted 15 minutes ago; you can assume the database didn't restart after a server crash or reboot. At this point you can check database logs to see if the instance tried to restart and failed or no attempt was made to restart. Based on that, you can manually restart the database and get users back to work.

oerr utility

The oerr utility gets more information about an error message. This command-line utility is where you specify an error number and a problem cause and possible solution is provided. While not in-depth troubleshooting, it is very handy:

```
$ oerr ora 1034
01034, 00000, "ORACLE not available"
// *Cause: Oracle was not started up. Possible causes include the following:
//         - The SGA requires more space than was allocated for it.
//         - The operating-system variable pointing to the instance is
//           improperly defined.
// *Action: Refer to accompanying messages for possible causes and correct
//          the problem mentioned in the other messages.
//          If Oracle has been initialized, then on some operating systems,
//          verify that Oracle was linked correctly. See the platform
//          specific Oracle documentation.
```

Developing and applying a solution

How do you fix a problem? Sometimes it is a simple command that is obvious even to the most inexperienced administrator. More commonly it is a multi-step operation that may span both database and non-database areas. Consider these guidelines as you develop and implement your plan.

Clearly for very simple and obvious fixes, you are not going to apply every step listed in the following exhaustive detail. However, you should review the guidelines and see how they apply to what you are doing.

Technical fixes and software patches do not always work, which is outside your control. However, planning the repair process is something you can control and will greatly better the odds of your success.

Researching

You should *understand* what is happening and *why*. What is causing the problem and how is that best remedied?

- Review the error messages.
- Read the documentation.
- Search the Internet.
- Talk to other administrators.
- Get Oracle Support assistance.

It's dangerous to apply a fix when you don't know why something is occurring. Only through understanding will you have the confidence that whatever fix you apply is the right one and won't cause further damage.

Develop the pseudo-code list of steps that you will need to perform based on your research. This may cause more questions as it is developed, but that is good. The end product is a high-level plan of how to fix the problem.

Planning

How will you specifically fix the problem? Once equipped with your high-level plan, make it technically detailed.

- Identify the technical substeps for each high-level pseudo-code step.
- Know what commands need to be issued and by which account.
- Know the time necessary for each step to occur and dependencies between steps.
- If additional software or patches are required, make sure those needs are addressed.

Have another administrator review your fix-planning steps to make sure you haven't skipped anything.

Ramifications

If you perform the fix, what are the side effects?

- Will you have to restart and place the system in restricted session for a complex fix, kicking off system users?
- How long will the system be unavailable?
- When is the best downtime?
- Can you perform the fix solo, from end to end, or do you need help from other groups (such as networking or the system administrator)?
- Does the fix void your software warranty or break other components?

Coordinating with other groups and the user community for a fix is often a big hurdle when working on large, distributed, and complex systems. It's helpful to have management support as well as documented policies and procedures to support coordination efforts.

Testing

Don't tell me you're trying something in production before testing it first! If at all possible, re-create the problem in a test environment and apply the fix there before doing it in production.

Testing does these things:

- Ensures your steps are complete
- Provides accurate timeframes for the total fix

- Verifies your syntax with the opportunity to make mistakes
- Confirms the problem is actually fixed
- Verifies there are no unintended consequences

Many organizations are under mandate to test changes before going into production, and that is generally a good policy. With troubleshooting complex problems or operating on large amounts of data, it is even more important.

We've seen many ill-advised attempts at fixing something without it being tested, only to end in disastrous results. Don't let that happen to you.

Fallback options

The fix doesn't work and things go from bad to worse. You do have a fallback plan, right? A good administrator always has a workable fallback plan for when things go wrong. Those who don't sooner or later end up seeking other employment opportunities.

Before performing nearly any technical fix, do these things:

- Take another database backup or verify your most recent backups are valid and accessible.
- If backups are stored off-site for disaster recovery, recall those backups. You may need them before you start your maintenance operation.
- Consider taking multiple backup copies too, in case one copy is bad. Parachutists jump with a backup chute; shouldn't you?

Once large amounts of data have been modified, can it be undone without a backup? You may need to work with the application developers on data changes. Also consider other items that need to be undone outside the database. For example, a network change with DNS may take several hours to take effect. If you push a change to thousands of client workstations, how do you roll that back if necessary?

Support

Odds are you will be performing your maintenance over a weekend or late at night. If so, are the other people available and accessible to perform their parts of the fix?

- Do you have everyone's phone numbers?
- Are they willing and able to help you at 3 a.m. when you discover a problem?
- Are they authorized to make the change?

Verification

Who is going to test and confirm the fix actually worked? A test plan with testers or knowledgeable users is a good idea, particularly if data or application changes are necessary.

- Run through the plan first; otherwise you may discover broken parts of the application unrelated to the problem you are attempting to fix.
- Make sure these testers are available once you are done with your work.

Once you have developed, tested, applied, and verified your technical fix, what's the final step before turning it over to the users? Often, a full database or system backup. The benefit is that if something unrelated occurs and you need to restore, you don't need to go through the previous fix.

Troubleshooting Using Oracle Database Logs

You need to dive into the Oracle logs themselves. Each database has a set of directories where key log, trace, and dump files are stored.

Database log infrastructure

In versions of Oracle prior to 11, all logs were simply under several ORACLE_BASE/admin/<*database name*> subdirectories. These were flat files dumped into audit, background, or user dump subdirectories and it was up to the DBA to manage them. This was okay, but left room for some improvement.

Starting in Oracle 11, log file structure and management is modernized and referred to as the *Automatic Diagnostic Repository (ADR).* The file structure is slightly different than previous versions, but ADR promises the following:

- Integrated log management not just for the database but other Oracle products. Currently, Automatic Storage Management and listener will also write to the new log infrastructure.
- Event logging in terms of incidents with included diagnostic data and stored in zip files that can be reviewed and sent to Oracle support. The idea is to better compartmentalize error events and neatly package them so they can be sent directly to Oracle support.
- *Incident Flood Control* to intelligently limit the creation and size of trace files. If an event repeats at an extreme rate above a defined threshold, only the occurrence of the event is logged.

It is important to know where the key diagnostic files are located:

- The location for the diagnostic subdirectories (diag) is the ADR_BASE and is typically under the ORACLE_BASE.
- The location of the base for the log subdirectories is the ADR_HOME and is defined by database parameter DIAGNOSTIC_DEST.
- The ADR_HOME is beneath the ADR_BASE location and is under the database SID directory.

The structure for ADR_HOME for databases follows:

```
$ADR_BASE/diag/rdbms/<DATABASE NAME>/<DATABASE SID>
```

For example, here's the following structure for the devg11 database:

```
$ ls $ORACLE_BASE/diag/rdbms/dev11g/dev11g
alert  cdump  hm  incident  incpkg  ir  lck  metadata  stage  sweep  trace
```

The ADR_HOME location is the full path up to and including the second reference to devg11.

You see this same information neatly stored within the database and can be queried via V$DIAG_INFO:

```
SYS@dev11g>select name, value from v$diag_info;

NAME                     VALUE
------------------------ ------------------------------------
Diag Enabled             TRUE
ADR Base                 /u01/app/oracle
ADR Home                 /u01/app/oracle/diag/rdbms/dev11g/dev11g
Diag Trace               /u01/app/oracle/diag/rdbms/dev11g/dev11g/trace
Diag Alert               /u01/app/oracle/diag/rdbms/dev11g/dev11g/alert
Diag Incident            /u01/app/oracle/diag/rdbms/dev11g/dev11g/incident
Diag Cdump               /u01/app/oracle/diag/rdbms/dev11g/dev11g/cdump
Health Monitor           /u01/app/oracle/diag/rdbms/dev11g/dev11g/hm
Default Trace File
    /u01/app/oracle/diag/rdbms/dev11g/dev11g/trace/dev11g_ora_2942.trc
Active Problem Count     3
Active Incident Count    5

11 rows selected.

SYS@dev11g>
```

Within each database directory are subdirectories where different files are stored. Table 12-1 lists each primary directory and its purpose.

Table 12-1 Database Trace and Log Directories

Directory	*Purpose*
alert	Stores very important XML-formatted alert log for database.
cdump	Core dump location of memory stack when a process fails.
incident	Subdirectories relating to individual events or incidents.
trace	Trace and dump files for background and user processes. Also contains text formatted alert log.

This is a listing of each directory:

```
$ ls $ORACLE_BASE/diag/rdbms/dev11g/dev11g/alert
log.xml
$ ls $ORACLE_BASE/diag/rdbms/dev11g/dev11g/cdump
ls $ORACLE_BASE/diag/rdbms/dev11g/dev11g/incident
incdir_52994  incdir_52995  incdir_53178
$ ls $ORACLE_BASE/diag/rdbms/dev11g/dev11g/trace
alert_dev11g.log ashrpt.txt
dev11g_m000_13544.trc dev11g_m000_13544.trm tk_trace.txt
```

These directories can get cluttered with many files and eat up disk space.

Have a process to clean up the trace, cdump, and incident directories.

Database alert log

By far the most important file to review for a database is the alert log. This file is where database-level errors are written and operations such as startup, shutdown, and other events are logged. Oracle writes to this text-based file in a chronological order when the database is running.

The alert log is in the alert subdirectory and is named log.xml.

- Whenever a problem occurs, review the alert log file.
- Review the alert log file daily (if you're the DBA) to ensure errors are not occurring undetected.

Many DBAs even write scripts to scan the alert log for errors and have email messages sent to them if key events are detected. Also, many DBAs copy off their alert log weekly to prevent it from becoming excessively large.

Prior to Oracle 11g, the alert log was a text-formatted file. With 11g onwards, it is XML based, which allows easier viewing with web-based tools.

Here's a sample of an alert log file in XML format:

```
<msg time='2008-04-16T10:55:58.838-04:00' org_id='oracle' comp_id='rdbms'
 msg_id='kspdmp:13492:1735555342' type='NOTIFICATION' group='startup'
 level='16' pid='17067'>
 <txt>Starting up ORACLE RDBMS Version: 11.1.0.6.0.
 </txt>
</msg>
<msg time='2008-04-16T10:55:58.838-04:00' org_id='oracle' comp_id='rdbms'
 msg_id='kspdmp:13510:1323239670' type='NOTIFICATION' group='startup'
 level='16' pid='17067'>
 <txt>Using parameter settings in client-side pfile
/u01/app/oracle/admin/dev11g/pfile/init.ora
on machine classroom.perptech.local
 </txt>
</msg>
<msg time='2008-04-16T10:55:58.838-04:00' org_id='oracle' comp_id='rdbms'
 msg_id='kspdmp:13556:144004252' type='NOTIFICATION' group='startup'
 level='16' pid='17067'>
 <txt>System parameters with non-default values:
 </txt>
</msg>
```

This code shows routine database messages for a database startup.

A text-formatted version is still available for people using command-line editors like vi or Notepad. It is in the trace subdirectory and has the standard name format alert_<*SID*>.log (which is alert_dev11g.log in this example). Without the XML tags you can easily read it via a command-line utility.

Here's the same information as the XML file, but without the tags:

```
Wed Apr 16 10:55:57 2008
Starting ORACLE instance (normal)
LICENSE_MAX_SESSION = 0
LICENSE_SESSIONS_WARNING = 0
Shared memory segment for instance monitoring created
Picked latch-free SCN scheme 3
Using LOG_ARCHIVE_DEST_1 parameter default value
as /u01/app/oracle/product/11.1.0/db_1/dbs/arch
Using LOG_ARCHIVE_DEST_10 parameter default value as USE_DB_RECOVERY_FILE_DEST
Autotune of undo retention is turned on.
IMODE=BR
ILAT =18
LICENSE_MAX_USERS = 0
SYS auditing is disabled
Starting up ORACLE RDBMS Version: 11.1.0.6.0.
Using parameter settings in client-side pfile
 /u01/app/oracle/admin/dev11g/pfile/init.ora
on machine classroom.perptech.local
System parameters with non-default values:
```

Here's what an Oracle error looks like:

```
ORA-279 signalled during: alter database recover logfile

 '/u01/app/oracle/flash_recovery_area

/DEV11G/archivelog/2008_09_09/o1_mf_1_59_4df4td9j_.arc'...
```

Review and manage the alert log regularly.

Trace and dump files

When a problem event occurs (such as a failed process or failed memory allocation), log files for that event are written into the *trace directory.*

The format for the log file name is *<SID>_<process name>_<process ID>.trc:*

```
$ ls $ORACLE_BASE/diag/rdbms/dev11g/dev11g/trace
dev11g_m000_13544.trc dev11g_m000_13544.trm tk_trace.txt
```

Here are the contents of a trace file:

```
Trace file /u01/app/oracle/diag/rdbms/dev11g/dev11g/trace/dev11g_m000_13544.trc
Oracle Database 11g Enterprise Edition Release 11.1.0.6.0 - 64bit Production
With the Partitioning, OLAP, Data Mining and Real Application Testing options
ORACLE_HOME = /u01/app/oracle/product/11.1.0/db_1
System name:    Linux
Node name:      classroom.perptech.local
Release:        2.6.18-53.1.14.el5
Version:        #1 SMP Wed Mar 5 11:37:38 EST 2008
Machine:        x86_64
Instance name: dev11g
Redo thread mounted by this instance: 1
Oracle process number: 30
Unix process pid: 13544, image: oracle@classroom.perptech.local (m000)


*** 2008-08-27 16:01:46.547
*** SESSION ID:(118.2743) 2008-08-27 16:01:46.547
*** CLIENT ID:() 2008-08-27 16:01:46.547
*** SERVICE NAME:(SYS$BACKGROUND) 2008-08-27 16:01:46.547
*** MODULE NAME:(MMON_SLAVE) 2008-08-27 16:01:46.547
*** ACTION NAME:(JAVAVM JIT slave action) 2008-08-27 16:01:46.547

joxjitexe exiting
```

The difference between a dump and a trace file: A *trace* is an ongoing log of a problem event. The *dump* is the one-time dumping of information into a file for a problem event. As a DBA you should review these text files to diagnose what is occurring.

If a process crashes, a core dump can be created in the cdump directory. This is a binary trace file of the memory process and its contents at the time of the crash. Although many people consider these "hands-off" for a DBA to review, that isn't necessarily the case. The Linux and UNIX strings command can show the printable text of a binary file. If you opt to upload the core file to any support organization, you may want to review it first for username and password combinations as they are sometimes present in clear text in these files.

Listener log

You may have to track connections into the database via the listener. Every time a connection to the database occurs, that event (or failure) is stored in the *listener log*. Chapter 5 goes into greater detail of the database listener architecture.

Knowing where listener logs are generated is important to troubleshooting. You can find the listener log under the ADR_BASE/diag/ tnslsnr directory tree. (In this example it's /u01/app/oracle/diag/tnslsnr/classroom/listener/trace/listener.log.)

Here's a sample log entry:

```
21-SEP-2008 23:59:44 * (CONNECT_DATA= (CID=(PROGRAM=)
   (HOST=classroom.perptech.local) (USER=oracle))(COMMAND=status)
   (ARGUMENTS=64) (SERVICE=(ADDRESS=(PROTOCOL=TCP)
   (HOST=classroom.perptech.local) (PORT=1521)))
   (VERSION=185599488)) * status * 0
```

Key information is the time, host, and program for the incoming connections.

Here's a Quest TOAD (see Chapter 7) utility user connecting, most likely from her workstation:

```
05-MAY-2008 11:57:45 * (CONNECT_DATA= (SERVICE_NAME=192.168.2.121)
   (CID=(PROGRAM=C:\Program?Files\Quest?Software\TOAD\TOAD.exe)
   (HOST=LPT-MPYLE)(USER=mpyle))) * (ADDRESS=(PROTOCOL=tcp)
   (HOST=192.168.2.170) (PORT=3108))
   * establish * 192.168.2.121 * 12514
```

Finally, an error is occurring:

```
TNS-12514: TNS:listener does not currently know of service
         requested in connect descriptor
```

You can search for the *Transport Network Substrate (TNS)* error code in the listener log to see what errors are occurring. This is useful as there will (hopefully) be far more connections than errors and, like the alert logs, the listener log can grow large.

Benefiting from Other Diagnostic Utilities

As a DBA you should be grounded in the fundamentals of how your database works and where files are located.

Sometimes you'll have only a command-line interface into your database server and have to manually review log files. However, you also should know several easier, faster methods:

- Oracle Enterprise Manager
- Remote Diagnostic Assistant (RDA)
- Database diagnostic scripts

Oracle Enterprise Manager

Oracle *Enterprise Manager (EM)* lets you review alert messages on the database home page. This easy method of checking for critical errors lets you avoid manually sifting through text files.

Figure 12-4 shows the alert messages for dev11g under the section Alerts. You can see multiple error and diagnostic messages and the time they occurred. Clicking the message text itself provides additional information.

From within Enterprise Manager, you can enter the Enterprise Manager Support Workbench. Within that tool you can generate the collection of additional diagnostic information with the intent of uploading it to Oracle Support as a *Service Request (SR).* In Figure 12-5 you can see each error that has occurred and the number of incidents for that error.

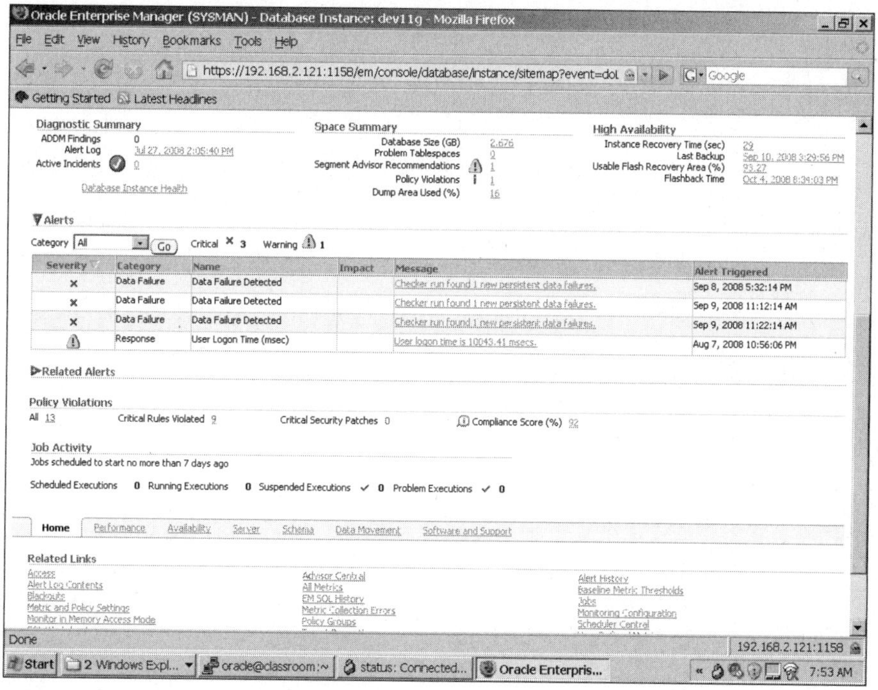

Figure 12-4: Viewing a database alert message.

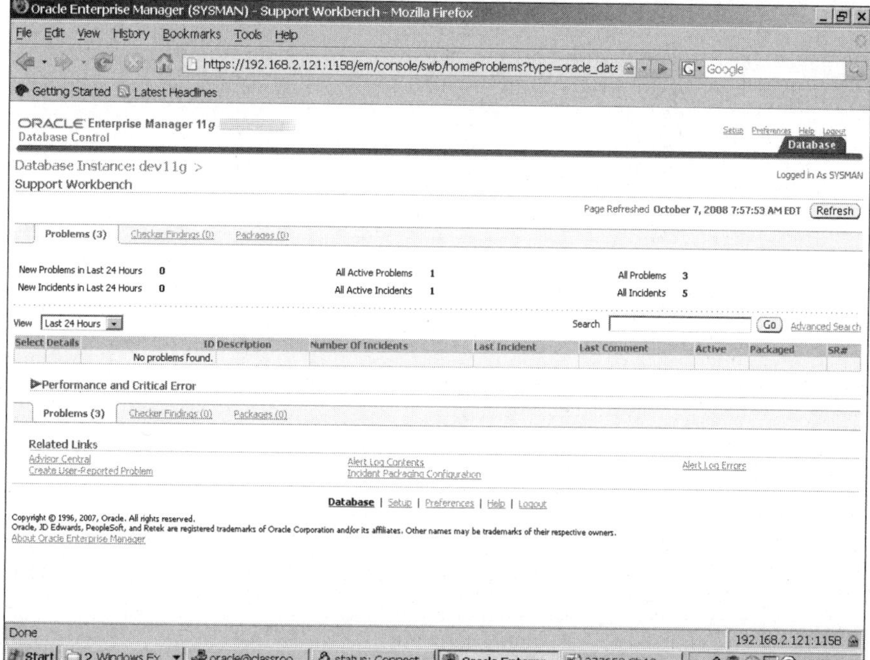

Figure 12-5: Checking out the Enterprise Manager Support Workbench.

Obviously you need to have an Oracle Support account and Customer Support Identifier to submit a package as an SR. This is a good way to streamline and automate your interaction with Oracle Support, which should allow for an easier troubleshooting process.

One benefit of formatting the alert log in XML is that you can easily view it via Enterprise Manager. The complete contents of the log and specific error messages can be displayed with timestamp ranges. You can see the most recent 100 entries in Figure 12-6.

You see the same information as in the alert log files via manual utilities, but the information is more cleanly presented via Enterprise Manager. It is the graphical representation provided by Enterprise Manager coupled with an intuitive interface and wizards that make EM a useful tool for the DBA.

Remote Diagnostic Agent

Oracle *Remote Diagnostic Agent (RDA)* is an Oracle support utility that captures Oracle-related information on an entire server and stores the results in a series of HTML files.

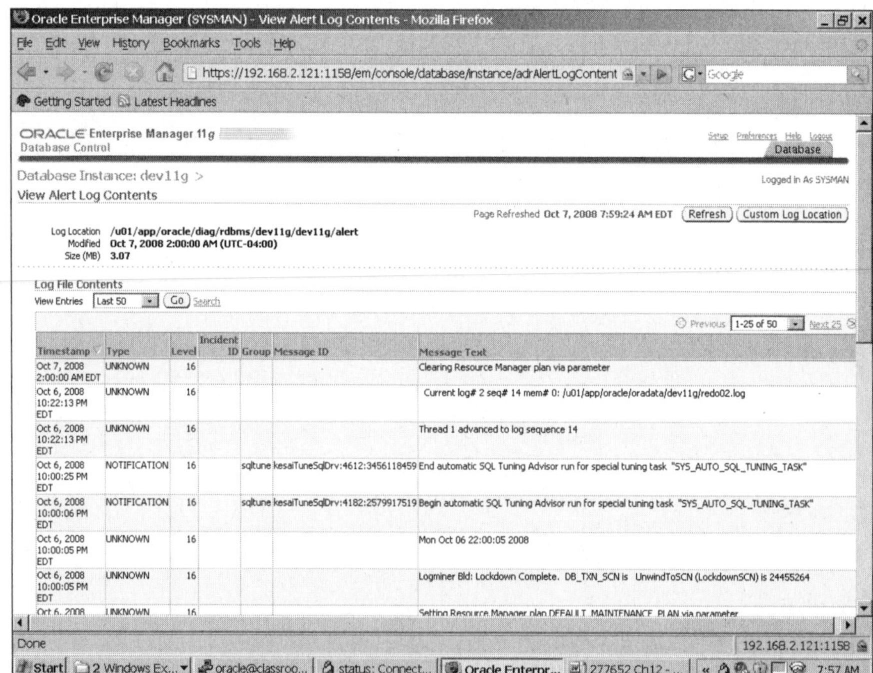

Figure 12-6: Viewing alert log contents.

The intent is to capture data about the operating system, hardware, Oracle software versions, database instances, listeners, and activities within the database in an automated manner. You can view that information as a series of static HTML pages to get fast graphical access to all Oracle-related information for a given server.

Not only is graphical information useful to DBAs, but when you provide an RDA to Oracle support it gives an accurate picture of your database environment. In fact, one of the first things many Oracle support analysts request is an RDA of your server.

Oracle RDA comes as a tar or zip file available for download via the Oracle Metalink support network. Once downloaded, it executes on the server as a Perl script. The output is a zip file that you can

- Upload to Oracle support
- Unzip into a series of HTML files that you can navigate to find key information

In Figure 12-7 you see the main index page of the RDA output where you can drill down into multiple useful areas.

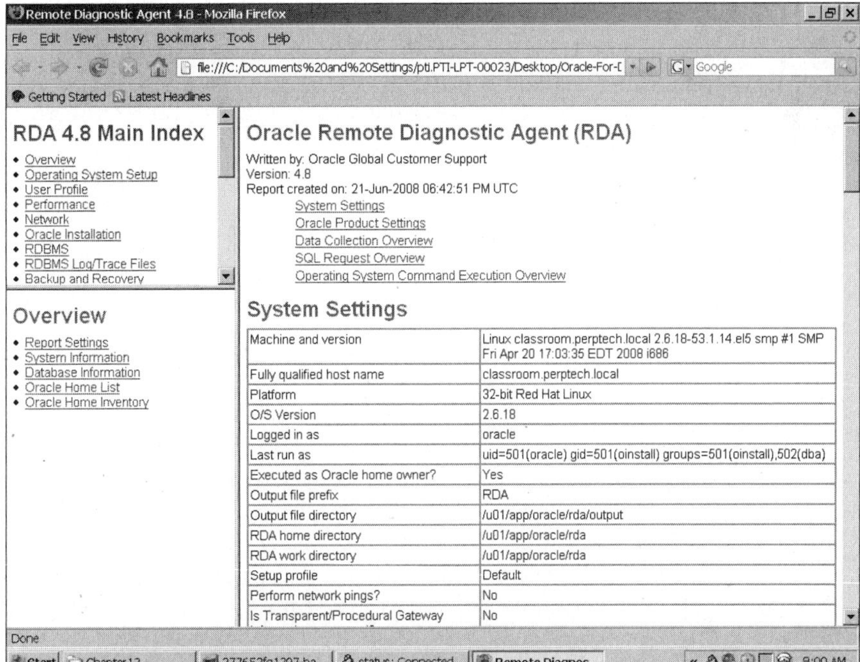

Figure 12-7: The RDA main index page.

RDAs are a great way to get a quick snapshot of a system even when there are no problems (per se). For example, if you are consulting and need a quick overview of a client's system, the RDA is very handy. Or if you are taking over an existing database server, the RDA will tell you exactly what is on that server and how it is configured.

Diagnostic database scripts

Most old-school DBAs from the Oracle 7 days lived and died by their toolbox of database scripts, and for good reason. Database scripts based on internal database views and tables provided the raw information for what is going on in a database. That raw data, coupled with a real understanding of how the database and application worked, often made for a very skilled administrator who could solve most problems. Towards that end, entire books are dedicated to database scripts, as well as many web sites with scripts available for download.

Oracle provides a set of database scripts in every $ORACLE_HOME/rdbms/admin directory. In it are core scripts necessary to create a database, build the data dictionary, and other maintenance operations which aren't very useful for troubleshooting.

However, the $ORACLE_HOME/rdbms/admin directory also has useful scripts such as utllockt.sql and utlrp.sql. Use them to search for database locks and compile invalid database objects. We encourage you to become familiar with the scripts in this directory and identify the ones that fit into your toolbox.

Many good third-party scripts exist both from books and Internet downloads. We can't validate everything out there, so use your own best judgment and don't run anything you don't understand or trust. However, there are some good scripts available so don't be afraid to seek out good sources and test them first on your *development* database.

And if all else fails, write your own. Here is one of our favorites we've used many times to see what is happening on a database and who is doing it:

```
SYS@dev11g>get show_session_short.sql
set linesize 180
set pagesize 20
col "Logon Time" format a11
col "UNIX Proc" format a9
col username format a15
col osuser format a13
col "Program Running" format a20
col sid format 9999
```

```
col "Connect Type" format a12
col serial# format 9999999
select s.username, osuser, status,
to_char(logon_time,'fmHH:MI:SS AM') as "Logon Time",
sid, s.serial#,  p.spid as "UNIX Proc"
from v$session s, v$process p
where s.paddr = p.addr
and s.username is not null
order by status, s.username, logon_time
SYS@dev11g>@show_session_short

USERNAME        OSUSER        STATUS   Logon Time   SID   SERIAL# UNIX Proc
--------------- ------------- -------- ----------- ----- -------- ---------
DBSNMP          oracle        ACTIVE   11:39:11 PM  125        12 29062
SYS             oracle        ACTIVE   12:18:25 AM  119       829 31376
SYSMAN          oracle        ACTIVE   11:40:39 PM  124        54 29264
SYSMAN          oracle        ACTIVE   11:41:19 PM  138        35 29359
DBSNMP          oracle        INACTIVE 11:37:51 PM  135        13 28749
SYSMAN          oracle        INACTIVE 11:40:26 PM  129        24 29258
SYSMAN          oracle        INACTIVE 11:40:49 PM  155        32 29273
SYSMAN          oracle        INACTIVE 11:40:59 PM  126        54 29275
SYSMAN          oracle        INACTIVE 11:41:29 PM  132        19 29357
SYSMAN          oracle        INACTIVE 11:41:39 PM  131        55 29355
SYSMAN          oracle        INACTIVE 11:41:49 PM  127       323 29361

11 rows selected.
SYS@dev11g>
```

While the script is useful, the actual point is to show you the power of a simple script and what it can quickly provide.

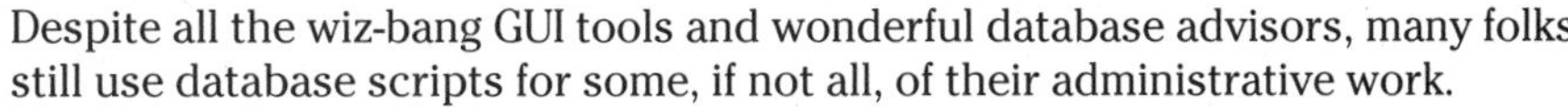

Despite all the wiz-bang GUI tools and wonderful database advisors, many folks still use database scripts for some, if not all, of their administrative work.

A toolbox of useful scripts coupled with modern Enterprise Manager tools provide DBAs with the best capability to manage their databases.

Chapter 13

Monitoring and Managing with Enterprise Manager

In This Chapter

- Working with Enterprise Manager Database Control
- Managing users
- Metering and Policy
- Setting up notifications

Whether you began by reading this chapter or started with Chapter 1, you probably know lots of ways to manage your Oracle database. This book offers a few ideas. You may have been approached by various software companies with their own solutions. The most popular database management approaches follow:

- Pure command line with SQL and OS commands
- Oracle Enterprise Manager (Database Control/Grid Control)
- Third-party software vendor tools
- Any combination of these

What works best for you? Whatever you're most comfortable with. Some methods are better than others for specific tasks. Most people end up with some sort of hybrid approach.

This chapter focuses on the Oracle Enterprise Manager method. This chapter gives an overview of the tool's unique features, as well as some navigation through many of its management pages.

Tasting Oracle Enterprise Manager Flavors

Oracle Enterprise Manager first became available way back in Oracle 7. It has gone through numerous changes since then. Without boring you with too much history, basically it started off as a desktop client and evolved into the web-based application it is today.

Oracle supports several current flavors of Enterprise Manager. It's important to know the differences between these tools. From now on, we refer to Oracle Enterprise Manager as OEM.

OEM Java Console

The Java-console version of OEM has been available from Oracle 8i through 10g. In 8i and 9i, it served as the main OEM management system. Not only was it a tool for simple management tasks, it connected to a central repository running on a remote central server, which expanded its capabilities to job scheduling and monitoring and paging.

As of Oracle 10g, OEM only shipped as the client version; there's no connectivity to a centralized server. It still has many useful features, though.

For quick, GUI-based tasks, you can install and run it on almost any OS with a supported Java Virtual Machine. It doesn't require a centralized management system. It offers all the basic features for managing the day-to-day operations of the database, such as the following:

- Tablespace/data file management
- Users/roles/privileges
- Startups/shutdowns
- Memory management
- Initialization parameters

On the other hand, and among other advanced features, it can't work with these:

- Scheduler
- Jobs
- Notifications
- Backups

- Data Pump
- Data Guard

It's a nice tool for backup and quick-and-dirty operations when you don't know SQL. But better versions of OEM can suit your needs.

The authors of this book were unable to find any information for or against using the 10g Java Console to manage an Oracle 11g database. We did some testing and it functioned quite well. However, keep in mind that the Java Console didn't ship with 11g. It was deprecated by Oracle for future releases starting with 11g.

We recommend using either Database Control or Grid Control if you're managing an 11g database.

OEM Database Control

OEM Database Control started shipping in Oracle 10g and above and serves as the junior replacement for the Java Console version that last shipped with 10g. It's the first major shift in graphical-based management options that Oracle has offered since Oracle 8i.

This is a web-based platform. All the commands you can type using SQL are translated into a graphical, point-and-click interface. Some users find this easier than learning and typing SQL commands. Database Control even supports clustering and RAC database management.

You must run a Database Control instance for each database you have. You have to start a Database Control stack for each database you want to manage. If you have many databases, you might find this method tedious and resource consuming. Grid Control steps in here.

OEM Grid Control

OEM Grid Control offers everything in Database Control and much more. The interface is similar when working on individual databases, it also acts as a central console for managing your entire environment:

- Oracle Software stacks
- Windows and Linux operating systems
- Microsoft SQL Server
- Other software products

With regard to databases, it can register and maintain Oracle versions from 8iR3 through 11gR1. As of this writing, Oracle hasn't shipped 11g Grid Control. However, they provided a patchset (10gR4) for 10g that certifies it for 11g database installations. Since 11g Grid Control has yet to ship, this chapter focuses on working with 11g Database Control.

Grid Control is installed on its own centralized server in your enterprise. Then you deploy the Oracle Management Agent to all the hosts which software you want Grid Control to manage. The install and setup can be a little intimidating at first, but if you have a diverse environment with many servers and versions of Oracle, it can be a lifesaver in the long run.

Configuring Enterprise Manager with the DBCA

The easiest way to set up database control is to configure it during database creation with the *Database Configuration Assistant (DBCA).* Chapter 4 briefly describes this option. Figure 13-1 shows where the DBCA asks if you want to configure your database with Database Control (for local management).

We recommend Database Control because it is the easiest approach. When you let the DBCA set up the database for you, it gathers the required answers for the installation while it takes you through different steps.

Once your database creation is complete, open a browser and log into Database Control to begin managing your database. Typically, this URL is most common: https://<hostname>:1158/em/console.

Figure 13-1: The Database Configuration Assistant offers its Enterprise Manager Options screen.

You can log in with any username that has *database administrator (DBA)* privileges. SYSMAN is the default user who owns the repository. You choose the password while you're making the database. Also, use the SYSDBA option if you want to do advanced DBA activities like backups or starts and stops. Just make sure your user has the SYSDBA privilege.

Creating and Managing Database Control Users

When you first create your database, three users are allowed to log in:

- SYS
- SYSTEM
- SYSMAN

However, creating your own users is best practice. This way each person can set up her own tasks and notifications and it's easier to identify who has made changes.

In Enterprise Manager Database Control, *all* users are super users. This means that they can do almost anything in the tool.

Follow these steps to create a user:

1. **Click Setup in the upper-right corner of any page within Enterprise Manager.**
2. **Click the Administrators link (on the left).**

   Figure 13-2 shows the link, which takes you to a list of users who are allowed to log into Database Control. You also see a Create button on top of that list.
3. **Click the Create button.**

   You see four fields.
4. **Fill in these fields:**
   - **Username**
   - **Password**
   - **Confirm password**
   - **Email address**

   You also see a flashlight icon next to the username. With it you can choose an existing user to assign Database Control privileges.

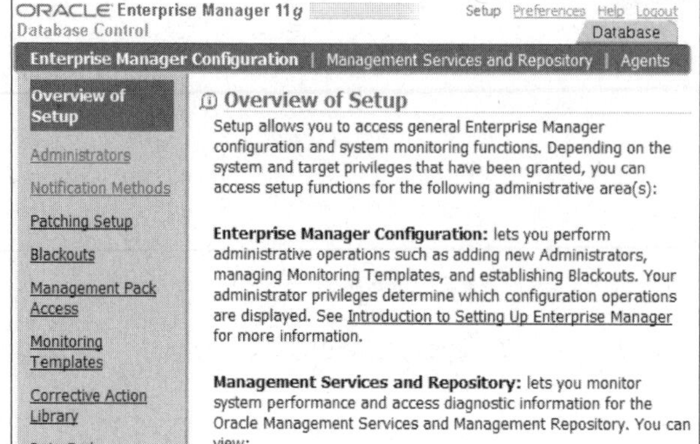

Figure 13-2: Database Control Configur- ation Page.

5. **Click the Review button on the bottom of the page.**

   Figure 13-3 shows an example of what you might see.

6. **Click the Finish button to complete the task.**

Removing users is simple. Click Setup in the upper-right corner of any page and then follow the Administrators link in the left sidebar. After that, click the radio button next to the username and then click the delete button on top of the user list.

Figure 13-3: Review the user you're creating in Enterprise Manager Database Control.

Create Administrator nbunker: Review

Properties

Name **nbunker**

E-mail Address **nbunker@perptech.com**

Super Administrator privileges with Full access to all targets, View access to all jobs and Full access to jobs granted by the job owner.

Database system privilege: SELECT ANY DICTIONARY

Database role: MGMT USER

When you remove a user via the Administrators page, the user is also removed from the database. So, if you created a Database Control user by choosing an already existing user, when they are removed from Database Control, they are gone for good from Database Control and the database.

Working with Metrics and Policies

One of Database Control's best features is automatic monitoring of your database with metrics and policies. This is a key component of your DBA job. Database Control uses metrics and policies to save you from having to write all kinds of programs by hand.

Metrics and *policies* are ways of monitoring in the system.

- **Metric:** A measurable point of data about the current operating database; typically associated with performance or availability. For example, you might want to know when free space drops below a certain point in your tablespaces or if the CPU exceeds 90 percent usage.
- **Policy:** A particular condition that users mustn't violate; typically associated with security. For example, you might want to know if someone logs into the database as SYSDBA or gains unauthorized access to certain features.
- **Target:** A component of the Oracle installation that Enterprise Manager can manage and monitor. Targets can be databases, hosts, listeners, applications, agents, and so on.

You can tell Database Control to watch metrics and policies, and alert you when certain conditions are met. Determine metrics and policies independently for each target type. Database Control organizes them this way so they're easier to administer.

Metric and Policy Settings are listed in the Related Links section under each target's main administration page.

This is how it's done for the target type database:

1. **Click the Database tab on the top of any screen in Database Control to take you to the database home page.**

   You're taken to the database home page.

   The Database tab is on every Database Control page. Figure 13-4 shows the tab at the top of the page.

2. **Once you're back on the database's home page, scroll to the Related Links section.**

   The related links section only shows up from the database's home page, which you access by clicking the Database tab at the top of any screen.

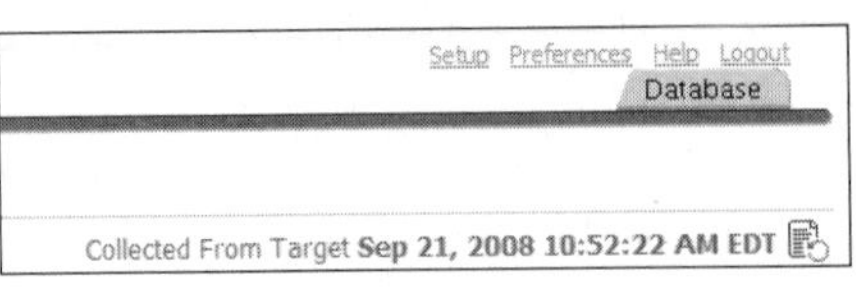

Figure 13-4: The Database tab is at the top right of any page in Database Control.

3. **Click the Metric and Policy Settings link in the Related Links section.**

   You're taken to the Metric and Policy Settings page, as shown in Figure 13-5.

4. **Click the Metric Thresholds tab.**

Figure 13-5: Top of the Metric and Policy Settings page.

5. **Choose All Metrics from the drop-down menu.**

   You can monitor literally dozens of data points. Many you won't care about; some are critical to you. Each metric has two thresholds:

   - Critical
   - Warning

   You can adjust these values independently of one another. If a threshold's exceeded, a notification appears under the Alerts section of the target's main page, and you can get an email.

6. **To review your policy settings, click the Policies tab.**

   Each policy has a description. Click the Edit icon to change a policy's threshold. Policy violations register on the target's main page under the Policy Violations section.

You don't have to monitor certain metrics or policies. For metrics, set the value for both Critical *and* Warning thresholds to Null. For policies, check the box next to the policy name and click the Remove button.

We could spend an entire book just explaining all the metrics and policies that are available by default. However, it is probably easier for you to access Oracle's free documentation available online for a complete reference.

Setting Up Notifications

One of the nicest features OEM offers is the ability to monitor and notify. You could spend weeks writing your own shell scripts to capture, measure, and evaluate hundreds of different metrics on the system. In fact, we've seen people do this. You could also spend thousands of dollars on third-party monitoring tools. No shortage of companies have developed fancy graphical interfaces for Oracle.

Despite all this, we encourage you to investigate what Oracle has to offer from within. Then make any decisions on third-party software. We aren't saying one is better than the other. Oracle also requires licensing fees. However, the convenience of having well-supported, built-in features has advantages.

Set up notifications with these steps:

1. **Log in to Database Control.**
2. **Click the Setup link.**

   You're taken to the Enterprise Manager configuration page. Here you see options for controlling your Database Control environment.
3. **Click the Notification Methods link.**

   You're taken to a screen for configuring your mail server settings.
4. **Fill in the fields, shown in Figure 13-6, with the correct information:**
   - **Outgoing Mail (SMTP) Server.** Name or IP address of your outgoing mail server.
   - **User Name.** Optional. In the event your SMTP server requires authentication to send messages, you can put the username in here.
   - **Password.** Optional. Some mail servers require authentication to send messages. This field is for the password.
   - **Confirm Password.** Optional. Some mail servers require authentication to send messages.
   - **Identify Sender As.** For indentifying the message. In Figure 13-6 the sender is simply Oracle.
   - **Sender's E-Mail Address.** For indentifying the message. In Figure 13-6 the email address is oracle@perptech.com.

   You may have to team up with your mail server administrator to get some of the required information.

5. **Click the Test Mail Servers button.**

   This helps make sure Enterprise Manager can communicate with the mail server.

6. **When you're satisfied, click the Apply button.**

Mail Server

Enterprise Manager requires the following information to send e-mail notifications by means of Notification Rules. When specifying multiple SMTP servers, separate each server by a comma or space.

Revert | Apply | Test Mail Servers

Outgoing Mail (SMTP) Server	192.168.2.121:25 Use the format SERVER:PORT (Example: SMTP1:587). Port 25 is used if no port is specified for the server. (Example: SMTP1, MyServer:587).
User Name	 Specify user name if your SMTP server requires authentication.
Password	 Specify the authentication password. The name and password will be used for all SMTP servers.
Confirm Password	
Identify Sender As	Oracle
Sender's E-mail Address	oracle@perptech.com

Figure 13-6: Notification Method set up in Enterprise Manager.

To combat spam, some mail servers reject messages that don't have a valid domain name. We've seen people use server names for the email domain. Usually, these servers *don't* match a valid domain name and they will be rejected by the mail server delivering your email. This could be a serious problem as you might not get important alerts.

Setting Up User Notifications

An important part of being a database administrator is keeping on top of problems or events in the database. You can't stay logged into Database Control watching the Alerts section for new events. Luckily, Enterprise Manager can email and page you when certain events occur.

You can alert different users for specific situations and on specific schedules. This option is especially nice when your company has a rotating schedule for who services these events.

You may have already configured notifications (when we discuss how to create users earlier in this chapter). However, if you didn't do it then, here's how to do it after the fact:

1. **On the Database Control home page, click the Preferences link.**

   Preferences are controlled by the user who's currently logged in. If you want to set up your own notification preferences, you have to be logged in as yourself.

   After clicking the Preferences link, you're taken to your account's General settings page. You see either a list of email address or an empty section for you to add them to.

2. **Click the Add Another Row button.**

   You see the output as shown in Figure 13-7.

E-mail Addresses

These addresses are used to send notifications to you. You can specify multiple addresses if you want to be notified in different ways, and the format to use for each address. Later on, you will need to define a Notification Schedule before any e-mail notifications can be sent to you.

Remove Test

Select All | Select None

Select E-mail Address	Message Format
☑	Long Format

Add Another Row

TIP Refer to on-line help for message format sample.

Revert Apply

Figure 13-7: Adding an email address for notifications.

3. **Type the email address in the E-Mail Address field.**

   You can only enter one address at a time. If you want to add an address, click Add Another Row.

4. **When you're finished adding addresses, click the Apply button.**

   Message Format offers a drop-down list. If you're emailing a pager, you might want to specify the short format. You won't get as many details, but it works better with a device that sends and receives only small messages.

   To remove addresses, just click the Select box next to the address and then click the Apply button. Then test the addresses.

5. **Check the Select box next to the address you want to verify; then click the Test button.**

6. **Make sure the account gets a test email from Database Control.**

   Now set the alert schedule.

7. **Click the Schedule link on the right of the page.**

   That link takes you to a calendar-type module.

8. **Click the Edit Schedule Definition button.**

9. **Choose one of the following options:**

   - **Rotation Frequency:** Customize the times and days within the rotation frequency to repeat cycles.
   - **Edit Existing Schedule:** Adjust a schedule you've already set up.
   - **Replace Existing Schedule/Start Date:** Start over with your schedule and decide when notifications should begin.
   - **Time Zone:** This is typically the time zone you live in, not the time zone where the database resides.

10. **Click the Continue button.**

11. **Complete the Email Addresses field.**
12. **Enter the times you'd like to be alerted.**

Alerts only work for one-hour increments. Click the Batch Fill-In button for tools that help with blocks of time. Figure 13-8 shows that author Chris Ruel will be on call Monday through Friday, from 5:00 p.m. until 9:00 a.m.

13. **Click the Finish button.**

You're shown your new schedule.

Figure 13-8: The Batch Fill-In screen completes blocks of time.

Optional Batch Fill-in

Click on 'Batch Fill-in' to use the same e-mail addresses across the specified hours, days, and weeks.

Start Time 5:00 AM PM
End Time 9:00 AM PM
E-mail Addresses chris.ruel@gmail.com

Days of Week Monday Tuesday Wednesday Thursday Friday Saturday Sunday

Batch Fill-in

14. **Click Subscribe for the events you want alerts for.**
15. **Click the Rules link.**

Enterprise Manager comes with a list of rule sets; you can subscribe to them. A *rule set* is a list of metrics and policies. Based on your metrics and policies settings, when thresholds are triggered, an alert goes to the people subscribed to that rule.

The supplied rules are convenient for quick setup. The supplied rules typically alert you to more than you might be concerned about.

Try making some of your own rules. You need to know if the database is down or a tablespace is filling up. Come up with a short list of critical situations that require immediate alerts and click the Create button (above the rule set). Use the tabs to add metrics, policies, and thresholds.

16. **Click the Subscribe (Send E-Mail) check box for anything you want notifications for.**
17. **Click Apply to finish.**

All metrics and policies show up in the Alerts section of the main page of Database Control. Check that list daily, if not more often.

Navigating Database Control's Main Page

The good news is the Database Control interface is fairly intuitive. You learn it quickly if you use it regularly.

The Help link at the top right and bottom-middle of every page is useful. Depending on what section you're in, the Help link takes you to data on that specific topic.

We offer a few tips for getting around the major sections.

Inspecting the Database Control main page

Figure 13-9 shows the top part of the Database Control main page as it looks when you first log in. You might call this the *dashboard.* It gives an idea of your database's overall health. Each monitored component in Database Control is a *target.* Each target has its own dashboard.

Figure 13-9: The top half of the Database Control main page is chock-full of data.

The database target is the dashboard you see when you first log in. All the other major sections are listed and separated, according to task, immediately under the target name.

As shown is Figure 13-9, tabs march along the database name:

- **Home:** Using this link will always take you to the main "dashboard" of that target.
- **Performance:** This tab will give you an overview of the performance of the database. You will see things like I/O, CPU usage, top sessions, locks, etc. It contains anything that might help when diagnosing performance problems on the system.
- **Availability:** This section deals with backup and recovery. It can be considered the GUI of the RMAN tool discussed in Chapter 8.
- **Server:** This section controls the "meat" of the operational portions of the database. You control space, security, initialization parameters, resources, and scheduling tasks all from this section.
- **Schema:** As this section is named, it deals with all objects in the database. You can change objects, add new ones, and delete them from this section.
- **Data Movement:** This section contains all the tools necessary for loading and unloading data. It can be considered the graphical interface for tools normally used from the command line such as SQL*Loader or Data Pump. You can also clone databases and set up replication from within this section.
- **Software and Support:** This section is helpful for things like patching, viewing, and testing configuration changes and deploying new code.

Look at Figure 13-10 for the lower half of the Database Control main page for the target type database. Each section has links you can follow to investigate specific events. In some cases, a wizard is launched to interactively help diagnose problems.

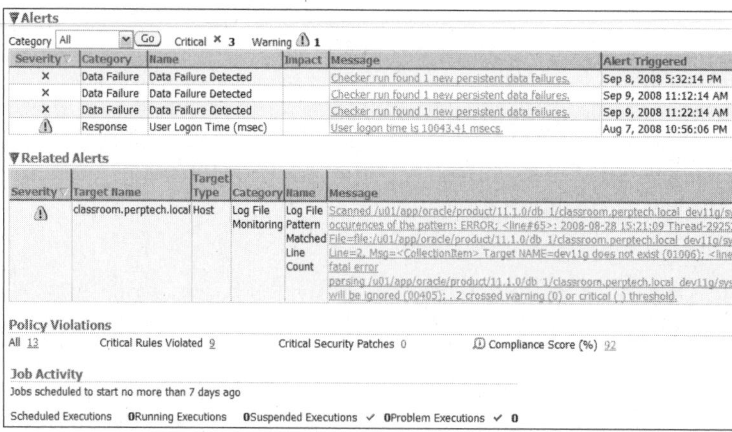

Figure 13-10: The Lower half of the main control page for the target type database.

- **Alerts:** A list of events triggered by the current target's metric and policy settings.
- **Related Alerts:** Alerts for metric and policy violations for other targets that are related to the current target.
- **Policy Violations:** Specific list of the current target's policy violations.
- **Job Activity:** Output or recent job activity.

Accessing other targets

As mentioned earlier, each target has its own dashboard page. From the database target dashboard, you can access the other targets that Database Control monitors.

Follow these steps to access the host or listener target dashboard:

1. **Click the Home tab for the database.**

   Under the General section on the top left, you see links for the host and listener.

2. **Click the links for the target you want to know more about.**

   You're taken to each target's dashboard.

Part IV
Inspecting Advanced Oracle Technologies

"Your database is beyond repair, but before I tell you our backup recommendation, let me ask you a question. How many index cards do you think will fit on the walls of your computer room?"

In this part . . .

Rolling back might become a necessity; every database crashes. Chapter 14 details tools you rarely see but that make your recovery easier. Chapter 15 helps ensure your database is up and running as much as possible, even when recovery is occurring.

Chapter 14

Flashing Back and Replaying: Advanced Features

In This Chapter

- Visiting the flashback database
- Flashing back to the data archive
- Replaying the database

This chapter details features that you don't see on most Oracle enterprises day to day. (Of course, someone out there will disagree and we apologize.) Regardless, most DBAs who are new to the sport probably won't start here; these features are for more advanced administration.

You might assume these things are related:

- Flashback database
- Flashback data archive
- Database replay

Each of these features is used to a different end. This chapter explains how these features can add value to your Oracle environment.

Rolling Back with Flashback Database

Have you ever wanted a time machine? No such thing exists. Or does it? The Oracle time machine known as *flashback database* lets you rewind, fast forward, and recover from situations with ease. *Flashback database* can sound intimidating, but the feature is simple.

You could argue that moving the database forward and back with Oracle Recovery Manager with good backups is possible. However, restoring a large database to a previous point is time consuming and tedious. Also, if you don't go back far enough, you have to start all over from the beginning.

Flashback database works by recording extra information that allows you to roll back transactions without doing a full database recovery. Not only that, but it works very quickly. The flashback database has these quick features, among others:

- You can open the database read only to see if you went back far enough.
- Not far enough? Quickly roll back further.
- Too far? Roll forward again.

You can perform all these tasks with simple commands inside SQL*Plus or Oracle Enterprise Manager. To do them with RMAN, you're talking multiple full restores and lots of time in between.

Configuring and enabling a flash back

Oracle stores a file called a flashback log. *Flashback logs* have the data to roll back blocks to a previous time. Flashback logs are stored in the flash_recovery_area. Chapter 8 shows how to configure the flash recovery area.

Two variables come into play here:

- How far back do you want to go?
- How much data is changed in your database within that time period?

The further back you go and the more changes you have, the more flashback logs you generate. Be sure you have enough space to store those logs or you won't be flashing anywhere.

If you're considering implementing flashback database, you may need to enlarge the parameter db_recovery_file_dest_size. By how much depends on the two variables: how far back and how much data? If you want a good starting point, use this formula:

> New Flash Recovery Area Size = Current Flash Recovery Area Size + Total Database Size × .3

In essence, you are trying to reserve roughly 30 percent of your total database size in the Flash Recovery area for flashback logs.

From then on, you can monitor how much space the flashback logs are consuming. We show you how to do that shortly.

Once you configure the flash recovery area, turn on the flashback feature in the database:

1. **Consider how far back you want to be able to flash back.**

   Configure this setting with the parameter db_flashback_retention_target. The default value is 24 hours (or 1,440 minutes). Say you want to be able to flash back up to 48 hours.

2. **Log into SQL as SYSDBA and type the following:**

   ```
   <alter system set db_flashback_retention_target
           =2880;>
   ```

   You should see the following for any amount of time you choose. In this example time is set to 2,880 minutes.

   ```
   System altered.
   ```

3. **Shut down your database and restart it in mount mode.**

4. **Put the database in flashback mode by typing this:**

   ```
   <alter database flashback on;>
   ```

   You should see this:

   ```
   Database altered.
   ```

5. **Open the database by typing this:**

   ```
   <alter database open;>
   ```

   You should see this:

   ```
   Database altered.
   ```

   Now that the database is in flashback mode, you can flash back to any time within your flashback window.

You might want to flash back for these reasons:

- **Repeated testing scenarios:** Say you have an application that you're testing in your development environment. Every time you run the application, it changes your data. You will want to reset the data back to its original values before the next test. Flash back is an excellent tool for this.
- **Logical Data Corruption:** Perhaps someone accidentally ran the wrong program in your production environment; you need to return to a point before the mistake occurred. You could do this with a data recovery, but flashback is quicker and easier.
- **Deployment procedures:** Perhaps you're releasing a new version of your code that updates all sorts of objects in your production schema with both DDL and DML. You can easily roll it back if the application isn't working properly in target performance parameters.

Using restore points

Flashing back a database is time based. Normally, you select a time and tell the database to go back to that time within the flashback window. However, another convenient feature — a *restore point* — is a named, easily identified point for locating a specific instance in the past.

Say you're doing a code deployment and want to mark when the database will be returned to if you have to back out the change. You could record the time, but Oracle may not get it exact when you flash back. Buck the margin of error and create a restore point — an exact time.

Oracle has a margin of error of plus or minus a few seconds.

To create and name a restore point, follow these steps:

1. **Log into the database as SYS.**
2. **Type the following with your restore point name:**

```
<create restore point pre_deploy_15SEP2008;
```

In this example the restore point is called pre_deploy_15SEP2008. You should see this:

```
Restore point created.
```

Restore points come with a few other handy options:

- **Get a list of all the restore points you created:**

```
< select scn, time, name
From v$restore_point;>
```

You should see this:

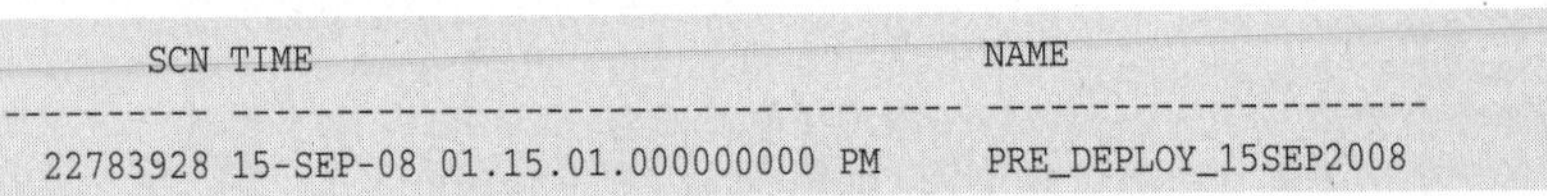

```
       SCN TIME                                NAME
---------- ----------------------------------- ---------------------
  22783928 15-SEP-08 01.15.01.000000000 PM     PRE_DEPLOY_15SEP2008
```

- **Create a restore point that's guaranteed forever.** Be careful using that method: Your flashback logs grow until the restore point is dropped.

```
<create restore point pre_deploy_15SEP2008_g guarantee flashback database;>
```

You should see this:

```
Restore point created.
```

- **Drop the restore point when your code release succeeds:**

```
drop restore point PRE_DEPLOY_15SEP2008;
```

You should see this:

```
Restore point dropped.
```

Flashing back your database

When the database must be flashed back, don't worry. The process is relatively easy.

Flashing back a database removes any change that occurred after the point in time chosen to return. Don't take this consideration lightly.

To start off, say you haven't created any restore points and want to see how far back you can go. Type this:

```
< select oldest_flashback_time
from v$flashback_database_log;>
```

You should see something like this:

```
OLDEST_FLASHBACK_TIM
--------------------
14-SEP-2008 06:34:03
```

db_flashback_retention_target should be about the limit of that time frame. You may find it to be longer if space isn't a concern and the database hasn't yet purged old flashback logs.

Say a user accidentally dropped the HR schema from your database about an hour ago.

1. **Shut down your database.**
2. **Restart it in mount mode.**
3. **Type the following, where 1 is the number of hours you want to flash back:**

   ```
   < flashback database to timestamp sysdate - 1/24;>
   ```

   You should see this:

   ```
   Flashback complete.
   ```

4. **Check the flashback before making it permanent:**

   ```
   < alter database open read only;>
   ```

   You should see this:

   ```
   Database altered.
   ```

5. **If you're satisfied with the result, go to Step 6. If you're not satisfied with the time, skip to Step 9.**
6. **Shut down the database.**
7. **Start the database in mount mode.**

8. **Open the database with Resetlogs:**

   ```
   < alter database open resetlogs;>
   ```

   You should see this:

   ```
   Database altered.
   ```

9. **Restart the database in mount mode.**

10. **Type the following:**

    ```
    <recover database;>
    ```

    You should see this:

    ```
    Media recovery complete.
    ```

11. **Start your database in mount mode.**

    If you want to flash back to a timestamp, go to Step 12. If you want to flash back to a previously created restore point, go to Step 13.

12. **Type the following:**

    ```
    <flashback database to timestamp
    to_timestamp('23-SEP-2008 13:00:00','DD-MON-YYYY HH24:MI:SS');>
    ```

    You should see this:

    ```
    Flashback complete.
    ```

13. **Type the following if you want to use a restore point:**

    ```
    <flashback database to restore point pre_deploy_15SEP2008;>
    ```

    You should see this:

    ```
    Flashback complete.
    ```

Using Flashback Data Archive

Flashback data archive is a database mechanism that allows you to periodically or indefinitely store all row versions in a table over its lifetime. You can then choose a time to view the data as it existed at a specific point in time.

No need to code complex triggers to move rows to history tables. You also won't need to code complex application logic to retrieve the data. The archiving is completely transparent to developers and end users. Oracle has sometimes referred to this feature as *Oracle Total Recall.* (No, that's not a reference to some cheesy 1990s movie.)

When you enable flashback data archive, the row versions are automatically compressed to conserve space. You can also specify the retention period.

You can't do certain operations (such as DROP or TRUNCATE) on tables where you've enabled flashback data archive. Furthermore, you can't modify historical data; this ensures the validity and consistency of the archive data.

Flashback data archive is a totally online operation. No downtime is required to enable or use this feature. It's enabled on a table-by-table basis. You can also group objects according to retention periods for easier management. Indexes aren't maintained, but you can create your own index to facilitate searching.

After the specified retention period expires, data is automatically purged to conserve space. If space is a concern, you can set quotas to limit archive growth. Also, to best organize your flashback data, create tablespaces to store flashback data for specific retention periods.

If an archive quota is exceeded, new transactions are blocked. Keep an eye on space usage and periodically check the alert log for space warnings.

Here's how you might use a flashback data archive:

1. **Create a tablespace that holds data for a one-year retention period:**

   ```
   <create tablespace fbda_1yr datafile
   '/opt/oracle/oradata/dev11g/fdba_1yr_01.dbf' size 100M
   Autoextend on next 100M maxsize 10g;>
   ```

   The tablespace in this example is named for documentation purposes. You see this:

   ```
   Tablespace created.
   ```

2. **Create a flashback data archive object in your tablespace with a one-year retention and a 10GB space limit:**

   ```
   <create flashback archive FBDA1
   Tablespace fbda_1yr quota 10G retention 1 year;>
   ```

3. **Enable flashback data archiving on the table to keep row history:**

   ```
   <alter table emp flashback archive FBDA1;>
   ```

   You see this:

   ```
   Table altered.
   ```

4. **Query the table to see what it looked like:**

   ```
   <select *
   From emp
   As of timestamp sysdate - 180;>
   ```

   In this case you're serching for emp 6 months prior. You see the row images as they existed 180 days ago.

You can't DROP, TRUNCATE, or modify any historical rows in this table as long as flashback archive is enabled.

To remove the flashback archive status, deleting all historical data, type this:

```
<alter table EMP no flashback archive;>
```

You see this:

```
Table altered.
```

Oracle Database Replay

The Oracle Database Replay feature evolved from the need to be able to do realistic application testing. Before database replay, if you wanted to test any kind of changes against performance or workload, you had to buy a third-party tool or do massive amount of coding to fake a workload. In most cases, neither was truly representative of your real workload. Also, making changes to a production environment without testing them can be risky.

Database replay is one more tool in your shed to cover all the bases.

In essence, database replay allows you to record your workload real time and then play it back. Furthermore, you could play it against

- Another database
- A different version of Oracle
- A different OS

Database replay captures the workload at below the SQL level. The workload is stored in binary files. You can then transfer these files to a test environment, run the workload, and then analyze, fix problems, and test again. The same workload is repeatable. In conjunction with a tool like flashback database, you can repeatedly test changes in quick succession. Ultimately, it helps reduce the chances of something breaking when environments are changed.

Database replay provides a mechanism to help with these kinds of situations:

- Testing
- Configuration changes
- Upgrades

- Downgrades
- Application changes
- Debugging
- Storage, network, and interconnect changes
- Platform changes
- OS changes
- Conversion to Real Application Clusters (RAC)

Using database replay

Here's how to use database replay:

1. **Log into SQL*Plus as a user with the SYSDBA privilege.**

   Oracle requires a directory in which to write the replay files.

2. **Create a directory to a location on the OS with plenty of space:**

   ```
   <create or replace directory capture_dir as
   '/opt/oracle/admin/orcl/capture';>
   ```

   You see this:

   ```
   Directory created.
   ```

3. **Start a capture:**

   ```
   <exec dbms_workload_capture.start_capture ('CAPTURE_DEMO','CAPTURE_DIR');>
   ```

   This example uses the name capture demo.

   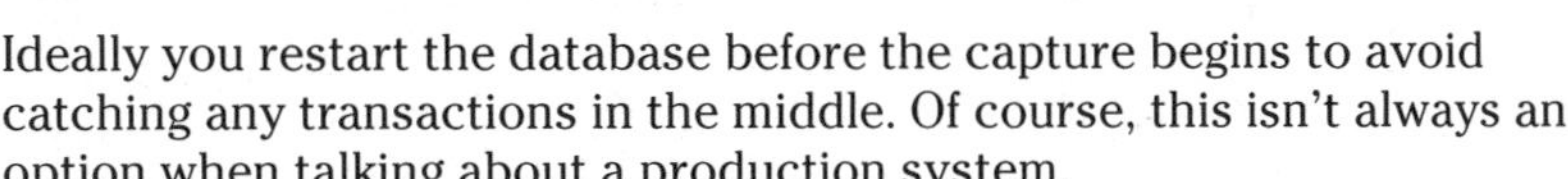

   Ideally you restart the database before the capture begins to avoid catching any transactions in the middle. Of course, this isn't always an option when talking about a production system.

   You see this:

   ```
   PL/SQL procedure successfully completed.
   ```

4. **Execute your workload.**

   If it's just normal application behavior, let it run for the amount of time you wish.

5. **Once the workload is complete or your time target has passed, stop the capture process:**

   ```
   <exec dbms_workload_capture.finish_capture;>
   ```

   You see this:

   ```
   PL/SQL procedure successfully completed.
   ```

According to Oracle documentation, capturing a workload can add up to 4.5 percent of processing overhead to the system as well as 64k of memory overhead for each session. Futhermore, if space runs out in the capture directory, the capture will stop. All the captured data up to that point will still be useful.

The step is to "replay" the workload. In our experience, the workload is usually replayed against a different database, such as a test environment. However, this is not always the case.

If your database environment is one where lengthy maintenance windows can occur (such as over a weekend) you might find yourself doing these things:

- Enabling flashback database
- Creating a restore point on Friday morning
- Starting a workload capture for four hours from 8 to noon
- Restricting the system and creating another restore point after the employees go home on Friday evening
- Restoring the database to the restore point Friday morning
- Deploying database or application changes
- Replaying your workload to test the changes
- Flashing back the workload to Friday evening
- Deploying database or application changes to take effect when the workers come back Monday morning

Replaying the workload

Follow the steps to replay the workload:

1. **Create a directory for the replay capture files:**

   ```
   <create or replace directory capture_dir as
   '/opt/oracle/admin/orcl/capture';>
   ```

   You see this:

   ```
   Directory created.
   ```

   This example assumes the replay is taking place on another database. If it's on the same database, there is no need to create a directory and move the capture files because they will already be in the correct location.

2. **Move the files from the capture directory on the source system to the directory on the replay system.**

3. **Begin the replay process on the database:**

```
<exec dbms_workload_replay.process_capture ('CAPTURE_DIR');>
```

You see this:

```
PL/SQL procedure successfully completed.
```

4. **Initialize a replay session called replay_demo:**

```
<exec dbms_workload_replay.initialize_replay
 ('REPLAY_DEMO_4','CAPTURE_DIR');>
```

You see this:

```
PL/SQL procedure successfully completed.
```

5. **Tell Oracle to prepare the replay files:**

```
<exec dbms_workload_replay.prepare_replay ;>
```

You see this:

```
PL/SQL procedure successfully completed.
```

Start *replay clients,* which are processes that execute and manage the workload. These processes are launched from the OS's command line.

6. **The following example starts a replay client with oracle as the password:**

```
<wrc system/oracle>
```

You see this:

```
Workload Replay Client: Release 11.1.0.6.0 -
Production on Wed Sep 24 09:33:19 2008
Copyright (c) 1982, 2007, Oracle. All rights reserved.
Wait for the replay to start (09:33:19)
```

7. **Tell the database to start the replay:**

```
<exec dbms_workload_replay.start_replay;>
```

You see this:

```
PL/SQL procedure successfully completed.
```

8. **Check on the status while the replay runs:**

```
<select id, name, status, duration_secs
  from dba_workload_replays;>
```

Basically you're querying the DBA_WORKLOAD_REPLAYS table. You see this (or something like it):

```
        ID NAME                 STATUS      DURATION_SECS
---------- -------------------- ----------- -------------
        10 REPLAY_DEMO          IN PROGRESS           369
```

You can create a replay report by using the commands shown in Figure 14-1.

Figure 14-1: Create a database replay report in SQL*Plus with these commands.

```
SQL> set serveroutput on
SQL> set long 99999
SQL> select dbms_workload_replay.report(10, 'TEXT')
  2  from dual;

DB Replay Report for REPLAY_DEMO
---------------------------------------------------------------------------------

---------------------------------------------------------------------------------
| DB Name | DB Id      | Release    | RAC | Replay Name   | Replay Status |
---------------------------------------------------------------------------------
| ORCL    | 1172537040 | 11.1.0.6.0 | NO  | REPLAY_DEMO_4 | COMPLETED     |
---------------------------------------------------------------------------------
```

When everything is done, you should clean up the replay metadata.

1. **Capture ID info on the source system:**

   ```
   <select id, name
     from dba_workload_captures;>
   ```

   You might see something like this:

   ```
           ID NAME
   ---------- -----------------------------------
            4 CAPTURE_DEMO
   ```

2. **Delete the capture information:**

   ```
   <exec dbms_workload_capture.delete_capture_info(4);>
   ```

   You see this:

   ```
   PL/SQL procedure successfully completed.
   ```

3. **Find the replay id on the replay system:**

   ```
   <select id, name
     from dba_workload_replays;>
   ```

   You might see something like this:

   ```
           ID NAME
   ---------- -----------------------------------
           10 REPLAY_DEMO
   ```

4. **Delete the replay information:**

   ```
   <exec dbms_workload_capture.delete_replay_info(10);>
   ```

Chapter 15

Using High-Availability Options

In This Chapter

- Using Real Application Clusters (RACs)
- Understanding Data Guard

A *high-availability architecture* combines hardware and software solutions to help reduce the impact of outages during planned and unplanned downtime. Your data's availability is of utmost importance. However, the level of availability varies by business. Some can deal with a little downtime here and there with minor business interruptions. A minute of downtime for others can cost tens of thousands of dollars. Luckily, Oracle helps harden against the forces out there that want to make your database unavailable.

Implementing a high-availability architecture may not be cost effective for everyone. It can be expensive in terms of hardware and software licenses. However, if downtime costs you thousands of dollars in short intervals, look at some of Oracle's high-availability options.

This chapter is about a couple of Oracle features that you can configure for high availability. Each feature has its strengths and weaknesses. You sometimes can combine features to get the best result. And because licensing Oracle options seems to change constantly and varies from site to site and version to version, we're deferring any questions about the licensing of these features to your friendly Oracle sales rep.

Lastly, entire books and weeklong classes deal with these technologies. We give an overview within this chapter. Unfortunately, we can't prepare you for an enterprise installation and configuration of these options. Consider this a guide with tools that help you investigate.

Gathering Real Application Clusters

If you've visited Oracle's web sites in the last eight years, you've seen their marketing byline: "Unbreakable." That tag line relies on *Real Application Clusters (RAC).* Of courses, a lot of elements are involved, but RAC has the spotlight.

RAC is Oracle's clustering solution. In a sense, it works on the theory that there is strength in numbers. RAC lets you have parallel database instance operating environments. These instances cooperate to share work and back up each other in the event one has an outage. RAC can help with both planned and unplanned outages. It allows you to shift your processing from server to server with little to no interruption to your end users and applications.

Determining whether RAC is right for you is a big decision. Implementing RAC requires lots of resources and money. Just like many things, sometimes spending a little more up front will save you later.

Consider what RAC can offer:

- **Scalability.** The technology is based on computers and resources that team up as one. With RAC, you can purchase and license hardware as you need it. Furthermore, you can plug the new hardware in as you go without taking down your database. If you've exceeded your computing capabilities for the server, seamlessly add one to your configuration.
- **Uptime.** RAC can harden your computing environment against planned and unplanned downtime. You can transparently remove portions of the application for planned downtime (such as maintenance, patches, and upgrades) with little to no interruption to end users. Furthermore, if one of your environment's computing resources fails, RAC automatically transfers application connections to other resources in the framework.
- **Performance.** Some might argue with this point, but you have to carefully define RAC's performance capabilities:

  - Because RAC is a complicated environment, your application has to be designed to best take advantage. If you ignore this fact, RAC can actually hurt performance. Keep that in mind.
  - RAC can offer performance benefits when it comes to the divide-and-conquer methodology. You can split large jobs across computers. If you know an underpowered machine is limiting your company, reconfiguring the job to run on multiple machines can offer great benefits. It's called *parallel processing* and it's part of RAC fundamentals.

RAC versus OPS

RAC, which has been around for many years, was previously known as the *parallel server option.* Before we get flamed about when RAC was RAC, we're perfectly happy to admit that before the RAC moniker, Oracle Parallel Server (OPS) was far from the capabilities that RAC has to offer. Oracle significantly hardened the architecture, made it more accessible and easier to set up. They also focused on the components of the environment that minimize downtime. So, you could say that RAC is a new breed of OPS that far surpasses prior capabilities.

Exploring RAC Architecture

RAC works through a complex organization of hardware and software configurations. Mostly throughout this book we talk of Oracle databases as a single set of files (the database) and a single set of memory and process components (the instance) that work together for you to access and maintain your data. That is the most typical configuration for an Oracle installation. In this configuration, the database files can only be mounted and accessed by one machine and one Oracle instance at a time.

With RAC, those files are sharable so many machines and instances can access the same files. There can be (depending on certification and versions) 100 database instances accessing the same shared database. Just like you might have two DBAs in your office:

- One can vacation while the other works (read: high availability).
- Both can work together on a large project to split the workload and meet an aggressive timeline (read: performance).
- Add a third person to meet workload requirements as the Oracle responsibilities grow (read: scalability).

Many components are required in a RAC setup. To give you a general idea on what the architecture looks like, refer to Figure 15-1.

Hardware considerations for RAC

RAC has some hardware requirements.

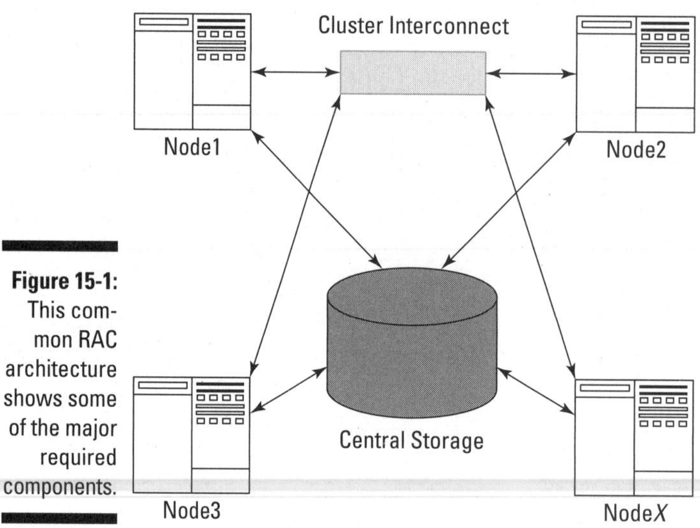

Figure 15-1: This common RAC architecture shows some of the major required components.

Nodes

A *node* is a server that runs an Oracle instance. A true RAC configuration has at least two nodes.

The number of nodes in your RAC configuration depends on hardware and software limitations. According to Oracle's documentation and support web sites, Oracle software itself can support up to 100 nodes, but other forces may limit you to fewer.

If you're getting into lots of nodes (more than eight), check with all your hardware and software vendors to see what your limit is.

Add nodes as you scale your cluster. You can add and remove them with minimal or no service interruption to your application. This ensures high availability. Typically, each node will have its own installation of the Oracle software.

You can have one central, shared software directory for each node to use. However, a configuration like this limits your high-availability capabilities.

For example, one advantage to installing the Oracle software on each node is the ability to individually patch the nodes by taking them down one at a time. This *rolling patch* avoids a complete application outage. You can't apply all patches this way. Check with patch documentation to be sure. On the other hand, one central installation requires you to shut down the entire cluster to apply the patch.

Each node should have its own Oracle software code tree if you want high availability.

Central storage

Some RAC configuration central storage requirements are discussed here:

- **All your database files, control files, redo logs, archive logs, and spfile should be on shared storage.** This way, each of the nodes has access to all the required files for data access, recovery, and configuration.
- **Attach the central storage to each node in the form of some high-speed media.** Lots of high-speed connections (fiber channel or iSCSI, for example) are available from different storage vendors. Make sure the storage and attachments are approved for Oracle RAC before making your decisions. (For example, NFS mounting drives to each server isn't typically a certified configuration.) You can use almost any shared storage configuration with decent education and testing results.
- **When choosing a storage vendor, consider your applications' performance needs.** Your disk subsystem should be able to scale as easily as your RAC nodes. As you add nodes, you may need to add physical disks to support the increased demand on the storage subsystem. You should be able to do this with little or no downtime.
- **The disk on the shared storage subsystem must be configured for shared access.** You may have up to four choices for this:
  - **Raw file system** (unformatted disks)
  - **Oracle Cluster File System (OCFS)** (available on Windows and Linux only)
  - **Oracle Automatic Storage Management (ASM)** (an Oracle-supplied volume manager of sorts for database-related files)
  - **Third-party solution** (such as Veritas)

You may have to combine options. For example, you might use Oracle ASM for your database files, but you need something other than ASM for cluster software-related files.

Cluster interconnect

The *cluster interconnect* is a dedicated piece of hardware that manages all the inter-instance communication. A lot of communication across instances occurs in a RAC configuration: maintaining consistency, sharing lock information, and transferring data blocks.

Oracle uses Cache Fusion for managing data transfer between nodes. Cache Fusion requires an extremely reliable, private, high-speed network connecting all the nodes.

Cache Fusion is a critical component for getting RAC to perform well. The interconnect needs to be gigabit speeds or better.

When you have cluster communication performance issues, the interconnect's ability to provide the required bandwidth is questioned. It's a necessary expense to set up a RAC environment appropriately. Would you spend thousands of dollars on a race car and then put street tires on it?

Network interfaces

Make sure you have the right network interfaces on the server for proper communication. This includes multiple network interface cards:

- One for the public or user connections to the machine
- One for the private interconnect for the cluster to share information across the nodes.

At the very least, a RAC configuration should have two network interface cards:

- One is for the private network for cluster interconnect traffic.
- One is for the public network.

The public network is the connection for all cluster connections, from your applications and end users (including you and the sys admin).

Software considerations for RAC

Before you set up RAC, investigate the software it needs to run smoothly. Consider the following areas of software.

Operating system

Though nearly all popular OSs run a RAC installation, you need to

- Verify that the OS is certified.
- Make sure the right release and patchsets are confirmed as RAC certified.
- Ensure your Oracle version is certified with your OS configuration.

Oracle's support web site (http://metalink.oracle.com) provides a matrix to help you identify certified combinations.

Furthermore, an uncertified OS may be certified later. It can be complicated at first, but getting this right off the bat goes a long way down the line.

Clustering software

Arguably, clustering software is the most important piece of software. Without clustering software, there is no cluster.

The software tracks cluster members such as databases, instances, listeners, and nodes. Lots of other cluster components run on each of the nodes and require maintenance for the clusterware to work properly. The clustering software tracks these components and facilitates internode communication and health.

Depending on your experience level with different types of clustering software, you might choose one over the other. Oracle provides clustering software in the form of Oracle Clusterware. Since Oracle 10g, Oracle Clusterware is available for almost all the major operating systems.

If you go with third-party clustering software, make sure it's certified by Oracle for RAC. Veritas and Sun Cluster are examples of certified third-party clustering software. However, make sure they're certified for your OS.

Oracle database

The Oracle database software is nothing special when it comes to RAC. You don't need to download any special components or anything to make an Oracle database RAC ready. RAC is built in to the database software. When you go to install Oracle RDBMS on a cluster, it will recognize that a cluster exists and ask if you would like to do a cluster install. It's as simple as that.

Optional software

You might want to use some optional pieces of software:

- **Oracle Agent:** If you manage your database with Oracle Grid Control, you need to install an agent on the cluster. Like the database software, the agent recognizes that it's being installed on a cluster and configures itself appropriately.
- **Oracle ASM:** Though included with the database software, it's generally good practice to install Oracle ASM into a home separate from the databases that run on the nodes. That way it can be maintained separately. With ASM in a separate home, you only have to shut down the one database you have to patch; uptime is preserved for everyone else. Of course, if all the databases use the same home, this option might not work.

Preparing for a RAC Install

Each OS has its own configuration for a RAC install. It's virtually impossible to cover everything here.

However, we can offer a few pieces of advice:

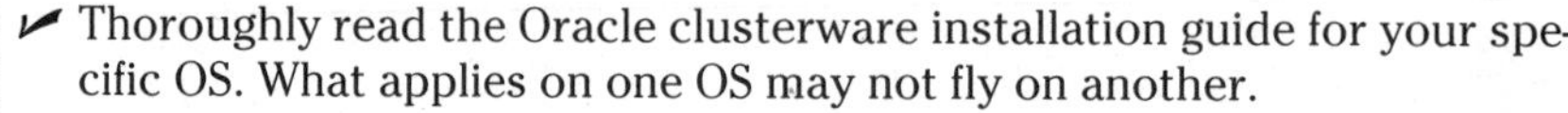

- Thoroughly read the Oracle clusterware installation guide for your specific OS. What applies on one OS may not fly on another.

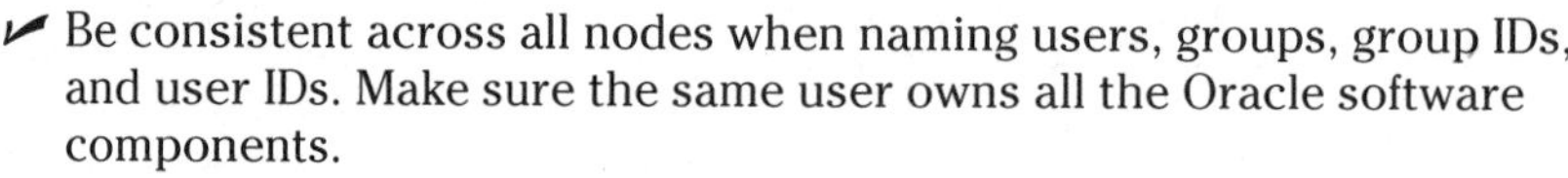

- Be consistent across all nodes when naming users, groups, group IDs, and user IDs. Make sure the same user owns all the Oracle software components.

  For example, on Linux, *oracle* is typically an account that owns the Oracle software installation. Create this user exactly the same way as you go to all the nodes. Linux has at least two OS groups for Oracle (*dba* and *oinstall*). These must be identical. For the users and groups, this goes for the group ID (*gid*) and user ID (*uid*) as well. gid and uid maintain permissions at the OS level. If they're not identical across nodes, permissions won't be maintained correctly and the cluster won't function.

- Set up the hosts file correctly. This goes for all RAC installations. The clustering software uses the *hosts file* to install the software and maintain communications. The domain name server, or DNS as it's sometimes referred to, doesn't substitute for this. You can add the host configuration to the DNS if you want, but make sure the hosts file is properly configured.

  Here is an example of what a two-node RAC host file may look like:

  ```
  127.0.0.1 localhost.localdomain localhost

  192.168.100.11 node1-priv.perptech.com node1-priv # node1 private
  192.168.100.12 node2-priv.perptech.com node2-priv # node2 private

  192.168.200.11 node1.perptech.com node1 # node1 public
  192.168.200.12 node2.perptech.com node2 # node2 public

  192.168.200.21 node1-vip.perptech.com node1-vip # node1 virtual
  192.168.200.22 node2-vip.perptech.com node2-vip # node2 virtual
  ```

  - Each cluster node connects to another through a *private* high-speed network *(cluster interconnect).*
  - The *public* IP used for all user communication to the nodes isn't related to the interconnect.
  - Each cluster node also has a *virtual* IP address that binds to the public NIC. If a node fails, the failed node's IP address can be reassigned to another node so applications can keep accessing the database through the same IP address).

- When using Oracle Clusterware, install it in a directory that's *not* a subset of your Oracle base. For example:

  ```
  ORACLE_BASE=/u01/app/oracle
  ORA_CRS_HOME=/u01/app/crs
  ```

  You must set many permissions under the clusterware home for special root access. You don't want those settings to interfere with the database software installation.

- When using Oracle Clusterware, correctly set the permissions:
  - Make sure permissions are right for the directories with the voting disk and the cluster registry. This step is easy to miss.
  - Make sure the permissions on those directories are set to stay the same on system boot up across all the nodes.

  Otherwise, you can't complete the clusterware installation or a node reboot may either cause the clustering services to not rejoin the cluster or the node to continually reboot itself.

- Configure the nodes in your cluster to be able to use the following:
  - **rsh** or **ssh** (ssh is recommend if you're on 10gR1 or greater.)
  - **rcp** or **scp** (scp is recommend if you're on 10gR1 or greater.)
  - **User equivalence for non-password authentication**

The communication and copying features are for software installation and patching. They aren't required for RAC to work after the fact.

Tools for managing a RAC installation

Oracle supplies several tools for managing a RAC installation. Some of the tools are RAC specific, while others are also for non-RAC databases. All the tools for both RAC and non-RAC databases become *cluster aware* when you launch them in the presence of a clustered environment. This means that they will see the cluster and all the nodes in it.

Cluster awareness is extremely handy because a lot of the things you do in one node have to be done across many of the nodes. Cluster-aware tools help you accomplish those tasks more easily.

Oracle Universal Installer for clusterware

If you choose Oracle Clusterware as your clustering software, right off the bat the Oracle Universal Installer (OUI) makes the software stack installation easy.

As long as you meet these two criteria, the OUI begins by installing the software from one node and then replicates across the entire cluster:

- Correctly configure the hosts file across all the nodes
- Enable user-equivalence, ssh/rsh, and scp/rcp for the Oracle user across all your nodes

This way, you only have to install the software once. (You still have to run a couple of configuration scripts on the remaining nodes after the initial install on the primary node.)

Furthermore, if you ever want to add a node to the cluster, with OUI you can use the primary node to clone the software across the network to the new node.

Oracle Universal Installer for other software

After you configure the clusterware on the nodes, the OUI is cluster aware for all installs thereafter. That means every time you go to install Oracle software, it asks you to choose the nodes you want to do the install on. This is very nice when you do your database and agent installations. Furthermore, all patch-sets that you apply also give you the option of pushing out to all the nodes.

Of course, if you're patching in a rolling method, you can apply it one node at a time (hence, *roll* from one node to the next).

Database Configuration Assistant (DBCA)

You use this tool to create a database in Chapter 4. When the DBCA is launched from a node in a cluster, it too is automatically cluster aware. It begins the database creation and configuration by asking on what nodes you want to perform operations. To create a four-instance cluster across four nodes, you only have to log on to one of the servers and do it all from the DBCA. This huge time saver automatically sets all the special initialization parameters for each node in each instance.

Network Configuration Assistant (NETCA)

When it comes to managing listeners and tnsnames files, NETCA is also cluster aware. If you need to add a listener or tnsnames entry, any action taken on one node is automatically propagated with appropriate settings across all the nodes. Configuring all the listener.ora and tnsnames.ora files across a multimode cluster would take a week by hand.

Server Control (srvctl)

Server Control is probably your day-to-day main command-line tool for managing your RAC environment.

To see an abbreviated list of all the things you can do with this tool, open a command-line prompt on your OS and type this:

```
<srvctl>
```

You see something like this:

```
Usage: srvctl <command> <object> [<options>]
    command: enable|disable|start|stop|relocate|status|add|remove|modify|getenv|
             setenv|unsetenv|config
    objects: database|instance|service|nodeapps|asm|listener
For detailed help on each command and object and its options use:
    srvctl <command> <object> -h
```

The server control utility lets you manage nearly all the resources across the entire cluster from one session. Say you're logged into node1 and want to shut down the instance prod31 on node3 for the database prod3. This is what you'd type:

```
<srvctl stop instance -d prod3 -i prod31>
```

You should see this:

That's right: Nothing. You see nothing if it works correctly. If you get errors, research appropriately.

You can use Server Control to do the following and any combination therein:

- Stop all instances of a database
- Stop two of five instances for a database
- Start all instances
- Stop one or all listeners

You can easily script Server Control into operating scripts. That's one of its big benefits. Tools like SQL*Plus and the listener control utility (which require an execution on each node for multi-node operations and multi-line inputs) make for more complex scripts. With Server Control, everything is contained in one line for whatever operation you want to accomplish.

Cluster Control (crsctl)

Cluster Control is another command-line tool that controls the cluster-specific resources. It can start and stop the cluster components on individual nodes.

Type this to launch cluster control and get a list of the command options:

```
<crsctl>
```

You see something like this:

```
Usage: crsctl check crs - checks the viability of the Oracle Clusterware
       crsctl check cssd
              - checks the viability of Cluster Synchronization Services
       crsctl check crsd        - checks the viability of Cluster Ready Services
       crsctl check evmd        - checks the viability of Event Manager
       crsctl check cluster [-node <nodename>]
              - checks the viability of CSS across nodes
       crsctl set css <parameter> <value> - sets a parameter override
…output snipped…
       crsctl query crs activeversion - lists the Oracle Clusterware operating
If necessary any of these commands can be run with additional tracing by adding
              a
              'trace'
 argument at the very front. Example: crsctl trace check css
```

We cut a large portion of the output because this tool has a lot of options.

Patching the OS is one situation when Cluster Control is useful:

1. **Stop all the cluster resources on that particular node with Server Control.**
2. **Stop the cluster specific components:**

   ```
   <crsctl stop crs>
   ```

   You see this:

   ```
   Stopping resources.
   Successfully stopped CRS resources
   Stopping CSSD.
   Shutting down CSS daemon.
   Shutdown request successfully issued.
   ```

   You might be required to reboot the node once or twice during the OS maintenance; you don't want the cluster to restart.
3. **Prevent the cluster services on this node from restarting:**

   ```
   <crsctl disable crs>
   ```
4. **Do all the reboot you want.**

   You don't have to worry about the cluster services interfering.
5. **Re-enable the cluster services:**

   ```
   <crsctl enable crs>
   ```

6. **Restart the cluster services:**

```
<crsctl start crs>
```

All the cluster resources start, including the database-related resources on the node.

Oracle Interface Configuration Tool (OIFCFG)

If you need to change the cluster (changing server name or IP addresses, for instance) you must use the Oracle Interface Configuration Tool to reconfigure those changes in the internal cluster configuration.

Avoid making these types of changes. Put some thought into your network naming and IP choice ahead of time.

Oracle RAC application for high availability

RAC helps with *high availability (HA)* by providing redundancy in your environment — specifically, redundant Oracle instances. One instance in a multi-instance environment can be removed for OS, hardware, or Oracle software maintenance without disrupting the application.

Extended RAC

Recent developments are happening in a movement called Extended RAC. This RAC solution can protect against total site loss while providing all the other RAC features. As network transmission speeds increase over time, some people think that RAC is possible with instances in remote locations.

This configuration requires high-speed SAN mirroring and a network transmission media called dark fiber. *Dark fiber* is a private, direct connection between two remote sites that can handle multiple network transmissions at once over the same cable using varying light frequencies.

At press time Extended RAC appears to have distance limitations. The farther apart the sites, the higher the latency. Latency turns into cluster performance degradation. We've been unable to find any definitive documentation on the distance limits. Degradation appears to factor heavily into your type of connection. Some sites use repeaters to extend even further.

In the mean time, if you need a remote site configured for disaster recovery, you may want to consider Data Guard. It can offer a lot of the features that Extended RAC does but at a fraction of the cost with no real distance limits.

However, make sure your expectations meet what it can deliver:

- RAC doesn't cover all points of failure. It definitely helps harden against node failure and instance failure. Unfortunately, it can't help with SAN, interconnect, or user error.
- RAC isn't typically considered a disaster protection solution. If your entire site was compromised by wind, fire, or water, RAC is going with it.

Defending Oracle Data Guard

Data Guard is Oracle's true disaster protection technology. In it you have two databases:

- A database called a *primary*
- A database called a *standby*

The two databases are connected by a network that ships all transactions from the primary and then applies them to the standby. In essence, you have one active database and one database in constant recovery.

Data Guard has options for multiple standby sites as well as an active-active configuration. See Figure 15-2 for a general architectural layout.

Data Guard architecture

Start a description with the primary database is easy because it differs very little from any other database you might have. The only difference is what it does with its archived redo logs.

The primary database writes one set of archive redo logs to a flash recovery area or a local disk. However, you may configure one or more other destinations in a Data Guard environment.

The LOG_ARCHIVE_DEST_n parameter may look like this for the configuration in Figure 15-2:

```
LOG_ARCHIVE_DEST_10='LOCATION=USE_DB_RECOVERY_FILE_DEST'
LOG_ARCHIVE_DEST_1='SERVICE=PHYSDBY1 ARCH'
LOG_ARCHIVE_DEST_2='SERVICE=LOGSDBY1 LGWR'
```

- **LOG_ARCHIVE_DEST_10** is configured to send archive redo logs to the local flash recovery area. One local destination is required for all archive log mode databases.
- **LOG_ARCHIVE_DEST_1** is configured to ship the archive logs via the archiver process (discussed in Chapter 2) to a remote site PHYSDBY1. The service name for this remote site has an entry in the tnsnames.ora file on the primary server.
- **LOG_ARCHIVE_DEST_2** is configured to ship the archive logs via the LGWR process to a remote site named LOGSDBY1. The service name for this remote site has an entry in the tnsnames.ora file on the primary server as well.

Why the difference in ARCn versus LGWR shipping methods? That has something to do with protection modes. A Data Guard environment has three protection modes.

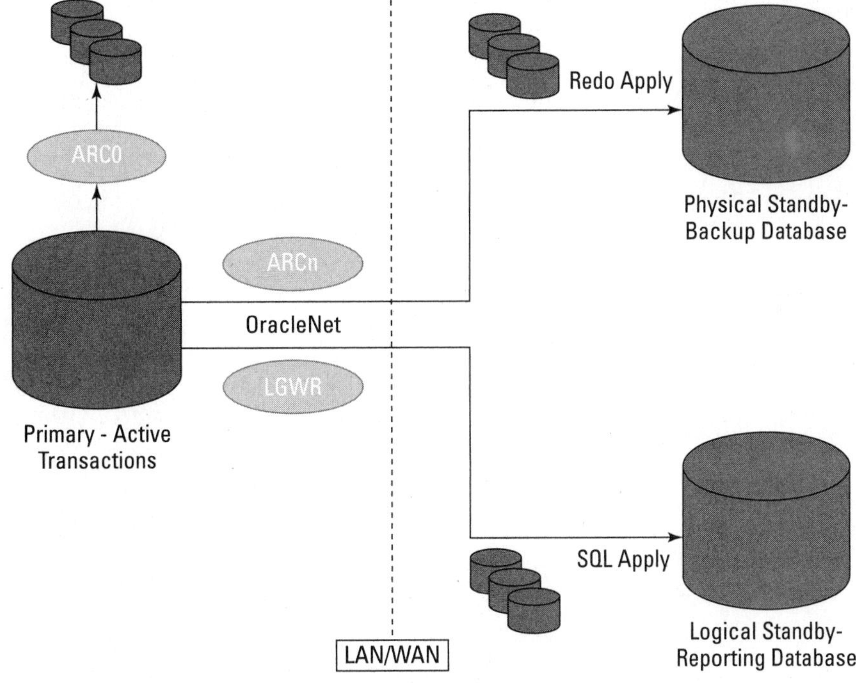

Figure 15-2: This Data Guard architecture has one physical and one logical standby database.

Maximum availability

This protection mode compromises between performance and data availability. It works by using the LGWR to simultaneously write to redo logs on both the primary and standby sites. The performance degradation comes in the form of processes having to wait for redo log entries to be written at multiple locations. Sessions issuing commits have to wait until all necessary information has been recorded in at least one standby database redo log. If one session hangs due to its inability to write redo information, the rest of the database keeps moving forward.

Maximum protection

This protection mode is similar to maximum availability except that if a session can't verify that redo is written on the remote site, the primary database shuts down.

Configure at least two standby sites for maximum protection mode. That way, one standby site becoming unavailable won't disrupt service to the entire application.

This mode verifies that no data loss will occur in the event of a disaster at the cost of performance.

Maximum performance

This protection mode detaches the log shipping process from the primary database by passing it to the archive log process (ARCn). By doing this, all operations on the primary site can continue without waiting for redo entries to be written to redo logs or redo shipping; it has to wait for these events with the other protection modes.

Maximum performance provides the highest level of performance on the primary site at the expense of *data divergence:* Archive redo data isn't shipped until an entire archive redo log is full. In a worst case scenario, an entire site loss could result in the loss of an entire archive redo log's worth of data.

Physical standby database

A *physical standby database* is a block-for-block copy of the primary site. It is built off a backup of the primary site and is maintained by shipping and applying archive logs to the standby site in the same way the transactions were committed on the primary site.

Physical standby databases can't be open for changes. You can stop recovery on the physical standby site and open it for read-only transactions. During this time, the standby site falls behind the primary site in terms of synchronicity. All the transactions are saved until the standby site's recovery is reactivated after reporting operations are done.

If you want a standby site available for reporting operations, consider setting up dual standby sites. That way, one can stay in recovery mode and you perhaps can open the other for reporting operations during the day; then close it at night for catchup. That way if you ever need to have a standby site activated, you won't have to wait for it to catch up first.

Here's a high-level overview of the steps to configure a physical standby database. In this example the primary site name is prod_a and the standby site name is prod_b.

1. **Set various initialization parameters in the primary database to prepare it for redo log shipping:**

   - **instance_name** (different on each site)

```
instance_name = prod_a
```

   - **db_name** (same on each site)

```
db_name = prod
```

   - **remote_archive_enable** (enables sending of logs to remote site)

```
remote_archive_enable = true
```

   - **log_archive_dest_1, 2**

```
log_archive_dest_1 = 'LOCATION=/u01/arch/prod'
log_Archive_dest_2 = 'SERVICE=prod_b.world ARCH'
```

   - **log_archive_format** (tells primary how to name local and standby logs)

```
log_archive_format = arch_%S.arc
```

   - **standby_file_management** (makes adding data files easier)

```
standby_file_management = true
```

   - **fal_client** (tells primary where to re-ship "lost" archive logs)

```
fal_client = 'prod_a.world'
```

Regarding Steps 1 and 6: Set all the parameters on both sites to facilitate failover/switchover operations.

2. **Create a standby copy of your primary control file by logging into SQL*Plus on the primary and typing the following:**

```
<alter database create standby controlfile as
'/u01/app/stdby_control.ctl';>
```

   You should see this:

```
Database altered.
```

3. **Move this copy to the standby site and put it in the directory of your choice.**
4. **Modify the initialization parameters on the prod_b instance to point to the new control file.**

   You can rename it however you want.

5. **Restore a backup of your primary site to the standby site.**

   You can do this with RMAN or traditional hot/cold backup methods. To simplify things, put the files in the same locations on the standby site as the primary. If you can't do that, you have to rename the files once you mount the database, or use the following initialization parameters on the standby site so the instance can convert the locations. Say the files were in /u01/app/oracle/oradata/prod on the primary and /disk1/app/oracle/oradata/prod on the standby:

```
DB_FILE_NAME_CONVERT = '/u01/','/disk1/'
```

   Oracle finds all instances of /u01 in your data file name and replaces them with /u02.

6. **Set the initialization parameters on the standby site:**
   - **instance_name** (different on each site)

```
instance_name = prod_b
```

   - **db_name** (same on each site)

```
db_name = prod
```

   - **remote_archive_enable** (enables receiving of logs on remote site)

```
remote_archive_enable = true
```

   - **standby_archive_dest** (tells standby database where to find logs)

```
standby_archive_dest = /disk1/arch/prod
```

   - **log_archive_format** (tells standby how to interpret log names, set same as primary)

```
log_archive_format = arch_%S.arc
```

   - **standby_file_management** (makes adding data files easier)

```
standby_file_management = true
```

- **fal_server** (tells standby where to search for "lost" archive logs)

```
fal_server = 'prod_a.world'
```

7. **Mount the standby database:**

```
<alter database mount standby database;>
```

You should see this:

```
Database altered.
```

8. **Start recovery on the standby database:**

```
<recover managed standby database disconnect;>
```

You see this:

```
Media recovery complete.
```

9. **Log out of the standby site.**

Let the recovery run in the background.

Logical standby database

A *logical standby database* works by copying your primary site with a backup. Then a process called SQL Apply takes the archive logs from the primary site and extracts the SQL statements from them to apply them to the logical standby database. During this time, the logical standby database is up and open. It's like having the best of both worlds. People can have updated data with the primary site for reporting purposes.

Because the standby database will be up and open, you must protect the data from being modified by anyone other than the SQL Apply services. If the data is modified outside of this procedure, the standby database will diverge from the primary. If you ever need to switch over to it for disaster recovery purposes, it won't match the primary.

To prevent replicated objects in the standby site from being modified, issue the following command in the standby environment:

```
ALTER DATABASE GUARD STANDBY;
```

Another unique feature of a logical standby database: the ability to only replicate certain objects. By default, all objects are replicated. However, you can force SQL Apply processes to skip certain objects. In addition, you can configure those skipped objects to allow modifications to them.

Performing switchover and failover operations

You can switch processing to your standby site two ways:

- **Switchover** is a planned switch that can occur if you want to do maintenance on the primary site that requires it to be unavailable. This operation may require a few minutes of downtime in the application but if you have to do maintenance that lasts for an hour or more, it could be worth it. It is called a *graceful* switchover because it turns the primary site into your standby and your standby site into your primary. Also, you can easily switch back to the original primary site without having to re-create it from scratch.
- **Failover** occurs when the primary site has been compromised in some way. Perhaps it was a total site loss or maybe you discovered physical corruption in a data file. Not always, but usually after a failover, you have to either completely re-create the primary site or recover it from a backup and re-instate it. You usually perform a failover only when you've determined that fixing the primary site will take long enough that you prefer not to have an application outage for the entire time.

To perform a switchover, follow these steps:

1. **On the current primary, log into SQL*Plus and type the following:**

   ```
   <alter database commit to switchover to physical standby;>
   ```

   You should see this:

   ```
   Database altered.
   ```

2. **Shut down the primary database:**

   ```
   <shutdown immediate>
   ```

   You should see this:

   ```
   Database closed.
   Database dismounted.
   ORACLE instance shut down.
   ```

3. **Start the primary database in nomount mode:**

   ```
   <startup nomount>
   ```

   You should see something like this:

   ```
   ORACLE instance started.
   Total System Global Area  789172224 bytes
   Fixed Size                  2148552 bytes
   Variable Size             578815800 bytes
   Database Buffers          201326592 bytes
   Redo Buffers                6881280 bytes
   ```

4. Mount the database as a standby:

```
<alter database mount standby database;>
```

You should see this:

```
Database altered.
```

5. Start recovery:

```
<recover managed standby database disconnect;>
```

You see this:

```
Media recovery complete.
```

6. Log into SQL*Plus on the current standby and type the following:

```
<alter database commit to switchover to physical primary;>
```

You should see this:

```
Database altered.
```

7. Shut down the standby database:

```
<shutdown immediate>
```

You should see this:

```
Database closed.
Database dismounted.
ORACLE instance shut down.
```

8. Make sure all appropriate initialization parameters are set for this database to behave properly as a primary.

9. Start it normally:

```
<startup>
```

You should see something like this:

```
ORACLE instance started.
Total System Global Area  789172224 bytes
Fixed Size                  2148552 bytes
Variable Size             578815800 bytes
Database Buffers          201326592 bytes
Redo Buffers                6881280 bytes
Database mounted.
Database opened.
```

10. Make sure the users and applications can connect to and use the new primary instance.

Part V
The Part of Tens

"They can predict earthquakes and seizures, why not server failures?"

In this part . . .

Implementing a database takes many steps. Chapter 16 leads you through the top ten things you should do during installation. Chapter 17 gives you the top ten things you should do when implementing.

Chapter 16

Top Ten Oracle Installation Do's

In This Chapter

- Reading documentation
- Seeing the Oracle Optimal Flexible Architecture
- Profiling
- Getting the wrong bit
- Forgetting to mask
- Becoming an Oracle
- Fighting stage fright
- Patching
- Fawning over user and group IDs
- Backing that thing up

In this chapter we focus things you shouldn't overlook when installing Oracle. Getting off to a good start with a solid, proper installation is key to success. By recognizing the common pitfalls up front, you experience less heartache and pain later on.

Read the Documentation

Every OS that runs Oracle has a corresponding documentation set. This documentation covers things like operating system packages, kernel parameters, network configuration, and other installation prerequisites.

Every operating system is different. Even if you think they're the same, you're wrong. UNIX is UNIX, right? Wrong. HP-UX, AIX, and Solaris each have very distinct prerequisites. Go to Oracle's documentation on the Internet and download the latest and greatest install guide for your OS. Read it thoroughly before you begin. We even recommend listing all the little things that have to be checked before you begin. If you make this a practice, you will find far fewer problems during and after installation.

The quickest way to get to Oracle's documentation is here:

1. **Go to** http://docs.oracle.com**.**
2. **Select the version you're interested in.**
3. **When you enter the 11g documentation set, open the Installing and Upgrading folder.**

   The folder's on the left side of the screen.
4. **Click the OS of your choice to enter the OS-specific installation guide.**

Observe the Optimal Flexible Architecture

The *optimal flexible architecture (OFA)* is an Oracle guideline that lays out how software and databases should be installed on a system. The OFA has these main purposes:

- Find Oracle files in explicit locations, even when on multiple devices
- Set up a software tree that allows easy patching and upgrades
- Mirror Oracle installations across all environments so they're the same or similar
- Keep separate Oracle files and installation types
- Facilitate routine management tasks
- Facilitate backup and recovery
- Manage and administer growth
- Facilitate layout for best performance

We recommend you fully read and understand Oracle's documentation to best implement the OFA.

There are many rules and guidelines: too many to cover here. Oracle's documentation gives explicit examples and suggestions for a variety of operating systems and storage. Furthermore, OFA has evolved over the years. The main ideas remain, but some have been tweaked. For each release of Oracle, don't hesitate to refresh yourself.

Configure Your Profile

The profile probably applies more to UNIX-type environments. However, by learning the key elements needed inside the profile, you can also see that they may apply to Windows.

The *profile* is the program (for lack of a better word) that runs every time you log into your operating system. It is typically found in your home directory. Depending on the shell that you use, it might be named any of the following ways:

- .profile
- .kshrc
- .bash_profile

By configuring this script, you can take better advantage of the operating environment and your Oracle software. Different types of users also may have different profiles. Furthermore, you may have multiple profiles depending on what you will do when you log in.

The profile sets up variables, execution paths, and permissions and sometimes limits in your session. The Oracle documentation recommends specific settings for your environment. Some are OS specific, others apply to almost all Oracle installations.

Definitely include these elements in your profile:

- Oracle base variable
- Oracle home variable
- Path variable
- Default file-permission settings
- Aliases
- Library variables

Without a properly configured profile, you have to change these every time you log into the system. We want to say having a profile is a requirement, but technically it's not. However, you should make it part of your standard practice.

Running the Wrong Bit

More operating systems are offering 64-bit versions. When you install Oracle, take advantage of the appropriate bit version. The fact is, 32-bit software usually runs fine on 64-bit operating systems. It doesn't work the other way around.

Don't spend all kinds of money on a 64-bit OS and hardware, and then install the 32-bit version of Oracle. This limits you in several ways:

- Your SGA can't exceed a certain size.
- You can't take advantage of the server's faster 64-bit architecture.
- Multitasking can be limited.

For what it's worth, this mistake is made more often in Windows environments.

When you order or download your Oracle software, ask the system administrator what binaries you can use. In almost all cases, 64 bit is preferable. That goes for when you are provisioning out a system as well; 64 bit offers more scalability and increased computing power.

Set umask

If you read and follow the Oracle documentation, this should not be a problem. Linux/UNIX environments have a umask setting.

Forgetting to properly set the umask parameter means a difficult, if not impossible, Oracle installation. The result doesn't typically affect the Oracle software owner, but the users who log in to the OS and try to use the system.

umask sets the default permission modes on files and directories that are added to the system. This can affect files copied to the system during installation, as well as things like log files, which are created as part of normal operation.

The Oracle-recommend umask is 022. This results in files being read+write for the owner, and read for all others. If you put the umask setting in the profile it sets each time you log in.

Become Oracle

On a production system the Oracle database software should be installed by a user specifically created for the task. This user is typically named *oracle*. Imagine that. Now, this isn't a hard and fast rule, but we recommend that you seriously consider this — especially if you're a beginner. This is how you find it in most systems as well as training materials and documentation.

Naming the user oracle avoids this scenario: The Oracle software is installed as another named user or by a user associated with a different software package. You don't want Craig installing the Oracle software stack under his own ID. He may leave the company someday and now you have a problem.

It's not best practice to let login IDs exist for people who no longer work at the company, which is a security concern not to mention confusing.

Set up a dedicated ID (we recommend *oracle*) to install software with. This makes maintenance and training easier, and it eases personnel transitions. This recommendation also comes from Oracle.

Stage It

If you download the software, you don't need it on disk for installation. We recommend keeping a hard copy somewhere for recovery reasons, but that's about it.

Even if you bought the installation CDs, copy the material to the hard drive before the installation.

- The install is faster if reading from disk.
- You don't have to worry about someone else in the server room ejecting the disk and it disappearing forever.
- Having a copy of the software helps if you want to add a feature that you hadn't installed at first. It's easier to find it in a staging area than hunting down the disk.
- If the Oracle binary files are corrupt and you need to reinstall a portion of the code tree, it's right there.

You can get software from Oracle two ways:

- Order it from the Oracle store.
- Download it from their web site.

Both copies are identical. The downloadable software isn't a trial version. Anyone can download and use it, provided you contact an Oracle sales rep and pay for it.

Patch It

You just downloaded and installed your brand-new Oracle database. Now we're telling you it needs to be patched. What?! Whether you order the CDs or download the software, you're probably not getting the most recent version. If you're licensed for Oracle — and you should be — log into their Oracle Support web site and search for the most recent patchsets to apply to your database.

1. **Go to Oracle's support web site at** http://metalink.oracle.com**.**
2. **Enter your login ID.**

   If you do not have one, click the Register button and follow those instructions.
3. **Enter your Customer Support Identifier (CSI).**

   You get this when you purchase support from an Oracle sales representative.

   Once you log in, you see tabs across the top of the page.
4. **Click the Patches and Updates tab.**
5. **Enter the following information:**
   - Your OS
   - Software package
   - Database version
   - Type of patch or patchset

We recommend being on the latest, greatest maintenance release of the Oracle software — but make sure the software is compatible with or supported by your application.

Many times we've discovered a client with an older version of Oracle. When we recommend a patch they announce they have some third-party software vendor who only certifies on a certain patch level.

Despite the problems with third-party software, there are benefits to being on the latest Oracle patchset:

- Oracle keeps creating patches to fix bugs in the release as long as your patch level is supported. Otherwise, you're out of luck.
- Quarterly Oracle security patches are usually available for the most recent patchsets only.
- The patchsets are maintenance releases in essence. This means that bugs found in previous releases are fixed.

Despite all the good things about being on the latest Oracle patchset, read the patchset documentation before you apply the patch. Unfortunately, sometimes bugs are introduced with a patchset. Make sure that any new issues don't affect the functionality your application works with.

Mind the User and Group IDs

This bit of advice pertains more to Linux/UNIX operating systems. When a group or user is created on Linux/UNIX, they're assigned a user ID number.

All file ownership and permissions are based on this number. By default, the OS chooses the first available number. This isn't where problems occur.

Problems occur when you install Oracle on multiple servers — especially systems using Oracle RAC or DataGuard. Due to file sharing, if the user and group IDs don't match across the systems, they're not going to function properly. Furthermore, if you're shipping Oracle files across the network (transportable tablespaces or cloning, for instance), you'll have problems reading these files when they arrive.

It is best practice to specifically assign a number to your Oracle user and its associated groups when they're created. Document this number in your company's Oracle operating procedures manual. If you have multiple DBAs or Oracle installers, use the same ID numbers across all systems.

Back It Up

You finally configured your OS, set up all the Oracle users and groups, configured your profile, staged the software (and its patches), installed Oracle, patched Oracle, and created your first database.

Wow, that's a lot of work.

Now back up your work! Now test your backup to make sure it's usable; see Chapter 17 for more.

Besides just a backup at the end, you could do multiple backups as you go: after the OS prerequisites are done, after Oracle is installed, after the patch, and so on. That way, you can easily go back without completely starting over.

Chapter 17

Top Ten Database Design Do's

In This Chapter

- Using Oracle's built-in constraints
- Spreading out your I/O
- Learning data normalization
- Improper or inconsistent naming conventions
- Setting up roles and privileges properly
- Cutting down on ad-hoc queries
- Enforcing password security
- Avoiding too many DBAs
- Storing code in the database
- Testing recovery strategy

In this chapter we focus on some of the mistakes or shortcomings we've seen in Oracle databases over the years. Most of these are honest mistakes due to inexperience with Oracle or databases in general and can easily be overcome. After all, if it weren't for things like this, DBAs like yourself wouldn't have anything to do!

Using Oracle's Built-In Constraints

Constraints enforce rules against your data. Oracle offers some of these built-in constraints:

- **Primary keys** identify a column or columns in the table whose data for the values stored is unique and non-null.
- **Foreign keys** enforce something called *referential integrity*.

- **Check constraints** are customizable constraints that check the data entered into a column.
- **Not Null constraints** disallow an empty column to be empty.
- **Unique constraints** are a column or group of columns whose values together are unique for the row.

Constraints seem like a very useful and almost required feature in any database. Odd as it may seem, some software vendors don't natively include a system of constraints in the database software. This requires developers to code their own in the application. This can be extremely difficult and a nightmare to maintain. Not to mention the fact that they will only be enforced through the application itself. Anybody gaining access via a tool like SQL*Plus won't be required to obey the application constraints.

In some Oracle databases the designer or primary developers came from a database that required the constraints to be created and managed in the application. Make sure you don't fall victim to this situation: Use the built-in Oracle constraints.

Spreading Out Your IO

When laying the files down on your system, you should make sure to evenly balance the files across the available disks. Some people might argue that their hands are tied.

For systems using local storage inside the server, buy as many smaller disks as possible so you can balance your IO. These days, it seems that manufacturers are offering ever large devices for storage. This makes your job difficult. Keep in mind that when you work with the storage/server vendor, the machine is for storing and retrieving data. By having several locations to store your data, you get more tuning capabilities.

The rules for storing Oracle files can be broken down an infinite number of ways. Here are some basics:

- Separate tables and indexes across different drives
- Store your redo log groups and members separately
- Store unrelated to application data separately
- Store table partitions separately
- Store system files separately
- Store the Oracle binaries on their own device

You can break this down even further depending on your data access behavior. By using Oracle's data dictionary and available monitoring tools, you can fine-tune the storage layout for your specific application.

Knowing Data Normalization

Data normalization is how you lay out your application storage needs in your tables. Before you begin designing a database from scratch, know the rules of normalization.

Some developers fall victim to data normalization shortcomings because of previous experience with other databases. For example, we have seen people design data models based on their experience with Microsoft Excel or Lotus Notes. These flat file-type databases have different rules for design. Normalization is a set of rules designed for relational type databases. Spend some quality time with an Oracle data-modeling book or class before you get too far in an application design project.

Using Naming Conventions

This topic boils down to good data-modeling skills. When creating objects in your system, it is important to follow rules. If you do your research or take a class on data modeling, you know the guidelines. Best practice is to adhere to those as best as possible. However, the most important thing is to follow some sort of documented, repeatable guidelines everyone can easily understand.

Avoid these common mistakes:

- **Don't use keywords.** Don't name your table *table*.
- **Don't let the system give default names.** This is usually the case with constraints. Take the time to come up with something descriptive.
- **Don't use quotes with column names and table names.** Many over-the-counter developer tools do this. Problem is you can end up with objects that have mixed-case names. Next thing you know you have tables named EMP, emp, and emP — all different.

Create a document that outlines the standard practices your company will use. This will aid in the training of new hires and make sure the IT department is on the same page when working collaboratively on an application.

Setting Up Roles and Privileges Properly

While it's tempting, make sure you don't fall victim to taking the easy way out when configuring object access. Don't grant everything to everybody because the design team doesn't want to put a system of roles and privileges in place. It's especially tempting when you need to meet a project deadline and a developer is dead in the water.

Do your best to come up with different roles for your developers, application users, and application owners. This makes management and security much easier down the road. Chapter 9 deals with configuring roles and privileges in your database. This is a very important chapter not only for security but manageability.

Keeping Ad-Hoc Queries to a Minimum

Okay, this piece of advice is difficult to swallow. Dozens of companies offer tools that show managers how easy it is to go into a database and design all kinds of fancy reports with graphs and colors. They promise increased revenue and efficient information transfer. The problem is that these products are marketed to managers, not the technical team.

We aren't saying that there is no place for a tool like this. Quite the opposite. After all, the whole point of having a database is to serve up data. However, having some control over what type of reports are allowed is going to make the DBA, the system administrator, and the end users happier overall.

Allowing unsolicited ad-hoc queries in your database to run any time, in any form, is asking for trouble. Not only can they run slowly, but the entire database can become unusable during their execution.

In an ideal world, reports are designed, qualified, and approved before they're run. A team of developers can work with DBAs and managers to list information needs. Those can be skillfully and efficiently transformed into canned reports available at the click of a button. They can be scheduled to run at specific times to avoid impacting the system.

Enforcing Password Security

When you create a user in Oracle, you're forced to set a password. This is good. However, not until 11g did Oracle force you to make sure that password was secure. During database creation, it asks if you want to revert to the pre-11g security requirements, which were minimal. One of the first things we recommend is an overhaul of the password security system.

Some common problems are easily remedied with Oracle password profiles:

- Lack of password complexity
- No regular password expiration schedule
- Reusable passwords
- Shared logins
- Default passwords

Implementing password security through a user profile is extremely easy. Unfortunately, one of the side effects of this is that the users will hate you for it! People seems to hate having to remember a password that's something other than their username. This is critical.

Limiting the Number of DBAs

Make sure that only company-approved people have access to the DBA role on the database. Not only does it threaten security but it reduces accountability. Tracing problems is much easier when the source isn't a group of dozens of users. Most problems we encounter are due to user error.

Again, expect resistant users. Every company has that person who's been with the team for 20 years and knows the business and application inside and out. He has always had DBA access. Problem is, he hasn't had any formal Oracle training or experience.

Do what you have to do to convince management that few people should have the keys to the kingdom. Also, make sure those people are trained and accountable for the actions they take.

Storing Code in the Database

SQL is the primary language for accessing and manipulating Oracle data. You can embed it in applications or store it in the database in the form of stored procedures.

Not all SQL needs to be stored in the database, but consider designing the application so the bulk of the business processes is made up of stored code.

Unless the developers are trained to take advantage of Oracle's stored procedure mechanisms, you don't have the best, most efficient database possible.

- **Stored code enforces security.** A stored procedure can be encrypted (*wrapped,* in Oracle terms). Users can run procedures without access to the base objects with which the code works. Stored procedures are executed with the owner's permissions, not the user who is calling it.
- **Stored code performs better.** It is pre-compiled in the database and can be stored in memory without parsing and compiling. This decreases CPU usage and increases system scalability. Stored code is easier to maintain because it's in one place. If you're adding functionality or changing business rules, the application can immediately take advantage of the changes without releasing a new version.

Testing Your Recovery Strategy

With a little training, it's easy to design a backup process for your system. Testing is a key element to a robust backup and recovery strategy. Running an error-free backup every night doesn't mean you can recover with it.

Now, we don't want to be doomsday preachers. Using RMAN and getting backups with no errors mean you have a significant chance of recovery. But what if you need those backups and they don't work? You could be, as they say, caught with your pants down. You might even be out of a job.

This extends to training. Do you know what commands to issue for a recovery? Do you know the fastest way to recover given the specific type of failure? Will you use RMAN or Flashback database?

Testing your recovery strategy checks the backup itself, and lets you practice for situations where a speedy recovery is required. You don't want to spend an hour reading the Oracle documentation. Know how to reduce the liability of your skill set by testing and practice.

Appendix A

Quick Start Install of Oracle 11g on Linux

In This Appendix

- Setting up the operating system
- Installing the Oracle software

To get you started, we included an appendix on installing the Oracle 11g software on Linux, which is a readily available, free operating system. This chapter gives you the necessary steps to install Oracle not only on the many flavors of Linux, but also applies to some UNIX systems as well. This appendix's example uses RedHat Enterprise Linux 4 (RHEL4).

This Oracle installation can test most of the features discussed in this book. We recommend having at least 2GB of memory and 10GB of free hard-disk space to do any work.

Setting Up the Operating System

Unlike installing Oracle on Windows, Linux environments have some installation prerequisites. This appendix goes over the basic prerequisites as specified in the documentation set Oracle Database Quick Installation Guide for 11g Release 1 (11.1) for Linux x86.

To view this documentation set, follow these steps:

1. **Go to** http://docs.oracle.com.
2. **Click Oracle Database documentation, 11g Release 1 (11.1).**
3. **Click the + next to the Installing and Upgrading folder.**
4. **Click Linux Installation Guides.**

   You see Quick Installation Guide for Linux x86 on the right. That is the document you want.

The next section assumes you will complete the required tasks logged in as the user *root.*

Checking your operating system version

Oracle is only *certified* to run on particular versions of Linux. If you have trouble with your database and need Oracle support, they may insist that you be on a certified version of Linux before they help you.

Use a certified version of Linux if this installation if you're planning to purchase Oracle support.

The supported versions of Linux for Oracle 11g follow:

- Asianux 2.0
- Asianux 3.0
- Oracle Enterprise Linux 4.0
- Oracle Enterprise Linux 5.0
- Red Hat Enterprise Linux 4.0
- Red Hat Enterprise Linux 5.0
- SUSE Enterprise Linux 10.0

To see what version of Linux you are on, follow these steps:

1. **Open a command prompt on your OS.**
2. **Type this:**

   ```
   <cat /proc/version>
   ```

   You should see something like this:

   ```
   Linux version 2.6.18-53.1.14.el5
   (gcc version 4.1.2 20070626 (Red Hat 4.1.2-14)) #1 SMP
   ```

Checking your kernel version

The *kernel* is essentially the core operating version of Linux operating system. It's kind of akin to a service pack in Windows. For Oracle to be certified, you also need to be on a certified kernel version.

RHEL4's required kernel version is 2.6.9. To see your kernel version, type this:

```
<uname -r>
```

You should see something like this:

```
2.6.9-55.0.0.0.2.EL
```

Checking your OS packages

Packages are modular pieces of the operating system that you can install to activate certain features. For Oracle to run on Linux, it requires particular packages.

RHEL4 requires the following packages:

- binutils-2.15.92.0.2-18
- compat-libstdc++-33.2.3-47.3
- elfutils-libelf-0.97-5
- elfutils-libelf-devel-0.97-5
- glibc-2.3.4-2.19
- glibc-common-2.3.4-2.19
- glibc-devel-2.3.4-2.19
- glibc-headers-2.3.4-2.19
- gcc-3.4.5-2
- gcc-c++-3.4.5-2
- libaio-devel-0.3.105-2
- libaio-0.3.105-2
- libgcc-3.4.5
- libstdc++-3.4.5-2
- libstdc++-devel-3.4.5-2
- make-3.80-5
- sysstat-5.0.5

To see if a required package is installed, to use RedHat Package Manager (rpm). For example, to check the *make* package, type this:

```
rpm -q make
```

You should see something like this:

```
make-3.81-1.1
```

If you find some packages not installed or that do not meet the required version, get them from the Linux distribution installation media or the appropriate Linux vendor's download site.

Creating Linux operating system groups and users

Linux best practices entail creating specific groups and users to install, own, and maintain the Oracle software.

Oracle requires two operating system groups for the software:

- **dba** controls what users can connect do on the database using operating system authentication.
- **oinstall** controls which users are allowed to modify the Oracle software. *Software modification* includes installs, upgrades, and patching.

To perform the commands that follow (as well as some that precede this), log in to the Linux computer as a Linux super user (root).

To create the groups, type this:

```
<groupadd dba><enter>
<groupadd oinstall><enter>
```

These commands have no output if the groups add successfully.

Do *not* add any users to Linux groups unless they're approved database administrators. Members of these groups can see almost any data they want or damage the database and Oracle installation.

Creating the Oracle Software Owner

On a Linux installation of Oracle, it is best practice to create a special user to own the Oracle software. While you can name the user whatever you want, best practices show that user is typically called *oracle* or some name with *ora* in it (such as *ora11g*).

The following command creates

- A user called oracle
- With the primary group *oinstall*

- The secondary group *dba*
- With a home directory /home/oracle
- Korn shell as the default shell

```
useradd -c "Oracle Software Owner" -d /home/oracle -m -g oinstall
-s /usr/bin/ksh -G dba oracle
```

After you create this user, change its password to something that you will remember.

To change the password for the user oracle, type this:

```
<password oracle>
```

It prompts you for the new password.

Configuring the Linux Kernel Parameters

The Linux operating system has a set of kernel parameters that control how memory and processes function on the system. Installing Oracle typically involves adjusting these parameters. The parameters are found in the /etc directory in a file called sysctl.conf.

Edit the sysctl.conf file and modify the following parameters to have the specified values:

```
fs.file-max = 512 * PROCESSES # Processes should be to the total number of
                                # sessions you expect to have on your system *
              20%.
kernel.shmall = 2097152
kernel.shmmax = 2147483648 # This parameter is typically set to the same size as
                            # the memory (RAM) you have on your system in bytes)
kernel.shmmni = 4096
kernel.sem = 250 32000 100 128
net.ipv4.ip_local_port_range = 1024 65000
net.core.rmem_default = 4194304
net.core.rmem_max = 4194304
net.core.wmem_default = 262144
net.core.wmem_max = 262144
net.ipv4.tcp_wmem = 262144 262144 262144
net.ipv4.tcp_rmem = 4194304 4194304 4194304
```

If one of the parameters doesn't exist, add it just as it looks here. To make the changes take effect, type the following command:

```
/sbin/sysctl -p
```

Creating the ORACLE_BASE directory

The ORACLE_BASE directory serves as the starting point for all your Oracle installation files. Choosing this directory carefully is important. Ideally, it will be on its own drive or mount point.

A typical ORACLE_BASE might be /u01/app/oracle.

1. **Create the ORACLE_BASE directory:**

   ```
   mkdir /u01/app/oracle
   ```

2. **Change the ownership of the directory so the owner is Oracle and the group is oinstall:**

   ```
   chown -R oracle:oinstall /u01/app/oracle
   ```

3. **Change the permissions on the directory:**

   ```
   chmod -R 775 /u01/app/oracle
   ```

   Now the owner can read, write, and execute; all other users can read and execute recursively.

Configuring the Oracle user's environment

When you create the user oracle, the user has the korn shell. The korn shell is controlled by a .profile file in the user's home directory.

To set up the user oracle's environment follow these steps:

1. **Log in to an OS terminal window as the user** oracle.

   You are in the home directory /home/oracle.

2. **Edit the file .profile and add the following lines.**

   ```
   export PATH=/usr/kerberos/sbin:/usr/kerberos/bin:
           /usr/local/sbin:/usr/local/bin:/sbin:/bin:/usr/sbin:/usr/bin:.
   export ORACLE_BASE=/u01/app/oracle
   export ORACLE_HOME=/u01/app/oracle/product/11.1.0/db_1
   export ORACLE_SID=dev11g
   export LD_LIBRARY_PATH=$ORACLE_HOME/lib
   export PATH=$ORACLE_HOME/bin:$PATH
   ```

   If the file already exists, make sure to add the lines to the bottom of the file.

3. **Save and exit the .profile file.**

4. **Run the following command to make the changes take effect:**

   ```
   <. .profile>
   ```

   There is no output.

5. **See if the changes worked:**

   ```
   <env |grep ORA>
   ```

   You should see something like this:

   ```
   ORACLE_SID=dev11g
   ORACLE_BASE=/u01/app/oracle
   ORACLE_HOME=/u01/app/oracle/product/11.1.0/db_1
   ```

   Congratulations! You are ready to install the software.

Installing the Oracle 11g database software

The following steps walk you through a quick start installation of the Oracle 11g database software. The steps at this point are almost identical across all operating systems so your skills will translate very easily from OS to OS.

1. **Download the software from the Oracle web site at** http://technet.oracle.com.

   You can order it from the Oracle store. We recommend downloading it because it's free and the same stuff you would get from the store. You can always burn it to DVD later on.

2. **Copy the entire disk to the hard drive.**
3. **Create a directory to hold the software.**

   Choose something like one of these:

   - /u01/app/oracle/stage
   - /u01/app/oracle/software/stage

   If you downloaded the software, unzip it first into the directory you created. After unzipping, you should see a folder called database.

4. **Open a terminal window and go to the software directory.**
5. cd **into the database directory and execute the runInstaller program:**

   ```
   <./runInstaller>
   ```

   It might take a minute or two depending on your machine speed. You're welcomed by the screen shown in Figure A-1.

6. **Select the Basic Installation radio button.**
7. **Choose an Oracle base directory.**

   We chose /u01/app/oracle. This directory serves as the base of the Oracle installation. It also corresponds with the examples in Oracle's official documentation, as well as the OFA standards. See Appendix B for an overview of the OFA standards.

Oracle Database 11g Installation - Select a Product to Install

Select Installation Method

ORACLE DATABASE 11g

Basic Installation

Perform full Oracle Database 11g installation with standard configuration options requiring minimal input.This option uses file system for storage, and a single password for all database accounts.

Oracle Base Location: /u01/app/oracle Browse...

Oracle Home Location: /u01/app/oracle/product/11.1.0/db_1 Browse...

Installation Type: Enterprise Edition (3.3GB)

UNIX DBA Group: dba

Create Starter Database (additional 1482MB)

Global Database Name: orcl

Database Password: Confirm Password:

This password is used for the SYS, SYSTEM, SYSMAN, and DBSNMP accounts.

Advanced Installation

Allows advanced selections such as different passwords for the SYS, SYSTEM, SYSMAN, and DBSNMP accounts, database character set, product languages, automated backups, custom installation, and alternative storage options such as Automatic Storage Management.

Help Back Next Install Cancel

Figure A-1: The Oracle Universal Installer screen welcomes you.

8. **Choose an Oracle Home directory.**

   All the Oracle executables are installed here. It should be a subdirectory of the Oracle Base. The location we chose is consistent with the OFA.

9. **Select Enterprise Edition.**

   This ensures you have all the features in this book.

10. **Decide whether you want to create a starter database.**

    We recommend *not* creating a starter database when you're first installing the database.

    Isn't getting the software installed a big enough milestone? After you make sure the software installed correctly, go to Chapter 4 and create the database yourself. This gives you more control and the opportunity to understand the database creation process. If you let the installer do it, many of the steps are left behind the scenes.

11. **Click the Next button.**

    The prerequisite checks are initiated. If you're on a typical desktop or laptop (non-server), you might see the warning shown in Figure A-2. This tells you that the IP address is DHCP.

12. **For testing, choose the check box next to the warning.**

    In a production environment, you should have a dedicated IP address.

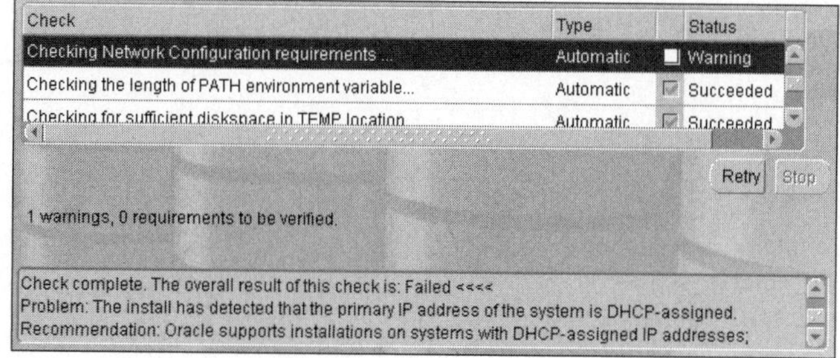

Figure A-2: You might see this warning for DHCP.

13. **Click the Install on a Summary Screen button.**

    A screen shows the progress and a slideshow tells you about all the great features you'll soon have at your fingertips. Depending on your machine's speed, the install can take anywhere from five minutes to one hour.

    When installation is complete, you should see a window telling you so.

14. **Click the Exit button to close the installer.**

Index

• *Symbols and Numerics* •

• *A* •

• B •

• D •

• F •

• G •

• H •

• I •

• J •

• L •

• M •

• N •

• O •

• P •

• Q •

• R •

• S •

• T •

• U •

• V •

• W •

• X •